ROBERT DOVER

foreword by Tami Hoag

The Gates to Brilliance

How a Gay, Jewish, Middle-Class Kid
Who Loved Horses Found Success

TRAFALGAR SQUARE
North Pomfret, Vermont

First published in 2021 by
Trafalgar Square Books
North Pomfret, Vermont 05053

Disclaimer of Liability
The author and publisher shall have neither liability nor responsibility to any person or entity with respect to any loss or damage caused or alleged to be caused directly or indirectly by the information contained in this book. While the book is as accurate as the author can make it, there may be errors, omissions, and inaccuracies.

Trafalgar Square Books encourages the use of approved safety helmets in all equestrian sports and activities.

Library of Congress Cataloging-in-Publication Data
Names: Dover, Robert, 1956- author.
Title: The gates to brilliance : how a gay, Jewish, middle-class kid who
   loved horses found success / Robert Dover.
Description: North Pomfret, Vermot : Trafalgar Square Books, 2021. | Includes
   index.
Identifiers: LCCN 2021011153 (print) | LCCN 2021011152 (ebook) | ISBN
   9781570769870 (paperback) | ISBN 9781570769887 (epub)
Subjects: LCSH: Dover, Robert, 1956- | United States Equestrian
   Team--Biography. | Dressage riders--United States--Biography. | Olympic
   athletes--United States--Biography. | Jewish gay men--United
   States--Biography. | Self-actualization (Psychology) | Success.
Classification: LCC SF309.482.D68 A3 2021 (ebook) | LCC SF309.482.D68 (print)
   | DDC 798.40092 [B] --dc23
LC record available at https://lccn.loc.gov/2021011153

All photos courtesy of the author unless otherwise indicated. An effort has been made to contact all photographers who could be identified. In some cases a photographer may not have been found. Should additional photographers be identified, they will be credited in future editions.

Book design by *Katarzyna Misiukanis–Celińska (https://misiukanis-artstudio.com)*
Cover design by *RM Didier*
Index by *Andrea M. Jones (www.jonesliteraryservices.com)*
Typefaces: *Source Serif Pro, Source Sans Pro* and *Hummingbird*

Printed in the United States of America

10 9 8 7 6 5 4 3 2 1

– for Robert –

the love of my life, my soulmate,
and my compass in all ways

FOREWORD

Nothing succeeds like success.
The trick is achieving
that success in the first place.

W hen I first met Robert Dover in the late 1990s, he had already represented the United States in four Olympic games, the World Equestrian Games, numerous World Cups, and many prestigious international competitions all over the world. I knew him by reputation only, by his achievements. The words that came to mind at the mention of his name were Olympian, icon, champion. He was ubiquitous at the elite level of the sport of dressage, a sport I was just stepping into at the time. His name was synonymous with success.

Hungry to learn what brought riders to the top and kept them there, I watched and listened, soaking up information like a sponge. I watched not only what riders like Robert did in the show ring, but in the warm-up, and learned as much as I could by observation and eavesdropping. I studied his habits in the training of his horses, his attention to detail, his quiet consistency, his precision and accuracy riding a test. I listened to him coaching his students in an attempt to absorb his philosophy of the sport.

My own trainer, Betsy Steiner, was a contemporary of Robert. They had many shared experiences in the sport, had trained with the same masters and shown on teams together. Their friendship led to my acquaintance with Robert, and I came a step closer for an even better view into the rarified air at the top of the sport. I listened with delight to the stories they told about their adventures in Europe. I started getting to know Robert as a person.

It's always fascinating to me to learn the stories of highly successful people. No matter their area of expertise, they all have certain qualities in common: passion, dedication, resilience, and focus. Robert is the perfect example of these qualities meshing together to form a champion.

In some ways, the story of his journey is almost a fairy tale. He was born at the perfect time and found himself—put himself—in the perfect places to learn from a literal who's who of modern dressage. If I could make a list of masters from which to learn this classical art of riding, it would include Colonel Bengt Lundquist, Willi Schultheis, George Theodorescu, Dr. Reiner Klimke, and Herbert Rehbein. It would have been a dream to train with any one of them. (Sadly, they're all gone now.) Robert made sure to learn from all of them. On that often bumpy road to the gates of excellence, the serendipity of being in the right place at the right moment plays only a small part. Determination drives the bus.

Over the years I've come to know Robert as one of the most determined people I've ever known. He is a tireless worker for any goal before him, whether in horse sport or fundraising for a cause or political activism. He simply doesn't consider the notion of defeat. He sets a goal, determines the steps to reach that goal, and never takes no for answer. Reading his story should be an inspiration to anyone, equestrian or not.

Robert is a unique human cocktail of determination mixed with an unflagging optimism, more energy than any three average people, and an essential twist of good humor that has carried him through good times and bad. And like anyone, he has gone through bad times. I find his willingness to share those stories just as readily as his triumphs, and to self-own his mistakes to be refreshingly honest and relatable.

We don't get success without failures along the way. It's a true champion who uses those moments as stepping stones to move on rather than anchors to hold him back. And those who can look back with love and humility, and embrace the whole journey are the ones who find contentment along with their success. That is Robert Dover in a nutshell. He wears his life experiences with the comfort of a favorite jacket. This is who he is, and who he is is fabulous every day!

Icon, mentor, coach, philanthropist, activist, friend. While Robert's achievements may seem larger than life, they are truly not larger than the life he has actually led. Enjoy his journey and let it inspire your own. ●

Tami Hoag
NEW YORK TIMES BESTSELLING AUTHOR OF *The Boy*

PREFACE

With all that has recently happened in the world, what better time to reflect on my life and my experiences. I have had and continue to enjoy a life of amazement! That doesn't mean that everything has been hunky-dory up until now, one hundred percent of the time, but looking back on it all, I recognize that, were it not for the trials and tribulations I have encountered along the way, I would never have learned the lessons that not only brought me the successes I have achieved but that also helped me become the person I am today.

The pandemic we all lived through in 2020 most certainly gave us reason to pause and reflect. In some ways it divided us while in other ways it taught us how connected we truly are as the world searched together to try to save humanity from a disease that touched the lives of everyone on the planet. I lost friends because of strong and differing opinions related to politics and the pandemic during this time, and I honestly hope that we will find our way back to common ground, heal our differences, and reunite in the days ahead. I feel more hopeful today than I have in recent years that the nations of the world will work together to tackle the most difficult issues we will face. While it may seem that each of us, alone, is powerless to change the course of history, I am positive that we all have our roles in the destiny and fate of the world.

Whether you believe in fate or that one finds one's own path and determines one's destiny, an important key to a successful and fulfilling life is figuring out what you are truly passionate about. Sure, there are highly successful people, but if they hate their jobs, they are not happy. Then there are those who are happy with very little to sustain them as long as they can do what they feel they were put here on this earth to do. I would prefer to be the latter over the former, though in this day and age, such a choice comes with great difficulties and challenges. The artist who knows she has no choice but to paint, the dancer who must dance, despite his raw and torn up feet, the writer whose words cannot help but spill out on page after page, despite knowing that in all probability, no one will ever read the book—*these* are the people who are living their passions and their dreams and who I regard as truly "successful." It is for them, and perhaps you, that I am writing this book, which is named after a quote from my mentor, Colonel Bengt Ljungquist. He said and wrote, *"The gates to brilliance are surrounded by a cloud of sweat and tears."* Now, fifty years later, I still use his words to remind my students and friends that only with great passion and determination can one achieve success, and even then, happiness may still be elusive. But this is what I know for sure—we were put on this planet to find happiness and LOVE, to share that LOVE, and to leave the world better than the one we were born into.

My hope is that by reading this book, you will be able to relate to many of my own reflections as I look back on my life and that some of my suggestions will help you find your very own path to happiness and success. ●

Robert Dover
WELLINGTON, FLORIDA

Childhood Games

Living with Purpose
by Defining Your Passion

1

CHAPTER

I grew up a very happy kid from a great family in a nice suburb outside of Chicago, Illinois. Our two-story home sat on a tree-lined, if somewhat busy road called Washington Boulevard. The house was typical brick, mid-century style, and big enough for my parents, me, and my three siblings. We had a nice backyard with an above-ground pool, and the neighborhood was loaded with other families—there were lots of kids our ages to grow up with as friends.

Although it was, for the most part, an idyllic childhood, as we all know, things aren't always as they seem.

I had a lot of nicknames as a kid, most of which referred to the fact that I was quite small, relative to my age. "Runt," "Rodent," "Schnunts," "Rocky" (for Rocky, the cartoon squirrel) were the most common. In fact, I weighed a massive 33⅓ pounds until I was six years old! I honestly had no issues with my nicknames and really just enjoyed the attention.

As the baby of our family, there is no doubt I was the most sheltered. My two sisters, Dale and Margo, are three and six years older than me, respectively, and my brother Al is eight years my senior. By the time I was out of kindergarten, Al was already in his teens, playing sports and hanging out with his friends, and because of this, I have very few memories of growing up with him. My sisters, on the other hand, held important places in my day-to-day life—Dale, most of the time, as my tormenter, and Margo as my lifeline when our mother was not there to rescue me from Dale. Poor Dale was equally tortured by Margo and Al, so it makes sense she would take out her frustrations on her little brother.

My dad was one of five kids—three sons and two daughters, all of whom lived very close by, as did my grandparents on both sides. One of my fondest recollections as a child is of Friday afternoons, seeing my grandma and my aunts and their kids coming down the sidewalk, pushing carts filled with food, which the ladies would, along with my mother, prepare for our Sabbath dinner. If you have seen the 1990 movie *Avalon*, you pretty much know the dynamics of our extended family! All the kids would be playing in the yard or in the basement—the older boys talking sports, the girls laughing about boys and the latest fads, while the babies accompanied their mothers to the kitchen. It smelled so good in the house, with chopped liver, brisket, potatoes, chicken, and matzo ball soup being cooked. The men of the family would arrive in time to eat. My dad, being the oldest of his siblings, would carve the meat for everyone, and we would all sit, adults in the dining room with us at the "kiddy table" in the adjoining family room. After dinner, my father and his brothers would retire to the den to loosen their belts, smoke cigars, talk work, and watch sports, while the ladies cleaned up and discussed their husbands and kids.

My great-grandfather, Mandel Dowel, had emigrated from his native Austria to the United States in 1896 and became a citizen on January sixteenth of that year at the Cook County Court in Chicago. His son Sam, my grandfather, grew up to become a very successful businessman, starting DoRay Lamp Company, a manufacturer of lighting equipment for buses and trucks sold primarily by after-market retailers across the country, as well as some manufacturers. My dad, as the oldest child, was to work for the company in any way my grandfather wished; however, Dad's life took a turn (as did everyone's) with the advent of World War II. He joined the Navy and was a gunner's mate on a ship off the coast of Africa and Europe. Like so many men of that era, he never talked much about his time at war, but he was incredibly proud to be an American and was known as a guy who would literally give the shirt off his back to anyone in need.

When he returned from the war, Dad went back to work for my grandfather. He also bought himself a beautiful pinto horse—more of a "parade horse" than what one sees today in Quarter Horses with color. He loved this horse, named "Tex," and rode him daily, taking part in festivals and annual parades. Dad met, fell in love with, and married my mom when he was 27 (she was 19). By the next year, Mom was pregnant with my brother and there was no doubt that, despite his love for Tex, it was time for my father to let him go in order to save the money he now needed to support his new family. Generous and socially conscious by nature, Dad donated his beloved pinto to the local American Cancer Society Auction, and Tex brought in $5,000 for the charity—a huge sum of money at the time. Dad always had an enormous love for horses and dogs—all animals, actually—something I definitely inherited from him.

My mom was a beauty and was "discovered" when she was only fourteen. She began to model and appeared in Off-Broadway, regional plays and commercials, singing and dancing. She also started the Village Players, a theater company in River Forest (where we lived until I was seven) that existed for decades. My mom acted in, directed, and choreographed many plays over the years. She made sure all but my brother Al took part in our local "Backyard Follies." River Forest was a lovely bedroom community outside of Chicago. It was a seemingly ideal place for raising kids, with good schools we could walk to and friendly neighbors. In retrospect, I can recognize it was a mostly WASP, fairly well-to-do neighborhood, in which the River Forest Tennis Club was the town center, housed in a historic Frank Lloyd Wright building and annually hosting the National Clay Court Championships. Just as well known was that the Club, at that time, did not admit Blacks, Jews, or Catholics (with a few exceptions for the latter if they were competitive tennis players).

Nearer to Chicago Avenue, there was more of an Italian community, including members of the Mob. The head of the Chicago Outfit Tony Accardo, as well as Paul "The Waiter" Ricca were in River Forest, and Sam Giancana lived nearby. I remember walking with my best friend David Lemmons, who lived next door and was my age, by a nearby home and wondering aloud to each other why a big man was standing out on the front porch with a machine gun in his hand. Still, we never heard gunfire or sensed fear in our community.

It was not until I was turning seven that my life got more complicated. David's older brother, Dicky, was in his mid-teens, and had never paid much attention to us, just as my own brother had not. Then, one afternoon, Dicky called me, telling me to come over. When I arrived at his house, I asked for David, but Dicky said he was out with their mom. He suggested we play a game and told me to follow him upstairs.

The attention and approval from a teenager felt awesome, and I followed him into his room. Dicky closed the door behind us. Being young and sheltered, I had zero chance of figuring out that I was being manipulated, and when Dicky told me to close my eyes so he could explain the game, I did as I was told. I heard him go into his closet and come out again.

My eyes still tightly shut, I listened as Dicky explained the object of the game was for me to touch the object he had brought out of the closet. If I got it right, I would win a prize. It seemed easy enough. To make sure I didn't cheat, Dicky tied a handkerchief around my forehead, making a blindfold.

"Wait a second," he said.

My friend's brother went back in his closet; when he came out again, he told me to put my hands together in front of me.

I suddenly felt what I thought was a wig...and then something else. Even though I was only seven, I asked him if it was his "pee-pee."

"Absolutely not!" he said, suggesting I keep trying.

I refused and began to take off my blindfold, hearing Dicky quickly re-enter his closet as I did so. When he came out, in his hands were a black wig and a football.

"Wow," I remember thinking. "How wrong was I!"

This was the beginning of six months of such "games."

One day Dicky brought me down to his basement, again blindfolded me, and told me that this time I needed to guess the object that he put between my legs, and I would only be able to feel it if I was undressed. I let him take down my pants.

A minute later I felt something trying to push into me. I was a very small child, and not only was it immediately painful, there was no logical way it was going to happen. I yelled out, pulling up my pants and bolting for the stairs. Dicky stopped me and reminded me of my promise to keep our game a secret. Otherwise, he said, he would have to tell my parents about all the times I was at his house without permission. I was devastated by the thought that I might get in trouble.

That was the last time I went next door. Shortly after, my family moved to Toronto, where my dad was opening a new branch of my grandfather's company.

It was not until I was in my thirties that I decided one day to find and call Dicky and confront him. I did end up speaking to him; I let him know that what he'd done was something that had an effect on my life, and were I not a strong and generally happy person, the scars might have been more traumatic and my life would have had a far different outcome.

Dicky said he had gone into the military, that he now had a wife and two kids and a job at a 7-Eleven. He said he was sorry. And that was that.

It was only in the last few years that I found out that my sister also was abused by another brother from the same family.

Honestly, it was only recently that I learned *most* of the facts about my parents, siblings, extended family members, and friends of my father, and what was happening during my childhood. My older brother Al explained that not only did my dad work for my grandfather, managing the company and opening new branches, he also held the job of "entertaining" members of the Mob. You see, my dad could get along well with virtually everyone, and people enjoyed hanging out with him too. Thus, everything at DoRay Lamp Company ran smoothly and without unnecessary interruptions.

When we moved after my grandfather asked my father to open a branch of the company in Toronto, it was then that I was introduced to horses—more specifically, it was when I had my first ride on a pony. When I was twelve, we were staying in a cottage on Lake Simcoe, a lovely place in southern Ontario, not far from the city. I went for a ride with the girl next door, and that's all it took: I was hooked on horses and riding.

I became as dedicated and focused as a young person can be. By thirteen, it became so obvious that horses were my passion that my parents relented and allowed me to use a thousand dollars of my bar mitzvah money to purchase my first horse. I bet you are thinking, "How could you buy a horse for a thousand dollars?" Actually, the story is even more interesting: Point of fact, mine was the very first bar mitzvah in the history of Freeport, Grand Bahama Island, where my family was now living.

My dad had decided he'd had enough of working for my grandfather and brought my family to Freeport, Grand Bahama Island, to work with a major real estate firm. The only horses ever brought to (little) Grand Bahama Island, up until then, had arrived by boat, literally throughout the centuries, as people from Western Europe and Great Britain sought to conquer and colonize that part of the world. My dad and I had gone to Florida and found the perfect first horse for me: Ebony Cash. I paid for him from my bar mitzvah "geld"—as mentioned, the sum of $1,000! Of course, my new horse then had to be flown to Freeport, which somehow was arranged quite simply and quickly. In retrospect, it all happened *too* quickly, for as the plane landed with my family and friends excitedly standing by, and even the local press on hand to welcome Ebony Cash to his new home, we realized the problem.

There was no way to get him off the plane!

As I mentioned before, neither horses nor other large livestock had ever arrived by air before; there was, therefore, no large machinery for unloading purposes—not even a ramp to walk my horse down.

You can imagine what went on next: lots of screaming, more than a few tears, airport staff looking for any possible way to get this horse off the plane! Could a horse walk down about forty stairs? Nope!

After much back and forth, the decision was to do something that, looking back, is hard to believe. With me holding the hay-string lead and halter attached to my incredibly sweet, beautiful horse, airport staff disassembled the crate he was standing in on the plane and reassembled it out on a very shaky forklift brought up next to the aircraft's door. Now, this crate had no "top" to it, so imagine a tiny corral about four feet wide with five-foot-high walls, sitting out on the raised forks of a regular forklift, which I was told to just "lead Cash out into."

Ignorance can sometimes truly be the best thing! I walked my good boy out into the rickety, open crate, and as Cash peered over the edge, twenty feet down to the ground, the forklift began what felt like the most unsafe, scary descent with literally everyone holding their breath. When we finally touched earth in one piece, cheers broke out.

Ebony Cash spent the next two years allowing me to learn dressage fundamentals, jumping, and the basic rules of polo. We tried foxhunting and even a couple fifty-mile endurance rides. One of my favorite activities was to take tourists, like the winning couple from *The Dating Game* television game show, for beach rides and swims in the ocean. At the time, The Bahamas were a playground for the rich and famous. We were so close to Miami that a lot of people would come for a day. One day the barn owner asked me to take a group of women for a ride on the beach. I had no idea who they were until they started talking. Apparently, The Supremes were playing a show at one of the resorts and had escaped for a little adventure on horseback. No one got hurt and they had fun. Sometimes the horses would try to roll on the beach—lucky for me, that didn't happen that day!

All of this was also thanks to my super first mentor, British Pony Club instructor Myra Wagener. Myra was responsible for not only molding the riding philosophies of all her "kids," but for teaching correct horsemanship in an environment where we truly had to learn every facet of care and be prepared to deal with emergency situations in a place where farriers and veterinarians were not always immediately available. Island life with horses—from that first day with Cash riding down on the forklift until my family moved to Florida a couple of years later—held miracles, nightmares, and everything in between. These early adventures created strong bonds, loving animals as I did. Myra has remained a lifelong friend, and we stay in touch to this day.

My passion for horses and riding showed no signs of waning, though my grandfather frequently voiced his hopes that I would "outgrow it" and follow my brother into law or a "real profession" that could support my future wife and children. Instead, when we moved to Hallandale, Florida, I took the $3,500 we received from the sale of my beloved Cash back on Grand Bahama Island, put $1,000 away in a savings account, and purchased a Thoroughbred mare right off the track from an acquaintance of my dad who owned racehorses.

Learning Moment 101: A fourteen-year-old boy does not need a three-year-old ex-racehorse with zero training and absolutely no brakes whatsoever! Several very scary runaway moments through thick clumps of trees and bushes over the next couple of weeks were more than enough to persuade me and my father to ask his "friend" to take back his mare.

I went out intent on finding a "more trained" horse. A short search and $1,500 later, I had Somerset Son, a horse of dubious talent as well as intellect and zero sense of self-preservation when the chips were down. My love for him, however, and my passion to learn to ride better and train my horse to do more just could not be stopped. I was now part of the US Pony Club and in a local group organized by someone who would become another lifelong friend, Margo Kirn. It would be Margo who introduced me to trainers who would have enormous and lasting effects on my career, such as Alex Konyot (one of the first dressage trainers in the United States and the father of Olympian Tina Konyot) and the man who would become my greatest mentor, Colonel Bengt Ljungquist.

I competed in Pony Club and combined training events throughout the South. These events were comprised of, first, a lower-level dressage test where judges scored Somerset Son and me on our performance of compulsory figures around a twenty- by sixty-meter arena. Once we completed this test, the next task was to gallop cross-country over a series of natural-looking obstacles, which, back then, did not fall down if the horse hit them. Finally, we jumped a course of fences in an arena in a phase called "stadium jumping," which was as much about seeing if the horse still had the stamina to jump (rather than plow straight through the obstacles) as it was to see how beautifully and harmoniously we cleared the fences within the time allowed. I loved all of it! And Pony Club was so much more than just competing. The care of the horses and our equipment, called "stable management," was considered equally important, and I and my fellow club members took written tests to constantly prove we were worthy to move up the levels, from "D" to—eventually—"A."

All through this time life was happening, too, and it wasn't all fabulous.

By now I understood that my father clearly had a problem with alcohol, and shortly after I purchased Somerset Son, he and my mom had a huge fight that ended with her announcing she wanted a divorce. As the baby of the family and the only one still at home to protest, I did so with such fervor that Mom relented and my parents stayed together...for me. (Naturally, years later when they finally did divorce, I was actually thankful and felt very guilty for making them stay married for those years on my behalf.)

With all that was going on at home, horses kept me sane as I felt less and less connected to others my age who did not share my love for animals. I kept to myself until after school when one of my folks would take me to the barn to ride.

When I was sixteen, we moved to Atlanta where I was fortunate to keep my horse in the stable of America's "Dressage Sweetheart," Elizabeth Lewis (now Lewis Page). Elizabeth was the star student of Colonel Ljungquist at that time, who I'd first met through Margo Pettus, which made riding with her even more fantastic. I secured an apprenticeship with Elizabeth, which allowed me to ride her gorgeously trained Grand Prix horses when she was out of town, and I am forever thankful for the training I received in her barn.

But I learned about things other than horses living in an Atlanta suburb back then—for example, I learned I was not welcome at certain parties held for the other boarders. I also will never forget the time my trainer and I pulled up to a gas station, and I was asked to take a picture of my trainer holding the gas pump for a car of African Americans at the next pump. I was most definitely in "The South," and as a young Jewish boy who had lived several years in The Bahamas where I was truly the minority and only trying to fit in and be worthy, I was appalled. I looked up to my trainer and consider him a friend. To this day, I believe he didn't exactly understand that what he was doing was wrong or hurtful. He was simply a product of his own parents' ingrained habits of discrimination, with views all too typical of those shared by so many in the South at that time. I also believe that he is a very different person today and has surmounted great personal struggles. I sincerely wish him happiness.

My parents, at the time, did not want me to make waves, so I remained silent when confronted with instances of prejudice, through those years—and too many after. Fortunately, there were people who did act with love in my life, and they, along with the animals and my family, kept me on the right path toward pursuing my passion.

— Find the Joy —

When asked by young people today how they should figure out "what they should do with their lives," I always suggest they look deeply into themselves, decide what they have a true passion for, and *follow it*. Certainly, they must be realistic and know they may need to do other jobs in order to make their passion possible, but finding and doing what you are passionate about will bring more happiness and fulfillment in the long run. ●

Getting Lost to Find My Way

Producing a Roadmap
to Your Goal

2
CHAPTER

I am famous for having absolutely no sense of direction. I can get lost anyplace. There is a show in Paris I've been to many times, and I know where the stables are in relation to the hotel where I always stayed. But there is one traffic circle that I always ended up driving around and around, at least eleven or twelve times, trying to figure out which exit would take me to the park where the show is held. Invariably, I'd take the wrong exit and have to turn back and go around again. The ten-minute drive always took me an hour.

It can even happen in Wellington where I've lived for years! One client sent me an address to a back gate entrance with a keycode to enter. I drove myself to the gate, but try as I might, the code wouldn't work. Luckily, someone exited as I was struggling to enter, so in I drove...only to find myself in an entirely different—and wrong—gated subdivision. I took a different route to my client's address for the next lesson, figuring there was no way I could get confused again...believe it or not, I ended up in the same (wrong) subdivision.

I *never* had a sense of direction. As eventing and Pony Club rallies became my life in my teens, I was a shoo-in to do well in the dressage arena, but once I broke into anything faster than a working trot out in the fields and forests, all bets were off. It didn't matter how many times I walked the cross-country course—I could pretty well be counted on to get lost somewhere along even the best-marked path, and the penalty points for time faults would come flying off my score!

Finally, when I was a young "A"-level Pony Clubber, our regional super-visor (who also happened to be future Olympian Lendon Gray's sponsor), Mrs. Peggy Whitehurst, took me quietly aside at my last national rally and said, "Robert, darlin', you're really good in the dressage arena, but you were just *not* made for runnin' about the countryside. You need to listen to me and stop this nonsense! Stay inside that rectangle, ya hear?"

Mrs. Whitehurst was absolutely right, and I did listen to her.

As a kid, I did not have, from the beginning, the goal of being an Olym-pic rider. Rather, I wanted to become a great rider and trainer, like my mentor, Colonel Ljungquist, and like other idols of mine: Willi Schultheis, Reiner Klimke, and Herbert Rehbein. I was very lucky to have trainers who "produced me"—early on I had no thoughts other than to follow their instructions and achieve that which they set in front of me as a plan. I was so in love with the process of riding, and improving and making my trainers proud, there was really no time to focus on long-term dreams. With each stage I got to, whether it was within the Pony Club—going from "C" to "B" and finally to "A"—or moving up in eventing or dressage, my goals were to excel and seek perfection at the level I was riding. My expectations of myself were similar in school and in all other aspects of my life. In other words, I was extremely focused, even at a very young age.

Looking back, it seems that my life was more driven by fate and circumstance than by my will or understanding. I also was fortunate to have great parents and other mentors, like Anne Reiley, who was like a second mother and allowed me to live with her and her super family in Virginia for stretches of time. We met the Reileys in Florida where Beth, their daughter who was my age, and I were both riding in Pony Club. My mother and Anne would take turns driving us to the barn, which was about forty-five minutes away from where we all lived. I was immediately comfortable with Anne, who had been an Olympic-level pairs skater (something I admired) and was both fantastic as a kind of "life coach" and an incredibly caring mom. The Reileys moved to Fairfax, Virginia, where they bought a farm on ten acres, and told my parents that I was welcome to come and stay there anytime and for as long as I wanted. To be sure, I took them up on this and was there practically half of each year, from the age of sixteen to eighteen.

Anne, my folks, my trainers, and my friends helped keep me moving forward on the correct path and were always there to push me in the right direction when I needed it.

When I was twenty, I trained at Patience Priest's Sugarland Farm in Poolesville, Maryland, where I had a great group of clients I thought of as friends. I was truly living hand to mouth and working very hard just to get by. With the farm as my home base, I drove my red 1972 MG all around the Capital Beltway to other barns, giving lessons for ten dollars an hour, half of what Colonel Ljungquist charged. I felt that this was fair and showed proper respect for what was clearly the difference between being trained by an Olympic coach and me, a very passionate and hard-working kid.

Inevitably and with regularity, my car broke down or ran short of gas, and I had to use all the money I'd earned that day—or sometimes even had to borrow from a client—to get myself and my car home, only to repeat the whole thing the next day. (Looking back, I would not have traded those times for anything, though I did finally trade in the MG for a nice, reliable Honda Civic.)

One day my client and good friend Ruth Barish and I took a drive down to November Hill Farm in Virginia where Gert Zuther was bringing in German horses to sell. He showed me a bay three-year-old that I instantly fell in love with and then talked about all the way home. I now had the dream of becoming great, and seeing this young horse made me realize that in order to become a top competitor, among the best in the country, I needed just such an amazing animal in my life. Ruth was a no-nonsense lady who was also a genius and not afraid to let you know it. She never hesitated to explain that while I was *fairly* intelligent, I should always remember that she was *extremely* intelligent! On this day her words of wisdom, which ultimately changed my life forever, were: "Robert, you had best toughen up and figure out a way to buy this horse!"

But even back in 1980, "this horse" was a whopping $20,000! The sum far exceeded the little I had managed to save, and I felt defeated and envious of those rich enough to buy top horses and make their dreams come true.

Upon our return to our farm, I proceeded to tell anyone who would listen about our day and the great young horse, "Federleicht," I had ridden, but how I could never afford him. And this is where fate and love interceded in the form of one beautiful lady, Caroline Muldoon.

Caroline was a student of mine. She, her husband Joe, and their three kids owned a string of dressage horses, polo ponies, and jumpers. Caroline always seemed to wind up with horses that other people didn't want—they often bucked her off, and over the years, broke almost every bone in her body, it felt like. But she always kept smiling and continued to love her horses, her lessons, and learning.

She also became the answer to my prayers when she followed me out to my car, asked me how much this super horse Federleicht cost, and proceeded to write me a check for $20,000.

INCREDIBLE!

I was speechless at first, and then promised I would pay her back, which I did over the next year.

Federleicht was extremely volatile, which made him hypersensitive and very trainable—as long as he was comfortable with me. When I tried him, it was pretty cold, and I thought after I rode him that I should throw a cooler over him. Well, just before doing that, I patted him behind the saddle...and we went flying through the air. The first competition I took him to was at the Potomac Valley Horse Show where there was a field of four arenas, marked off as most places did in those days, with white chain. A pretty famous judge and rider at the time was sitting in the judge's booth at "C" (which was the back of a horse trailer), and as I trotted around toward her, the brim on her large hat "flopped," Feder scooted and somehow managed to get his hind leg caught in the arena chain, and we proceed to go flying back to the ingate, the whole arena dragging behind us! The Pony Clubbers came and put it all back together, and Feder, just turning four at the time, re-entered the arena in what was far more of a high, prancing passage than a regular trot. He won his first class, he was so very expressive! And this perfectly illustrates how he was throughout his career.

Feder went on to become the horse that took me to an Olympics, World Championships, and two World Cups. He won the top title in the Western European League, as well as the Grand Prix Freestyle at Aachen (in 1987), where we stood in front of 50,000 spectators as they played the national anthem and the American flag was raised in the stadium. This horse, Ruth's advice, and Caroline's generosity gave me the direction I needed to choose a path toward a dream.

The final thing Feder would do for me was bittersweet. In 1989, I was still living day to day, trying to get by, but an Irish rider, Ite Young, wanted to purchase him and keep him with me in training. I had declined offers from more than a few Europeans for sums close to a million dollars before the 1988 Olympics in Seoul, South Korea, but after competing and placing twelfth at the Games, I decided it was the right time and the right person and agreed to approximately half that amount. I felt the money would truly be life-changing.

And it was.

— Three Ways to Find Your Way —

Today, I get asked two questions all the time:

- *"How can I become successful and make my riding dreams come true when I do not have the money I need for horses, training, and competing?"*
- *"How can I get a sponsor?"*

These are both legitimate questions, especially in a time when a great horse may cost hundreds of thousands, if not millions, of dollars.

I always consider the person who asks me these questions and that rider's ultimate goal, whether it is the Olympics or to be a good professional trainer in a specific area of the country. I explain the hard work, dedication, focus, humility, sense of humor, honesty, and grit required of anyone seeking to be excellent in any endeavor in life. I also emphasize the need to love and embrace the road being traveled—its highs and lows, successes and failures—in order to find true happiness along the way. Finally, I tell it like it is, explaining that there are normally two reasons someone chooses to sponsor a rider: Either the sponsor has an emotional attachment to that person and wishes to help as a parent might help a child, or the sponsor is attracted to the prior and potential achievements of the rider and wants to become a part of that success story.

Caroline Muldoon helped me in 1980 out of love and a belief in my potential. Later in my career, other wonderful people, including Walter and Mary Anne McPhail and Jane Forbes Clark, became my sponsors because they trusted in my ability to make US Teams and bring back medals. This is not to say they did not care about me—they were indeed great friends, but even the best of friends will generally only sponsor someone when they feel quite certain the results they wish will be achieved.

With the help of Mrs. Peggy Whitehurst, I realized early on that I had no sense of direction on the cross-country course. I was exactly the same way when it came to driving my car from barn to barn, giving lessons. My only way of dealing with it was to create a perfect roadmap, one where if I followed it without fail, I would always end up at my destination. Not only did this work for me behind the wheel, it ended up becoming the way I navigated myself and others through life, careers, and toward major goals.

But the question remains, "How do you create a roadmap to your goal in the first place?" A key here is figuring out exactly what your goal is. It took a drive with a friend to look at a horse for my larger goal to really come into focus.

I encourage you to look at the roadmap for your life and your goals in three ways:

• *Determine your goal for each day.* When I get on my horses or begin a lesson with a rider, I already have my plan in place to achieve a successful outcome. With a horse, I have a warm-up that loosens the animal and prepares him for the next part of a training session: *the gymnastics*. Gymnastics entail what I call the "Rubber Band Exercise," which ensures the horse is able to properly lengthen and shorten his frame and strides from back to front (longitudinally) with harmonious half-halts. With the half-halts coming nicely through, I move on to the "meat" of my lesson, in which I work on the predetermined exercises or movements I wish to improve in the horse that day. Successfully achieving my goal, I finish the session by once again loosening the horse and giving him a final stretch and a big pat on the neck and sugar for being so great that day. The point here is to make it clear that *I do nothing without a plan for success, day to day, month to month, and year to year.* I would use the exact same process I just described for training a dressage horse to achieve success in any sport, art, or business endeavor.

• *Determine your short-term goals.* When I worked with the Canadian and US Olympic Teams and their national federations, I created four-year plans with markers *for each year* that I drew out specifically to ensure successful championships, resulting in medals. Having done this for myself as a competitive rider, it was not hard to create roadmaps for these teams. In 2012, before I was hired to be Technical Advisor/Chef d'Equipe for the US Dressage Team, I wrote and shared a post that said if need be, I would drag the entire country, kicking and screaming, to the medal podiums at the upcoming Olympics in Rio de Janeiro. Fortunately, everyone involved with our Team was (and is) so fantastic that we were truly a village with the same goal and desire *to achieve* our goal. And that is exactly what happened. Practically every marker I had set on the roadmap, we met or exceeded.

• *Determine your long-term or life goals.* Say to yourself, "*Here* is where I am, and *there* is where I wish to be at the pinnacle of my life." This requires acknowledging your daily and short-term goals and meeting them (or not) over the days, months, and years you spend pursuing your bigger dream. Long-term goals may change as you evolve. I was sure I was going to be a veterinarian when I left for college, but one semester of organic chemistry and physics made it clear to me that my brain was not made for that kind of thinking. Rather, philosophy and English were both easy for me to excel in. Of course, ultimately, who I became was based on my greatest passion: horses!

Follow your passion, and set achievable and yet lofty goals, and you will be on your own roadmap to success. ●

The Yellow Brick Road

Following
the Right System

3

CHAPTER

My mentor Colonel Bengt Ljungquist used to tell me that we should not think in days or weeks or even months; we needed to patiently think in *years* as dressage trainers. We needed to understand the basic principles of our art and practice them again and again.

I would take my daily lesson with the Colonel and then watch him teach others at Linda Zang's Idlewilde Farm in Davidsonville, Maryland. It was an amazing time for me, a skinny teenage kid, surrounded by our country's top riders and training daily with the US Olympic Coach. I soaked up every minute I could.

One afternoon, just as Colonel Ljungquist was about to leave for a trip, along with his wife, to their home in Sweden, he took me aside near the arena. I had no idea what he wanted as he never had done such a thing before. Looking very serious, he put his hand on my shoulder and said, "Robert, it is your responsibility to remember and teach the people all that I have taught you—the basic principles of dressage—because," and he pointed to the arena where a number of people were still riding, "they are going to forget. Do you understand me?"

I was both flustered and honored, and naturally told him I would do as he said. With that, we said our goodbyes.

I had no idea that it would be the last time I would see the Colonel. While in Sweden, the Colonel and his wife were getting ready one evening to go out to a family event. Mrs. Ljungquist went out to start and warm up the car, and when he didn't come out after several minutes, she went back in and found him collapsed at the bottom of the stairs. He had suffered a heart attack and passed away. Somehow he knew that it was his last trip home, and he would never be coming back.

The Colonel also knew I had spent years devoted to his system of training; not only would I never forget, I would also feel the obligation to teach his methods and basic philosophies of training horses and riders in the art of dressage. I have kept my promise to him, but I have also added many layers to my system, as over the years I absorbed information and understanding from other great horsemen—like Schultheis, Rhebein, and Klimke—and of course, learned from good old trial and error.

From Colonel Ljungquist, I learned that animals and people do best when the rules stay the same from day to day. He would say, "Fifteen minutes of good work is better than an hour and a half of wandering aimlessly around." We would loosen and relax our horses, stretching them forward and down, and then give them a short break as a reward. Next, we would go on a twenty-meter circle and perform the "Rubber

Band Exercise" in all three gaits—walk, trot, and canter: For example, in the trot on a circle by A, near the entrance of the arena, we would ride a half-halt, calling the horse to a perfect state of balance and attention, asking the horse to bend the joints of his hind legs more and thereby increasing the collection of his energy and his frame. For a few strides, that intensified collection would create the appearance of a passage—a higher, prancing trot that is very beautiful to behold. Retaining that collected energy, as we left the wall for the open part of the circle, we would ask the horses to extend their trot, the hind legs pushing off the ground as the front legs reached out as high and forward as they possibly could, still in the same rhythm and harmony as the collected trot before. Upon reaching the wall again on our circle, the next collecting half-halt would be ridden, bringing the horse from back to front, back into collection. We practiced this exercise daily until the horse, like a rubber band, could contract and expand in perfect harmony, with a consistent rhythm and frame. This was the "gymnasticizing" portion of the lesson, after which we would work on a few key movements that we wished to elevate to a higher quality.

Through the Colonel's system, I came to understand that the half-halt was not simply a means to an end but rather the end in itself! If you can always bring your horse to a "perfect state of balance and attention," then all things are possible.

One of the greatest trainers and competitive riders was Dr. Reiner Klimke. He was famous for bringing many horses to the Olympic level and won both team and individual gold medals in Los Angeles in 1984 aboard his wonderful horse Ahlerich. While living in Germany in the mid-eighties, I was fortunate to gain his help and think of Dr. Klimke today as one of my greatest mentors. He taught me innumerable lessons in training, but more importantly, he taught me how to be a top competitor when it came to the more complicated facts about "show business."

On the day I moved my horses to his farm in Münster, Dr. Klimke came walking out of the stables followed by four other people. We shook hands, and he proceeded to introduce me to each of his staff members, one at a time: "Robert, this is my assistant trainer, this is my groom, this is my farrier, this is my vet. Anything that goes wrong when I am not riding my horse in the Big Arena is THEIR FAULT."

Dr. Klimke did not crack a smile, but neither did his staff members look outwardly nervous following this rather awesome statement. This giant of the sport knew very well he had the best team a professional could assemble, and they all knew how integral they were to his ultimate success. His was a system of excellence. It did not include a lavish facility with over-the-top elegance. To the contrary, Dr. Klimke's farm was more of a "public stables" on the rustic and workmanlike end of the spectrum. While I was there with a few other American friends, we couldn't help but notice that the mirrors in the indoor arena were so old we couldn't even see our reflections in them. I decided that, as a gift, we would replace them for him while he was off competing!

Dr. Klimke taught me a huge amount about competing and the press. Those days pre-dated the Internet—we didn't see immediate results from international competition, nor could we watch riders around the world in real time! I came home after winning a show with my horses and was greeted by Dr. Klimke in the stables. He asked what I had planned for my next show. When I explained that I was going back out the next week with two of my other horses (I was very lucky to have seven Grand Prix horses at that time in my life!), he said that would be a mistake and to wait at least two to three weeks until the magazines came out with articles, as they would, depicting my horses' and my success at the show we'd just completed.

"Let the judges read of your wins and your scores before showing again," he recommended, "and you will see how it benefits your next classes."

No one has ever been better at understanding the mental and political part of our subjective sport. It is a "who beats who where" sport, and even today, with all the incredible technological changes that affect how we handle business, competition, and publicity, Americans still have to travel in groups every year to compete against, and hopefully beat, the top combinations in Europe in order to ever contend for the medal podiums. Dr. Klimke's lessons on "becoming a winner" were among the most important parts of the overall system I used for myself and the riders and teams I have coached over the decades.

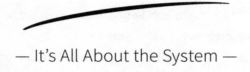

— It's All About the System —

I have known many great athletes from all sorts of sports—naturally, equestrians, but also others in the Olympic "family," as well as top NFL players. I also am fortunate to know people who have excelled in the arts and the business world. I have always been curious about what made these people achieve a level of success that eluded so many others. What were the common threads inherent in their stories, other than what they often say, when asked, was "a lot of luck"? Digging deeper, I have found that, among other qualities which highly successful people seem to share, they all had great trainers who guided them and submerged them in a system, which they then maintained in some form throughout their fantastic careers.

In his international bestseller *Outliers,* Malcolm Gladwell explains that reaching the 10,000-hour rule, which he considers the key to success in any field, means practicing a specific task hours a week for ten years.

In my opinion, I would add to that and say that 10,000 hours of practicing a specific task *under a great trainer's system and observation* will create a successful outcome.

For decades, I have watched and been amazed by how people who diligently practiced and stuck with a system, no matter how counterproductive it seemed to me in certain ways—that is, it might not have been the "best" system—eventually enjoyed quite a bit of success. The old saying, "There are many roads to Rome," speaks to the notion that, provided there are sound basics within the system one is using, sticking with that system in order to achieve consistency over time will, most probably, produce desirable results. If you have a very strong set of ideas, if you believe in it with a good enough horse, it can work. But I have seen those with a poor system, and a lack of conviction in what it is they are doing and what they are trying to achieve, flounder.

I am asked all the time, "What should I do to be as sure as I can that I will be successful?" Whether you are working to become a magician, a figure skater, or an equestrian, my answer is the same: Find and learn from the finest teacher/trainer/coach you can; get the very best magic hat, skates, or horse you can afford; and settle in with the understanding that you truly cannot think in weeks or months *but in years!* Find joy in the daily process of learning and training in your system, including not only the highs from the little and big achievements along the way, but also from the days that don't go quite as you wish, and even from the failures.

The truth is, a great system allows the student to learn from taking chances, many of which will result in failures. It is those failures that finally clarify the path toward success, provided the coach keeps the student positive and open-minded. *A great system provides a pathway, well traversed by those who came before, that—even with the hardships inherent in the daily struggle—will eventually pay off and produce desired outcomes.*

So, what do you do if the system you have chosen and to which you have dedicated yourself—and in the case of an equestrian, your horse—is not working? I cannot tell you how many people and horses I have met in my life where I thought, "If only they had been in a better system, the sky would have been the limit!" In a world where a reality-television personality can become president, it seems pretty much anyone can persuade others that they have the secret to their success, whether it is true or not.

How should you select a trainer or coach, then? First, know that being a novice does not mean you are not good enough or worthy of having a great coach with proven, beautiful, and excellent results. In fact, the most important time to have superb training is at the beginning of your journey. Then, the best way to figure out whether a trainer may be the right choice to help you achieve your goals is to look at the way the individual trained himself. One key to determining if someone is great at what he does is to see if he makes the sport—whether participating in it or coaching it—look very easy, without a lot of unnecessary energy being expended or what I call "noise." For instance, if you are considering taking ski lessons, perhaps look for the coach who makes it look beautiful and elegant while also showing the pure joy that the sport brings. Then, do your research and ensure that the coach is accredited and extremely well-thought-of in the skiing community. Naturally, if your goal is more than just to learn skills—you are hoping to make an Olympic Team, for example—then you should be looking for that rare and amazing coach who has "done it all," offering experience both as a competitor and a trainer of the very best in the world in the sport.

Compared to most people, I had relatively few trainers once I was at a place where I was committed to trying to be the best. However, the coaches I did have, not so surprisingly, were among the greatest of the last hundred years! German Olympian Gabriela Grillo had a wonderful saying about riding and especially competing: "Ride from half-halt to half-halt, movement to movement, point to point. If there is a mistake, toss it out over your shoulder and concentrate on going for the next 10!"

Finding a system that can bring you success is a lot like *The Wizard of Oz*. Dorothy and her companions are told to stay on the Yellow Brick Road in order to safely arrive at Oz. But they are warned that along the way, there will be other paths that look even better or like shortcuts. It is one of those paths, as fantastic as it initially appears, that takes them to the scary forest with the lions, tigers, and bears—OH MY! Many times, the scary or frustrating experiences are the result of not doing one's due diligence when selecting a coach and the system that coach will be providing. No one should have to start all over again after experiencing a failing system, especially one that caused undue pain or bewilderment! I am not telling you that it's a breeze to become great—no matter how fantastic the trainer and how talented you might be, there will be ups and downs and sweat, and yes, even tears. But if all the elements are there: a great trainer, the best equipment (or in the case of an equestrian, horse), and a super system, the chances of success over time multiply exponentially.

Remember, your life is not a dress rehearsal. If you do not believe you are going in the right direction, make the necessary change before it is too late. Find your way back to that Yellow Brick Road and stay on it all the way to OZ! ●

A Rather Silly Sport

Focus, Patience, Humor, and Humility

4

CHAPTER

When I was a kid, there were far fewer things around competing for one's attention. Today, between our cell phones beeping with a call or text message that just must be answered immediately, and the constant bombardment of ads to buy this or that so our lives will have meaning and be "complete," remaining focused on any given task has become extremely difficult, if not impossible. I actually feel lucky that, not only did I grow up when I did, but I was an introvert as a child. I was one hundred percent addicted to horses and riding, and for whatever reason, a perfectionist *about everything*—from school to the cleanliness of my room.

When I was around the age of eight, someone told my parents that I had "special artistic skills" and should be placed in a school for children with such aptitudes. I guess they thought I should paint because the next thing I remember is walking into a new building with a briefcase about as big as I was. That time was short-lived; my one work of art saved by my mother was a small oil painting of a flying horse. Interestingly, at that point in my life, I had not yet seen a real live horse.

My next endeavor was to be the best tetherball player at Camp Timberlane, which I attended in the summer. As I've mentioned, I was a very small kid, only weighing just over thirty pounds when I started grade school. Regardless of my small stature, I was determined that, using technique and timing produced through unending hours at the court, I could outplay even the biggest and strongest of my opponents. And truth be told, I won most of the time.

My focus was next aimed at an activity that was not so much a sport, though I am sure I considered it to be one! It was a game my sisters and their girlfriends played after school, and I honestly cannot recall if it had a name. Two people would each hold an end of a long, white, elastic band that was about half- to three-quarter-inch in width. The goal was to run toward it and leap, one way or another, over it with both feet and come down on the other side—sort of like high jumping with an elastic band instead of a hard pole. Each time the person made it over, the band would be raised to the next level. When you failed to get over, you were "out." Once again, although I was very small, I became technically good and very competitive against even the best of my sister's friends, something about which I was very proud.

My twelfth year, we spent the summer at Lake Simcoe, about an hour north of Toronto. My family had a Wire-Haired Fox Terrier named Skeeter. I loved him very much, even though my siblings had trained him to grab my pants and pull them down, something they all delighted in. One nice afternoon, Skeeter went to the neighbor's, pulled a nice, juicy steak, right off their grill, and brought it home to munch down. The couple next door took off after our dog, with good reason, and ended up in our yard, fortunately laughing it off with my folks. And there was their daughter Donna by their sides, about my age and with a big smile on her face. Well, we became best friends.

Donna introduced me to her world of animals, from guinea pigs and rabbits to a pair of ponies in a small field nearby. She had bridles for them and told me she'd teach me how to catch and ride them.

If you have never heard the term "Thelwell," it refers to a famous British artist and illustrator, Norman Thelwell, who drew many ponies in the fifties and sixties, depicting their intelligence, strong will, and general "orneriness" in what became very popular cartoons. Well, these two ponies were "Thelwellian" in every way. Just catching them could take most of the afternoon and end up with the two of us out of breath and covered in muck. But eventually, we always did get bridles on those ponies. Donna taught me how to jump on bareback, and the learning curve was steep as I tried to stay on while the pony dodged around. He would swerve one way, and I would slide off the other and have to chase him down to jump back on. It took me no time at all to completely fall in love with everything about it.

Donna said she wanted to take me to a "real farm" where they taught riding lessons. My dad, having had his own horse that he loved as a young man, was fine with this idea, and so we were off to Trakehnen Farm, owned and run by Gerda Friedrichs, one of the very first people to import German (Trakehner) horses to North America. To me, the farm was amazing! It had aisles full of horses and an indoor arena where a German man was giving lessons to both kids and adults. I could not wait to be put on one of those enormous animals and learn how to really ride.

I had on blue jeans and loafers, which had been fine for riding the ponies bareback, so the instructor wrapped my skinny legs, from my ankles to just below my knees, with leg wraps, just like the horses had on. I was led to the middle of the arena where a horse with a saddle and bridle awaited. A long line was connected to a leather halter-like thing on his head, which the instructor called a "cavesson."

The German gentleman proceeded to explain to me how to mount my horse. Now, I had been jumping on my pony and thought myself a pro at getting on by now, but much to my surprise, I had been doing pretty much everything wrong, which the instructor made abundantly clear. What was also clear was that my opinions were not being asked for; riding lessons meant listening and doing as I was told. But I was determined to learn this new and fabulous thing, horseback riding, or what everyone at the stable called *Dressur Reiten*.

Once mounted, the trainer explained that I had no need for reins or stirrups because my hands were not even close to being "good enough" to touch a horse's mouth through a bit. I would need to first learn true balance in walk, trot, and canter. And so began months of being on what I learned was the "longe line," going around in circles, sometimes losing my balance and sliding off into the thick sand and shavings which made up the footing below. I had no fear of falling off, probably because I had become quite good at it with the unruly ponies earlier in the summer. Plus, my instructor was teaching me basic vaulting lessons, as well, which when mounting consisted of grabbing onto the horse's mane and leaping off my left leg while throwing my right leg over the saddle and pulling myself up onto the horse. This I had to learn both at a standstill and while the horse was walking—or even trotting and cantering—around the circle, and I loved it! I was also taught to "go around the world," which meant I had to make a complete revolution in the saddle, one leg at a time, and end up facing forward again, and to hold my legs up in a split while keeping perfect form from the waist up and not bouncing in any gait, but especially in the trot. So difficult and yet awesomely fun!

Finally I was allowed to take my first group lesson with reins and stirrups. I was excited and a little nervous as I had only ridden the one horse on the longe line for so long. Out I went into the group of about six riders. Within minutes my horse, seeing another coming near, kicked out, and I heard a *snap* followed by a man's cry. My horse had broken the guy's leg!

I was beside myself, hyperventilating in the aisle after being taken off the horse. I thought I would never be allowed to ride again since I was clearly a danger to others! But nobody blamed me or was angry with me, and my riding lessons resumed.

In the winter of 1980, I was living in Pepperell, Massachusetts, working for an older, very successful, businessman and his lovely, much younger wife. My contract stipulated that, in the spring, I be sent for a month to Willi Schultheis, one of the greatest dressage trainers of the last hundred years, with whom I had taken a clinic a couple of years before on a horse he had trained, Lago Maggiore. Off I went on my very first flight to Germany with one large suitcase, my backpack, and my saddle. I knew only that Schultheis lived in a small town called Warendorf and assumed it wouldn't be that difficult to find in such a little country.

I landed in Frankfurt having spent six hours sitting upright in coach with kids on either side of me screaming most of the night. I retrieved my suitcase and walked from the terminal to the train station below, where I was confronted with corridors going every possible way and signs and announcements only in German. I did not then speak a word of German and quickly became overwhelmed by exhaustion and worry. All I could think to do was ask people I passed, "Warendorf? Schultheis?"

The universe came to my aid suddenly in the form of a sweet little haus-frau, who looked at me and said, "Schultheis? Warendorf? *Komme mit.*"

My savior took me by the sleeve and walked me to the ticket counter where she told the attendant I needed a ticket to Münster. To my good fortune, she was also going that way, so we sat together on the train for the next few hours, silent except for the few times I asked for reassurance that we were *actually* going to Warendorf and not somewhere else, like the place where her "sons" would meet us, tie me up, and hold me for ransom. But each time I looked to her, she would just say, "Ya, ya—War-endorf! Schultheis!"

Eventually, we arrived in Münster, and I obediently followed the wom-an from the train station to the line of taxis sitting outside. With bags and saddle stowed in the trunk, my hausfrau told the driver to take us to Warendorf and then said, *"Emshof."* I sat back, not knowing what she meant but too tired to care.

An hour later, we pulled up to a brick hotel. My companion paid the driver and motioned for me to get out and get my bags. At the front desk, she rang the bell on the counter and yelled, "Heinz!"

Out from the back room came a thin man who greeted my angel lady with a smile of recognition before eyeing me up and down. It would be much later that I learned what she told him next: that I was her American son and spoke no German but needed a nice room with its own bath and a bicycle to be able to get to Schultheis' in the morning.

My German "mother" gave me a big hug, turned, and left. Although I tried much later to find her and thank her, I would never locate her or see her again.

Heinz took me to my room. There was a little twin bed and an alarm clock on the table next to it. He set the clock for seven in the morning. So tired was I that I could not figure out how to get my sheets and blanket out of the white layer of fabric that I thought was to keep them hermetically sealed for my protection. (I had never before seen a duvet cover over a comforter!) Finally, I simply opened the side with the buttons and crawled in like it was a sleeping bag, where I fell immediately asleep.

It seemed like only minutes later that the alarm went off. Throwing on my boots and breeches after a quick shower, I grabbed my saddle and headed for the lobby. To my surprise, there were many people in riding clothes in the next room having breakfast. And there was Heinz, gesturing for me to leave my saddle by the door and go do the same. I was famished and felt so much better as I sat eating, even though I couldn't understand a thing people around me were saying.

When I finished, Heinz took me to my bike and pointed the way down the street, emphatically indicating with his hands that the Schultheis farm would be on the left-hand side. Off I pedaled, trying to keep my saddle from tipping over the handlebars of the bike while watching dozens of people pass me, traveling in both directions, some in riding boots like myself, and others—much older people— seemingly going to work or to shop. I had never seen so much biking in America!

I went by a huge stable on the right, which looked as if it was affiliated with the military. Germany had a mandatory two years of service for those turning eighteen, and if they were good enough horsemen, they could serve as cavalry riders. On the left, another big farm came up, the letters *DOKR* on the sign out front. This, I would learn, was the German Olympic Equestrian Headquarters, the equivalent of Gladstone in New Jersey in the United States.

A little farther down the road I came to the farm of Willi Schultheis and turned my bike toward the barn. The place was lovely and rather new-looking but not over-the-top: There was a sweet house to the left with a garden behind it. On the other side of the drive stood the barn and small indoor and outdoor arenas. A track traced the circumference of the farm—I learned this was for Schultheis' wife, who was a racehorse trainer and quite a rider in her own right.

Herr Schultheis could not have been nicer, greeting me with a big smile and handshake, but he spoke no English. He called out to someone and a young man, about my age, emerged from the barn and introduced himself as Dieter Laugks. A wave of relief came over me as he began speaking perfect English!

I followed them into the barn, where the horses seemed giant to me, until Dieter opened a stall door, and I saw the horse was standing on a week's worth of straw, easily a foot off the ground. It was explained to me that a bale of straw was thrown into each stall daily, and once a week the entire box was stripped completely, and the process would start again. This seemed logical at first, but I almost immediately began to notice all the horses had some degree of a cough, and upon entering some of the stalls, the stench from ammonia took my breath away. The other thing I would see in the coming days was that many of the horses had "thrush," an infection in the soft tissue of their hooves. This was no doubt because they stood in such dirty stalls all day and was probably exacerbated by the fact that they were all shod with "degree pads." A degree pad is put between the horse's shoe and his foot, raising the back of the foot higher than the front, thus taking pressure off the V-shaped "frog" of the hoof sole. Each time a horse steps down and the frog connects to the ground, blood is pumped back from the hoof toward the heart. Without frog pressure, the foot tends to shrink and become "boxy-looking," and thrush more easily finds a home in the hoof.

In other words, Herr Schultheis was the finest trainer in the world, but the stable management at that time left something to be desired.

The next weeks flew by as I found myself in a new routine. Even though I could not understand what my trainer was saying, I would sit in the arena or on the hill above it, watch every lesson, and take in everything I saw him and his riders do. With each day, I was put on more horses. Herr Schultheis would teach me, with Dieter translating, then would disappear into his house or his garden. He loved watching television and working in his garden or on his tractor. As much of a genius as he was on horses, it seemed he had lost, for the most part, his fascination with them. This man could jump on any horse, no matter how complicated, and in moments the horse would be dancing like an incredible star. Perhaps being that gifted made it all a bit boring and predictable.

It didn't matter to me, though. I was in heaven and obsessed with everything I was absorbing. And I learned as much from the horses he put me on as I did from him in the end.

One day, a young man named Michael Ripploh came by the farm and watched one of my rides. He spoke English well, and we quickly became friendly. I enjoyed what he shared about the town—the home for all German Olympic sports, not just equestrian. Michael invited me to stop by his home down the street and introduced me to his charming mother and father—both horse enthusiasts. Michael had several horses of his own, which he kept to train and sell in a private barn next to the DOKR. I appreciated the fact that he came by Herr Schultheis' farm every few days to see how I was making out.

The last week of my time with Schultheis, Michael brought another man along with him. They stood on the hill over the outdoor arena and watched me ride several horses while speaking with Herr Schultheis. Afterward, the man was introduced to me as Ulli Kasselmann. I shook his hand and went back to work without thinking any more about it.

My time with Willi Schultheis came to an end, and I found my way home to Pepperell. I had only been back in Massachusetts a few days when I received a call from Germany in the middle of the night. I picked up the phone, still half asleep, and heard Michael on the other end of the line, saying he was with Herr Kasselmann and they were offering me a job to go work for Performance Sales International's Chestnut Lawn Farm in Virginia. PSI was a breeding, training, and auction business that had been founded in Germany by former German show jumper Paul Schockemöhle, along with Ulli Kasselmann and a silent partner, George Theodorescu (who would coach French, Italian, Russian, and American dressage teams during his career). They thought the United States was a perfect expansion of their business, which was at the very top of the industry when it came to jumpers and dressage horses.

I thanked them both for the call and the offer but explained that I had taken my job in Pepperell only months before and was very happy where I was. (I did not mention I had also recently started dating someone in Boston who I really liked.) With that, I hung up and went back to bed.

The following night, at a slightly later hour, the phone rang and once again it was Michael and Ulli. This time, in broken English, it was Ulli who tried to persuade me that taking the job he was offering would be a good move. I reiterated that I was very happy where I was and, while flattered by the offer, I was not interested. I again thanked them and hung up.

Well, you know how they say "the third time is the charm"? The next night, even later still, my phone rang, and it was Michael and Ulli, and Paul Schockemöhle had joined them in their pitch. As I began to once again thank them for their offer and politely decline, Paul interrupted and insisted I just listen to their offer.

What he described that night became a deal I could not resist: I was offered way more money than I or probably any dressage rider was making at that time in America. I could live near downtown Washington, DC, and commute daily to Chestnut Lawn Farm, just outside the Beltway in Remington, Virginia. I would be sent eight horses from Germany to train, compete, and sell. My two personal horses, Chablis and Federleicht, could come with me and board at the farm for free. And finally, I was invited to return to Germany and select a top Grand Prix horse from their program to have as my primary competition horse and showcase PSI in the United States.

And with that, I was sold and giving my employer in Pepperell two weeks' notice.

Arriving at Chestnut Lawn Farm, I was not disappointed. The long drive, graced with beautiful chestnut trees on either side, brought me to a Colonial-style, brick-and-stone mansion with huge white pillars and multiple chimneys that suggested a time when fireplaces had been needed to warm the many rooms inside. Michael Ripploh met me outside. He had been hired to oversee the sales of horses sent over from Germany by Paul and Ulli. I was introduced to Hans and his family. Hans managed the farm and was to begin a breeding program to produce young sport horses in the United States, using mares, stallions, and semen imported from Paul's farm in Germany. Finally, I was greeted by Teri Rudd, a top international jumper rider and trainer Paul had brought on to train and sell show jumpers.

Teri and I had our own beautiful barns, each with about thirty stalls. Nearby was the indoor arena with a second-floor viewing lounge, all built with cedar tongue-and-groove. The arena wasn't large but it would do! I also had a lovely outdoor dressage arena, and Teri had a fantastic, ten-acre Grand Prix jumping field with every possible fence one would see at the Olympic Games. It was pretty much heaven for horses and horse people.

My two horses—eight-year-old Chablis and six-year-old Federleicht—were already settling in. There were also eight other horses, as promised, that had been sent over from Germany for me to work with and sell. Michael introduced me to each one, explaining age, breeding, level of training, and anything special I should know about. I could not wait to get to work.

It was an hour's drive to my apartment, right outside of Washington, DC, in Arlington, Virginia. My boyfriend David, who had come along from Boston, had already unpacked most of our belongings. David was not a "horse person," and in fact, didn't particularly care for them or the amount of time they kept me away from him. He was just out of college and starting a career in health care. He was cute but very emotional and could be tough when he wanted to be. But for the moment, we were both happy and excited to be starting a new life together.

The next two years, from 1982 to 1984, were full of EVERYTHING! I rode and trained my string of horses, all of which, other than my own two, were supposed to be sold as soon as possible. The problem was that they were either too young and untrained or they were older and had various issues. There was an eight-year-old that had obviously been abused because every time I applied any pressure, he would either rear up on his hind legs or bolt ahead, out of control. Others were so uneducated that they were hard to steer and just needed time. Michael saw this and did not pressure me but rather helped me get the young ones ridden and allowed me space to figure out the others.

PSI had already held a couple of auctions in the two years preceding my arrival at Chestnut Lawn, and now that I represented them at their US headquarters, I began receiving calls from friends and others who had purchased PSI horses. One by one, people told me of their woes—of soundness problems or character flaws—and one by one, I told them to bring their horses back to me and I would see what I could do. I mean, these were my American friends and colleagues, and I could not let them down or not live up to my own reputation or let PSI's be damaged.

People started to regularly come to see and try our horses. Michael would lead each horse down the aisle, explaining how fabulous this one and that one was and how much potential each had. Customers would smile at him and look at me as I tried my best to hide from Michael and either nodded my head in agreement or acted as if I was slitting my throat. I simply could not lie to anyone about horses that had problems, and truly, almost all of them had some! It was not that Michael was in any way a bad person, he was simply a good salesman—and I was most definitely *not*. (Michael is actually a lifelong friend and lovely person who has been in a successful relationship in Warendorf with another great friend of mine, Fran.)

Finally, about six months after I came to Chestnut Lawn, a fairly nice three-year-old was sold to a good rider who loved him—until we found out the horse did not pass the routine pre-purchase veterinary inspection. Michael and I made the dreaded call to Paul and Ulli, who were not happy and demanded to know what had happened. I explained that the vet had failed the horse because his X-rays showed the horse had two navicular bones (a tiny bone located in the hoof).

"Well, all horses have two navicular bones, so what could possibly be the problem, then?" asked Paul, extremely frustrated with me.

To which I blurted out, "IN ONE FOOT?"

The horse had obviously not been examined with X-rays in Germany before he was exported, thus no one noticed he had a congenital deformity in one foot.

So now, between the eight sales horses I'd been sent from Europe and the five auction horses I had taken back for retraining, it was becoming clear to me that this was perhaps not the life for me. Still, things were going well personally: I had found a nice person who loved my little Grand Prix horse, Chablis, and bought him. Federleicht was becoming a fantastic prospect for the biggest arenas, and PSI Romantico, the Grand Prix horse Ulli had given me to compete and showcase the business, was bringing me closer and closer to a berth on the 1983 Pan American Team. I began winning a lot of classes, beginning with the very first Palm Beach Dressage Derby, hosted by Gisela and Howald Pferdekaemper and Janne Rumbough. Romantico was extremely sweet but was not the easiest horse to ride in that his walk and canter were not naturally rhythmic. His walk tended to pace—a fault where the walk becomes two rather than four beats. Additionally, his canter was not very elastic and often became four instead of three beats if I did not perfectly maintain his energy. On the other hand, for that time period in dressage competition, he had a fantastic trot and super piaffe (trot on the spot) and passage (high, lofty trot), and those movements were scored with extra points for their degree of difficulty. I worked very hard to minimize Romantico's weaknesses and show him with clean tests. This effort resulted in our going to the final trials for the Pan American Games ranked Number One in the country.

The final selection trials for the 1983 Pan American Games were held at Gladstone, the official Olympic Training Center in New Jersey, about an hour from Manhattan. Interestingly, the Games, which were being held in Caracas, Venezuela, that year, were comprised of the Prix St. Georges (a test of medium difficulty that would determine the team medals), the Intermediate II (a test two levels harder that required the horse truly be trained to the highest degree), and the Grand Prix (which would decide the individual medals). Because of this, only combinations that were Grand Prix trained were competing for the Pan Am Team over two weekends. Classes were to be ridden like a real show under the strictest rules and judged by a five-member panel selected by the US federation. Of course, our Olympic coach was on hand to watch the classes and discuss the outcome with the selection committee.

Both weekends seemed to go great for Romantico and me with judges shooting me the "thumbs up" as we left the arena after each test. My confidence was high as our group of ten riders assembled in the trophy room to await the news to be delivered by the great Billy Steinkraus, former show jumper and US Equestrian Team President. The US Dressage Team Coach, who was at that time George Theodorescu, stood, smoking his pipe by the door as Billy thanked us all for our hard work and began announcing the members of the Team.

First to be named: Hilda Gurney! I was so pleased for her, as she had been a bronze medalist in 1976 with the fantastic horse Keen, and I knew she would be an awesome teammate on her stallion Chrisos.

Second name called: Kay Meredith! I loved Kay. She also was deserving, and I knew we would have a great time together in Caracas.

Third: Carol Grant! I had actually helped Carol during the week leading up to the competition because her horse, Percy, was acting up, so I was happy for her, even though the announcement meant that, since it was a three-rider team, I would only be the "Traveling Reserve" who comes along in case of injury or illness on the part of another Team member. It was my first ever Team placement, so inside I acknowledged I could live with that.

Then it came: "First Reserve, Dennis Callin!" Denny was my friend, so I couldn't be mad, but my heart sunk a bit lower. At least we could be the two reserve riders in our first effort together.

"Second Reserve, Kerry Schroeder with Marchenhoff."

What?

Wait!

Marchenhoff?

That could simply not be. There had to have been a mistake. I thought to myself, *Romantico could make more points without ever having to break from a trot than that horse!* (In truth, Kerry had done a lovely job of training and competing her stallion.)

Broken, I slipped out of the room in disgrace and fled to my dorm above the garages across the way. I lay on my bed and cried for hours.

My life was over.

Then there was a knock on my door and Pan Am Team member (and former US Dressage Federation president) Kay Meredith came in and sat on the edge of my bed. I have never forgotten her kindness as she consoled me, explaining that my not making the Team bound for Caracas was not because Romantico and I were not good enough, and it wasn't felt that we had under-performed over the last week. She said the decision had nothing to do with my riding, and I would learn the real reasons for the Team selection in the future, but now was the time to pick myself up and move forward with my life and my career.

This was a life-changing moment for me. That day I made a promise to myself that I would never base my happiness as a person on what happened—or didn't happen—in a rectangle where we pranced around on horses while wearing tails, top hats, and white gloves.

The next year Romantico and I were easy front-runners for what would be our first Olympic Team for the Games in Los Angeles, and I found out the reason we had not been named to the Pan Am Team the year before: My horse's gaits might have shown their flaws in the easier Team test (the Prix St. Georges) at the Pan Ams, and this might have been held against me when judged the following year at the Olympics. The decision had been based not on my competitive results during the Team selection trials but rather on the opinion of the Team Coach in consultation with Billy Steinkraus.

But just as it seemed my Olympic dream was about to come true, Paul and Ulli notified me that Romantico had to be sold immediately—and if I didn't find a buyer in the United States, they would find one in Europe. I was shocked when they said they wanted $175,000 for him, as there was no way I had anywhere close to that amount, nor did I know anyone who did. My only hope was to find a group of supporters who might form a syndicate or limited partnership to procure my horse for me. Incredibly, that is exactly what my sister Margo did. With the help of her friend, horsewoman Marnie Reeder and her husband Tommy Beckett, she came up with a group of about twenty people in Texas who generously bought Romantico, enabling us to take our partnership on to the Olympics. (I am sure I have never adequately thanked all of them, so if you are reading this book right now and were part of the Romantico Partnership, thank you from the bottom of my heart!)

Understanding the complex ways the competitive dressage world worked was another "Aha!" moment for me and an important building block in my career as both a rider and a coach. I would, later in my life, as an Olympic coach and a trainer, never play riders like pawns in my personal chess game.

As I have looked back on my life, I recognize that I was not curing cancer or ending world famine. I was riding a horse around a big rectangle with flowerpots sitting on top of letters. Yes, dressage is a beautiful art, but sometimes it is a very silly sport.

Now, understand—I am very grateful for the sport and always gave and still give a hundred and fifty percent to each and every achievement or goal. However, perspective is everything. Sometimes you win when you should lose, and sometimes you lose when you should win, but always you should be humble and keep your sense of humor. These qualities will serve you well throughout life and keep you a happier person. Whether the decision to keep me off the 1983 Pan American Games Team was valid or not, it was not the way to conduct a selection process, and it was a lesson I have never forgotten. Most importantly, it inspired a promise to myself that my happiness as a person would never again be determined by whether or not I made a team. It's great to represent one's country and go to horse shows, but life is short. When you only find joy in the achievement of transitory goals without truly loving the entire journey, you are missing the point of being alive in each moment.

Of course, there are more than a few moments in my life when I sort of forgot how important humility is, only to be jogged back to reality by the universe!

In 1998, I was in Montreal for an international competition leading up to the World Championships. I'd had really good tests with Lennox, a big bay gelding, owned by Kenn Acebal. After the show, I decided to have some "me time" and headed downtown for an afternoon of shopping, a haircut, and a nice meal. I looked up the city's "gay shopping area" and found it easily.

A couple of hours later, with a new pair of jeans and a cute haircut, I strolled down the pedestrian-only street on a gorgeous day, feeling like a million dollars. A few young guys were walking several yards behind me, and I could see they were looking at me and talking with each other and smiling. Naturally, I smiled back over my shoulder once or twice and could not help but think to myself, "Robert, you've got it going on today!"

I spied a charming restaurant for a late lunch and walked in the door. As I waited for the host to greet me, I noticed a couple of good-looking guys at a nearby table who, like the boys on the street, were definitely looking at and talking about me.

"What a fantastic day!" I thought. "I am so hot!"

Suddenly, it appeared one of the guys was motioning for me to come over. I turned around to be sure there was not someone behind me, but for sure, they wanted to speak to me! With confidence higher than ever, I swaggered to their table and said, "Hey, boys. How are you?"

In a very quiet and sexy voice, one of them replied, "Just so you know, you have tape on the inseam of your pants, from the top of your leg to your foot, with 30/32, 30/32, 30/32, all the way down."

I looked at my leg, now realizing why all the guys had been staring at me and smiling so much.

As I sat with my lunch that day, I had to laugh and promise myself that I'd always remember this moment when I was a little too full of myself and the universe put me in my place!

A similar lesson was related to my very bad habit of saying what I think without considering who I might be talking to or where I might be. On one such occasion, I was out with my husband Robert (yes, we have the same name!) and our best friend, Ron Davis, at the Broadway play *Taboo*, about the life of Boy George. As the lights came on at intermission, I began to share my opinion of the show with the others when Ron motioned me to "shush," reminding me that friends and family of cast members might be sitting next to us.

Fair enough.

We got up and went downstairs to the restrooms, and as we stood in the long line, I said, "Well, it's not the *worst* thing we've ever seen. I mean, it's not *Dance of the Vampires*."

Just as Ron nodded in agreement, a very elegant, mustachioed gentleman in a brown tweed suit tapped my shoulder and asked, "So, you did not like *Dance of the Vampires*?"

Confidently, I replied, "Are you kidding? It was definitely the worst show ever produced in the history of Broadway."

The man gave me a long look before saying, "I am sorry you did not like MY SHOW."

Oh my god! How could I backpedal from that? Taking a chance, I put my arm over his shoulders and offered, "I'm sure you've done many great things since then."

"No," he answered. "We lost four million dollars in the first week. It did a little better in Europe, though."

Seeing a free stall open, I rushed into the bathroom and closed the door, thinking, "Robert, you've done it again! Why do you have to open your mouth?"

I waited what seemed like forever before I cautiously exited the restroom and proceeded back to my seat. Just as I got to the top of the stairs, thinking I was out of trouble, I heard someone say, "Dear, that is the man who said he hated my show." I looked at the man and his wife, waved sheepishly, and walked away as briskly as I could.

The universe had more for me, though, when it comes to waiting in lines at restrooms! Robert and I were at a US Equestrian Team benefit in Manhattan at the elegant Asprey jewelry boutique, and they had just auctioned off an original illustration of a horse's head. I took a good look at it, right before heading to the restroom with Robert. As we waited, I said in my usual voice (which, if you know me at all, you know carries extremely well), "I can't believe they got $50,000 for that drawing of a horse head! I could sketch that in five minutes!"

Naturally, a second later, out came the artist, Fernando Botero, from a stall behind us, followed by the gentleman who had purchased the piece, from the next stall over. Robert gave me the look I have come to know so well that means, "I can't believe you have done it again!"

I always say that anyone worth anything in my sport has known the great successes as well as the most difficult of challenges and failures.

In the winter of 1995, having had a very good showing with Devereaux, a big chestnut gelding owned by Suzanne Dansby, at the World Equestrian Games in The Hague the summer before, we looked like a shoo-in for a medal at the World Cup in Las Vegas. We had won a lot and prepared a new and exciting end for our Freestyle, which had helped make us fifth in the world already. Everything was looking good, despite a quarter crack in one of Devereaux's feet that seemed to be under control.

Somehow, during the flight out to Las Vegas from Miami, Devereaux must have stepped on himself and broken open the crack because it was bleeding when we got him off the plane. I had our veterinarian and an excellent farrier meet us the minute we arrived at the venue; together they worked to close the crack and stop the bleeding.

Devereaux passed the mandatory vet check where all riders must trot their horses about twenty meters each way in front of the panel of judges and the official veterinarian from the competition. However, when I rode him, I could feel his hesitancy to step down hard on his foot, and when I stopped after about five minutes, it was clearly bleeding again.

The Grand Prix was the following day, and I had to decide if I was going to try to patch it up and take my chances after all the hard work and expense to get to the World Cup...or go to the organizers and retire from the competition. Devereaux was an amazingly sweet and generous horse and would have certainly tried his best, but I remembered a talk I'd had with gold-medal-winning show jumper Joe Fargis at my first Olympics. "If you do what is in the best interest of your horse, you can go to sleep that night knowing you did the right thing," he'd said.

The press caught wind that we were pulling out and rushed to me for a statement. Without skipping a beat, I told them that, while I was sad that we could not contest the World Cup and knew my horse would have been great, I was not there producing world peace. Even when a competition seemed incredibly serious, keeping it all in perspective was hugely important in maintaining my overall happiness, not to mention the happiness of my "dance partner."

We will all hopefully live to prance another day!

Robert Dover

— It's All About Perspective —

While I could not get enough of riding in my teens, I also played soccer and was one of the better dribblers on my team. This was the way I found I was with anything I set my mind to master. Even while I was spending almost every waking hour that I was not in school at the stables in The Bahamas, during lunchtime I took up playing pool and eventually could not only win most games but also make some rather amazing shots that dazzled my friends. These examples show how focus produces results. (What is also interesting is that I have absolutely no ability to play pool now! Nor could I win at soccer or tetherball if put to the test.)

Focus and the "doing of it" promotes the "doing of it" such that, with proper instruction, you can become good. However, loss of focus or time not doing something will definitely affect your ability to excel at it. Remembering how to ride a bike is not the same as being great at riding a bike!

Becoming proficient at anything requires patience, both with yourself and others. This is when a good coach will figure out a way to instill the understanding that everyone goes through difficult times, and it is actually surmounting these problems that teaches you how to succeed. Negative emotions like frustration cloud your ability to focus on figuring out the formula for success in any moment. Of course, telling someone, especially a kid who is riding an animal with a mind of its own (and sometimes a very stubborn mind at that), to be patient while the horse is literally dragging the kid back to the barn is not so easy. This is where maintaining a "sense of humor" is necessary!

Throughout life, there is no doubt that the universe will keep throwing roadblocks directly in your path toward success. Some of it will indeed be both hard and complicated and even worthy of fretting over. Sadly, there is no life without great loss and mistakes, and nothing I can write here will minimize the challenges you will go through. But just recognizing that everyone on earth has felt or will feel sadness or disappointment at some point can be helpful to remember. For all the things that set us back and maybe even devastate us in the moment, patience, perspective, and maintaining a sense of humor and humility are vital.

So...once you have your long- and short-term goals in place and your roadmap is drawn, stay focused! I remind people all the time that it is very easy to be tempted away from the Yellow Brick Road by a lovely-looking shortcut that seems so perfect but will end up leading you to the scary forest with the lions, tigers, and bears...

OH MY! ●

Scars on My Heart

Loss, Mourning, Grief, and Grace

When I was a child, no one sat me down and explained to me that there was a one-hundred-percent certainty that I would feel the terrible pain of loss and mourning. Perhaps that is one of the greatest hopes of all parents—that their children will not have to learn those lessons until they are much older, if not adults. No doubt, I was very sheltered as a kid, and I can't possibly say how much I love my parents and family for that.

But it was because I had not yet encountered loss that when, at fourteen, I heard my mom screaming at my very intoxicated father that she wanted a divorce, I pitched a hysterical fit. With them and a friend of my mother's in the room, I cried and ranted, making it unbearably clear that I could not live through my parents' separation. I had not the slightest concern for anyone's well-being other than my own, my needs, my life, and how this madness was affecting *me*. In the end, I was undoubtedly persuasive because my parents somehow made up that night, and they would stay together until my freshman year at college.

Naturally, looking back on those years now, I should never have pleaded with them to stay together in a marriage in which my mom was so miserable and my father was enabled rather than forced to face his demons and perhaps find true success. But I, barely a teenager, sensitive, a little insecure, could only see what I was about to lose so was determined to "fix it!" And I assumed I had. There would be no world in which I had to endure loss—or so I thought.

My life continued on as a kind of fairy tale on Grand Bahama Island. I went to school, played soccer, and went to the barn to ride my horse with my trainer, Myra Wagener, who as I've mentioned taught us island kids not only great basics of riding but so much more about "horse-mastership." When you live on a little island that relies completely on importation of *everything*, from feed and bedding to veterinarians and farriers who ensure the horses are healthy and well shod, pretty much anything that can go wrong does, at one point or another. Myra taught us how to pull a loose or sprung shoe, how to use a syringe both intramuscularly and intravenously, and how to deal with colics and injuries until a specialist could get there—sometimes not until days after the onset of the emergency.

Even more incredible, when I think back to those days, were the times when we had to think outside the box because the boat with our bedding or feed did not arrive. Out we went into the forest to collect pine needles to serve as temporary bedding. And I can remember feeding horses bread in order to sustain them until a shipment of grain arrived. Desperate times require desperate measures.

But I also recall so fondly the days we would ride bareback down to the beach and take our horses swimming, sometimes with one of us riding a horse while another kid held onto the horse's tail, literally feeling like he was flying through the clear blue Bahamian water. And celebrating Boxing Day (seeing as the island was a British commonwealth), lounging with our horses on the grass in front of the local pub, jumping them back and forth over picnic tables, and drinking water out of stirrup cups.

It was a magical time in many ways, for sure, until one day my father came home and told us that we had to move to Florida right away. And by *right away*, he actually meant in the next twenty-four hours! During the sixties, constitutional advancements gave The Bahamas full internal self-government, and a move was made by the ruling political party to increase Bahamian ownership of business enterprises and replace foreign workers with Bahamians. They were not going to allow Americans to steal all the best jobs any longer. Some families were given a week to get their things in order, but others, like ours, were given twenty-four hours to leave the island.

My parents told me I needed to quickly sell my horse, Ebony Cash, to someone staying on the island.

I was devastated. I could not understand how I was supposed to give up my best friend ever—suddenly and for a reason that, at fourteen, I could not comprehend, no less. But it was made clear there was no choice, and an arrangement was made with a family whose young son was a friend of mine.

We were off to our new home in Hallandale, Florida. I was, as most children are, resilient in the face of loss, and I was quickly focused on finding a new horse to buy with the money we had received for Ebony Cash. Soon after our move, our old family dog named Skeeter, one day was not there. When I asked where he was, my mom explained that it was time for Skeeter to leave us and that she had taken him to the vet to be put to sleep. As sad as this made me, his being there one day and gone the next did not actually make me dwell on his death so much as his absence from my life.

A year or two later, as I was living with my "second family," the Reileys, in Fairfax, Virginia, my mother called. On this day, I could see the concerned look in Mrs. Reiley's face as she spoke with my mom. As she handed me the phone, she told me to sit down and, "It will be okay."

As soon as I was on the line, my mom said, "Robert, Grandma has passed away."

I could tell she was trying to be strong for me but the shock and sadness in her voice was obvious. She explained that my grandmother had been mentally and physically ill and decided that her life was too difficult to endure. She had cleaned her apartment, put on her favorite nightgown, taken too many pills, and gone to sleep peacefully in her bed without any intention of waking up. I heard my mom say all this and saw the look on Mrs. Reiley's face as she waited for my reaction. Though I was sad, I did not cry. I understood my grandma was gone, but I had not seen her in a long time. Again, like with Skeeter, it was more like I felt only her ongoing lack of presence, not her death nor her anguish that led to it.

Only years later would I gain a better understanding of what Grandma had gone through. She had always been religious and very superstitious. I remember her once calling my mom in the middle of the night to tell her she'd had a dream and not to go near the stove in her chiffon nightgown. What I did not know as a child was that my grandmother had suffered from mental illness for many years—she'd had a nervous breakdown and had to be hospitalized for some time. She was a very sexual person, and after my mom's father died when I was only a baby, her sex life was apparently voracious. But that, set against her faith, which declared all her feelings and actions sins, caused her unending torment. There is a famous "family tale" about the time my grandmother got a knock on the door from an evangelical minister, hoping he could introduce her to his faith and save her from certain hell. Apparently, the outcome of that knock on the door was the two of them having sex in her apartment. (So the story goes.)

When my mom went to my grandma's condominium in Chicago to box her belongings after her death, Mom found a closet where my grandmother had set the icons of many religions—Jesus on a cross, Buddha, and other relics—on a table so she could pray to them all, just in case. Mom told me it was my grandmother's belief that she was about to suffer another breakdown that led her to the decision to end her own life. She did not want to be a burden on her family, and her quality of life was no longer worth her mental suffering. She went to sleep, and just like that, she was out of my life, as if she had gone on a long trip or moved to another country and was not coming back.

I made my first "long list" with the US Equestrian Team when I was eighteen years old. I owned a Thoroughbred I had bought from Elizabeth Lewis by the name of Jonathan Livingston Seagull. With Elizabeth's help and that of the Olympic coach at the time, Colonel Bengt Ljungquist, I trained Jonathan to Grand Prix. He and I would travel from Athens, Georgia, where I was attending the University of Georgia, and Davidsonville, Maryland, where Colonel Ljungquist was in residence at Idlewilde Farm.

It was an amazing time for me, and I thought everything was going my way until Jonathan began having some soundness issues. Arthritis of the area above his right front foot, known as "ringbone," was causing him intermittent discomfort. The vet said that while the ringbone would eventually make him incurably lame and unusable for dressage, for now, good shoeing and anti-inflammatories would keep him comfortable. Jonathan meant more to me than anything other than my immediate family. Truly, he was exactly that to me: my family and my best friend! He was beautiful to look at and wonderful to ride and learn on. He was also incredibly kind and gentle to be around, reminding me of my first horse, Ebony Cash. I was utterly committed to caring for him and keeping him healthy and happy.

Being named to the group to go to Gladstone for an Olympic training session was like winning the lottery. Not only did Jonathan and I reap the benefit of daily lessons from the Colonel, we had the privilege of living on the Gladstone premises for the first of what would be many times for me in the future. (Gladstone became my home from 1987 to 1989—but that's another story.) After returning to Linda Zang's Idlewilde Farm, it seemed like things were going really well: I was asked to be in an exhibition ride with other top US riders for the Washington International Horse Show, one of the most prestigious competitions in America. Jonathan continued to stay sound so I could ride and show.

One day, as I was walking Jonathan after a training session, he began to act strange, striking the ground with his front leg and acting as if he was coming down with colic, which is essentially a bad stomachache. Colic is very dangerous to horses because they are unable to throw up; in fact, it kills more horses than any other illness.

I immediately called my veterinarian but was very relieved to find Jonathan was back to himself well before the vet arrived to check him over. The vet thought it was probably a mild case of gas colic that had resolved itself as I walked my horse during his cool-down. With that, I went back to our normal training schedule.

A few days after the colic scare, I decided to ride Jonathan up the hill to the arena behind Linda's home and work him there. It was such a nice, crisp day. The sky was brilliant blue. t felt like the perfect time to work on the last part of the Grand Prix.

I had ridden about five minutes when Jonathan suddenly stopped and turned his head so that I could see his eye, a look of terror in it. He stumbled but caught himself long enough for me to jump from the saddle. A sound that was more like a scream than a neigh came out of his mouth as he stumbled again and fell to the ground.

I cried out at the top of my lungs, pleading for help, but we were too far from the barn down the hill for anyone to hear me.

I could see a truck pull into the entrance of the farm, and I recognized it was our farrier, Gene Freeze. I waved wildly, and he saw me and came running. Seeing Jonathan twitching on the ground, unable to stand up, Gene told me to get to the house and call the vet. I was hysterical and did not want to leave my horse, but finally did as he urged and ran the hundred yards to Linda's home, knocked hard, and pushed the door open. Linda's mother, seeing the panic in my face, immediately gave me the phone. I cried as the vet's office assistant told me to go back to my horse, the vet was on his way.

Running back to the arena, I could see from some distance away that Gene had already covered my horse's head with a blanket from his truck. I was overcome, in total shock. I could hardly stand.

Gene gently told me there was nothing more anyone could do. He said Jonathan had probably suffered a heart attack and had died before he hit the ground. He told me to go home—that he would take care of it.

Nothing in my life had prepared me for this moment. I drove home to my apartment, sobbing all the way. It felt as though my life was over. I had lost my best friend, my career, my everything.

I QUIT!

Deep in a depression, I spent the next few weeks moving aimlessly around my apartment. I kept waiting for the phone to ring, for me to pick it up and hear the voice of my trainer, Colonel Ljungquist, telling me it was all going to be okay and that he had my future in his hands and would take care of me. That call never came, and I was both angry and disappointed. How could I, his supposed "star student," be cast aside the moment I no longer had a top horse to ride?

Week after week, I mourned the loss of my Jonathan, moping around the apartment and not going out unless I had to buy food. After about three months, I realized the only person who was going to pick me back up was myself. I missed the horses and my friends from the barn, and I knew it was time to get my act together. I had to start all over again to find horses to ride, and I needed to begin giving lessons again.

I was warmly greeted by everyone back at Idlewilde Farm. They consoled me, acknowledging my loss and asking where I had been so long. Colonel Ljungquist gave me a pat on my shoulder and told me to get on with my riding. He also said he knew someone who might purchase a Grand Prix horse for me. I felt excitement build once again as he explained that his friend Eric Lette, National Champion of Sweden, was selling his top horse—Aintree, a chestnut Swedish Warmblood with lovely movement—and that we should immediately go try him. I asked the price and was floored when the Colonel told me the gelding was a whopping $30,000! It was unbelievable to me that someone would consider spending that much money on me. Colonel Ljungquist said we would leave the following Monday to try Aintree, as Eric was actually showing him this weekend.

This horse was hopefully a perfect "next step" for me. I was so excited over the weekend, preparing myself for my very first trip abroad, to try a Grand Prix horse and an expensive one at that, no less. (It is hard to imagine that the same $30,000 for an international Grand Prix horse, ten years of age and the Swedish National Champion, would be between one and five million dollars in today's market!) I arrived early to the farm on Monday morning, packed and ready to go, to find the Colonel in the arena...and the first thing he said to me was that we could forget going to try Aintree. Apparently, that weekend, Eric had ridden the chestnut down the centerline in the Grand Prix and the horse had blown up and bucked him off. So much for that horse. (Point of interest: Aintree was sold by Eric soon after to a Swiss rider who made the next Olympics, held in Los Angeles, with him.)

I was as disappointed in not having a first adventure across the ocean as I was in not getting to try the horse, but I was not without options. I had recently received the ride on not one but two very nice horses: One was an interesting gelding named Apollo and the other was more of a project owned by a fellow Grand Prix rider, Linda Oliver. Both horses were in Great Falls, Virginia, a lengthy commute around the Washington Beltway from Hyattsville, Maryland, where I was living.

The lady who bought Apollo for me to ride ended up being more difficult than the horse was worth it to have, and that partnership came to a close. Linda's gelding, Blue Monday, was quite difficult mentally, and so that also did not go anywhere, but I was growing a bigger clientele and riding a lot of horses for other people. Eventually I was offered a place to train out of in Poolesville, Maryland, called Sugarland Farm. Owned by the Priest family, the mother had a large landscaping company and her daughter, Patience, was an aspiring dressage rider. It was a perfect situation to reboot my career so that I would no longer have to travel one hundred and fifty miles around the Beltway each day, teaching people at their homes. The farm had a big barn, a new indoor arena, and plenty of acres to hack on. Patience and I set out to run the business as partners, buying young horses and selling them, as well as teaching and training. She had a few horses already and each day began with her lessons.

At this time, I was living with two new roommates in Alexandria, Virginia, both of whom were young, gay guys. I kept that side of my life private, even from Patience. It was 1979 and I was afraid that coming out would destroy my business and my career, and things were finally going way too well in my life to risk wrecking it. Every day, I would do my teaching and training, and each night, I would have my "other life," going out in downtown Washington, DC, with my roommates, Rick and Richard. My two lives were completely separate. Being a true Gemini perhaps made it easy for me.

Patience and I had sold a few horses when we heard that a super Grand Prix horse was for sale by Karen Stives, a former Olympic eventer who had turned to dressage. She had purchased the gelding, Lago Maggiore, from Willi Schultheis in Germany but was not going to pursue her career further and was therefore selling the horse. Patience and I took the trip up to Massachusetts to try him and fell immediately in love. A cursory vetting told us the horse was in good shape for a thirteen-year-old, though his teeth were badly worn down, so much so that we could only go by Karen's word in terms of confirming his age, since the horse had come to her without registration papers. He was black with a little white on one leg and a star and stripe on his face. Even more important, Lago was very sweet and very well trained, even if a bit on the dull or cold side.

It was so exciting for me to suddenly have this wonderful horse to ride—a horse that could even, if things went well, possibly try out with me for the 1980 Olympics!

At this point, the only other horse I was riding at that level was a horse that Linda Zang had given up on named Glen. Glen was a sweet but very difficult horse to train, partly because he was very spooky and also because his conformation made him complicated, especially for anyone lacking in physical strength or a great deal of experience. All that being so, I was very grateful to Linda for giving me the ride on Glen after I lost Jonathan. I had entered him into our, and my, very first Grand Prix, the most difficult dressage test used in Olympics and World Championships.

I did this knowing that I had still never been able to do one of the most challenging movements in the test: fifteen one-tempi changes on the diagonal, which is where the horse looks like he is "skipping" in the canter. Just days before the show, I looked up and prayed for Glen to learn this very complex movement. As if God was listening and granting me a miracle, that very same day we actually got all fifteen ones—and had them clean from that day forward.

With Glen and Lago, I thought I might have a real chance at making the Team.

Soon, however, I figured out Glen was just too spooky and difficult for my Team goals, so I pushed myself and Lago in preparation for the Selection Trials. I did pretty well in a couple of classes, though I admit to being exhausted halfway through the Grand Prix. Part of the reason for this was nerves: I was a young competitor in my first year of doing this extremely hard test and tension compromised my breathing. When an athlete, two- or four-legged, loses his breath because of nerves, oxygen is depleted in his muscles and cramps ensue. I remember getting to the walk in the middle of the test and having to take my foot out of the stirrup to stretch my leg as I was in agony with a terrible cramp in my hamstring.

As it turned out, Lago and I did well enough to be the Second Reserve Rider for the Team, and I was very happy with him and knew he would do even better the next year.

That summer, Dieter and Liz Felgendreher invited me to bring Lago for a clinic with Willi Schultheis—it would be the first time I met the man I thought was the greatest trainer of the century, and I was incredibly excited, especially riding the horse he had trained himself to Grand Prix! Lago and I arrived at the Felgendrehers' beautiful farm in Kentucky. I had brought one of my best friends, Simon Barber, along with me to help with the driving and grooming. Simon was a sharp trainer and a true horse lover. He was also a real character—he had a thick head of curly blond hair and a voice octaves higher than most boys who have gone through puberty. Simon was hilarious and always the life of the party.

Both days of the clinic went extremely well; though Herr Schultheis spoke no English, Dieter Laugks, who had been a long-time student of his in Germany as a young man, translated everything he said into English for the riders and the audience. I was happy and proud of my horse and myself. With Dieter next to me, I asked Herr Schultheis his opinion as to what to do next. He smiled and just said Lago was still looking good for his age. A little confused by that statement, I replied that, at thirteen, my horse still had many good competitive years ahead.

Herr Schultheis laughed and said, "Thirteen? That horse was already fourteen when he was sold to Karen six years ago."

I stood there, hearing what Willi Schultheis was saying but not really grasping it. Lago Maggiore, my lovely black gelding who I had been pushing so hard to get to the Olympics, was actually twenty years old, not thirteen?

It is difficult to recapture all the feelings and thoughts that were going through my head at that moment: Angry for being lied to. Stupid for not figuring out that the reason Lago's teeth were only nubs was that they had been filed down by whomever in Germany had sold him to Karen Stives. (Filing down the teeth or "bishoping" is done so that even a veterinarian cannot tell a horse's age by looking at them.) Embarrassed that I had not known the truth. Guilty for pushing this kind, old horse around the arena for my own ambitions.

At the end of the day, I learned a huge amount from Lago, who then went on to teach Patience Priest the Grand Prix and lived into his thirties. At a clinic at Patience's farm, many years later, I was teaching in the indoor arena and in walked Lago, the big black horse now white from his shoulder to the tip of his nose from advanced age. He was allowed to be at total liberty on the farm and walked right up to me, looking for a treat.

As always, I had a lump of sugar in my pocket (because you can't train a seal without fish!), which I gave to him. He nuzzled me for a minute, looked around, and strode nonchalantly back out of the arena to roam the farm and graze. That was the last time I saw him, but like all the horses in my life, I have great fondness in my heart for him to this day.

Living near Washington, DC, I continued to have my two separate lives—by day I was extremely dedicated to and focused on my riding and training career, while at night I was out with my friends at the gay bars. Meeting guys was not easy for me, a skinny, Jewish kid, with long, curly, black hair, a big nose, and a huge space between my two front teeth. While I would stand against a wall, too shy to speak with anyone, my best friend Rick would walk once around the bar and pick up the cutest guy in the room. Rick was also skinny, but he had a super personality and was fearless and self-confident around the boys. He was also a practical joker and troublemaker.

The fashion fad one winter was ultra-long scarves, tied once around the neck and then allowed to fall practically to the floor. One night Rick came running over to me at my usual spot against the wall and excitedly told me to watch the tall drag queen across the dance floor, standing next to a cocktail table covered with people's drinks. Unbeknownst to the drag queen, Rick had tied her scarf to the bottom of the table.

The next song came on, and naturally, it was a great one. The drag queen, hearing it, got very excited and took a huge step forward toward the dance floor...and as she did, down came the cocktail table with the thirty or more drinks with it. Screams ensued, as well as laughter, especially from the devilish Rick, who took my hand and we ran out the door.

As fun as that time was, it was also the beginning of the end of our carefree, gay life. It was 1982.

One night I met a very cute guy at the bar and brought him home. When I began to kiss him, he stopped me and said he needed to tell me something: He had flown into DC that day from California for an appointment at the National Institutes of Health. He had some sort of rare blood disorder that was attacking his immune system, and they wanted to see him there to try to figure out what it was and how to deal with it. He told me he really wanted to be with me but was afraid to have sex in case his condition might be contagious. I could tell he was scared, so we just cuddled, and I held him through the night. The next day, he left for his appointment, and I never heard from him again.

A month later, I found out the roommate of a boy I was dating was going to a specialist because he had strange lumps on the back of his neck and his primary care doctor had no idea what was causing them. The next day, he called and said he was going home to his parents...and that was the last time any of us spoke to him.

Of course, this was the beginning of the HIV/AIDS epidemic that would take so many of our friends and loved ones far too early. There was no place I could go without hearing that this person was now sick and that friend had died. Those first couple of years, it was still not understood that the "gay plague" was being spread by unprotected sex, and most guys were not wearing condoms. By the time everyone really understood the dangers of the disease and how to protect oneself from transmission, it was 1986.

That summer, I competed my horse Federleicht in the World Championships in Toronto with dismal results, placing thirty-sixth out of approximately sixty riders. German Olympic gold medalist Gabriela Grillo had come to spectate and was kind enough to tell me afterward how much she thought of me and my lovely horse. Gabby told me I was welcome to come to her farm in Mülheim to train with her. I had very little money saved up at the time, but I was determined to change my life and finally learn how to become a winner, so I began to figure out how I could make it happen: I had four or five clients who agreed to pay my training fee and the expenses to send their horses over. I won a spot to represent the United States in the upcoming World Cup, which just so happened to be taking place less than an hour away from Gabby's farm. This meant I would also receive a grant from the US Equestrian Team to take my horse to Europe.

My boyfriend at that time, David, was also a dressage rider. (He was my fourth David in a row; the one before him, I had broken up with right before the Los Angeles Olympics.) David had found a promising young horse and wanted to take him along to Germany.

Right before we left, I received a letter from an old acquaintance with a page from a Fort-Lauderdale-based gay magazine called *Hot Spots*. The page was an obituary of a handsome young man who had been a bartender at a local club. My heart sank as I recognized this guy who I had slept with one time. I did not even remember his name, but I remembered enough to break into a cold sweat. My life, and everything that I was so excited about, could very well be over. At that time, a diagnosis of AIDS was a death warrant. There was no cure for the disease that ravaged the body in the most gruesome ways imaginable. My fear of dying rendered me incapable of getting tested. The dread of knowing overwhelmed my will to find out. I could not bring myself to tell anyone, not even David, what I was going through. I was a ticking time bomb. Every waking hour I was waiting for a symptom to show: a lesion on my skin, a bad cold that would surely lead to pneumonia, a sudden clouding of my eyesight, or all of the above.

Just before we were scheduled to return to the United States in 1988, I broke down and told David what I had been going through. He, as usual, was not overly emotional and barely reacted. Other than explosions of his terrible temper now and then, our relationship had grown pretty cold, and we had never been terrific communicators with each other anyway.

A few weeks later, the day before we were to fly home with the horses, David walked into the house and dropped a sheet of paper in front of me.

"There," he said. "If I am not positive, you are not either."

On the table in front of me were negative HIV test results. After five years of our relationship, admittedly most of which was not happy, David had given me the best present I had ever received since my mother gave birth to me. He had given me back my life.

After two years training in Germany, David and I had no place to go when we returned to the United States, but because I was a Team rider, the USET allowed us to temporarily live at Gladstone in the apartments over the garages while we looked for a new place of our own. Knowing David's test results, I now finally had the nerve to go to a clinic and get tested myself, and of course, I was negative. That day, I promised I would give back to those less fortunate who were fighting to survive. You could not open a gay magazine without seeing multiple obituaries, all for people who should have been in the prime of their lives.

Then I received the news that my great friend Simon Barber, who had accompanied me and Lago to our first Schultheis clinic, was ill. His family had turned their back on him years before, but fortunately, he had a wonderful lady friend who had taken him in. She told me Simon did not have much time, so I went to see him.

Walking into his room, I found Simon, hardly more than a skeleton, his normally high, cheerful voice now a whisper. He told me was taking drugs that he was sure would make him well again, but I could see in his eyes that he knew he was dying and did not have long. He asked me all about my riding and travels, and for a moment, as I told him about Germany, I could see the light come back in his eyes. But then he was exhausted and wanted to sleep. I hugged and kissed him goodbye.

Simon died a week later.

While I was in Washington performing a demonstration ride following the Seoul Olympics, I called David Number Three, a short Italian guy I had broken up with in 1984, because his mother had reached out and told me he was HIV positive. David began crying on the phone and asked if I would come meet him in the city. I drove to his neighborhood in Dupont Circle, and the minute I walked into his apartment, he burst into hysterics. He told me he was sick, that after I broke up with him, he'd started to go out to the bars and bath houses and have unprotected sex. He said he'd known it was dangerous by then, but he hadn't cared. I felt devastated as I saw the fear in his face.

David told me he was moving back to Boston to live with his family and that he hoped a cure would come soon. But there was no cure. David died within months of Pneumocystis pneumonia (PCP), an infection related to a weakened immune system from HIV.

At this time, I was living in Wellington with a wonderful man and my future husband, Robert Ross. We felt we had to do something as we were literally losing friends every single day. In addition, many of our horse friends had no insurance and could not afford the very expensive care needed with an AIDS diagnosis. This would inspire the founding of The Equestrian AIDS Foundation with the help of other community-minded friends, an organization providing financial assistance to people in the horse industry who were stricken with AIDS.

My mother had breast cancer for the first time in her forties. She had a complete mastectomy and was pronounced healthy after five years.

During the seven years my parents were divorced, each got married again—my mom once and my dad twice. None of those marriages worked out, and when my parents met each other again at my brother Al's wedding to his sweetheart, Lynn, they decided to get back together. I guess they thought a life spent bickering with each other was better than one spent alone. They lived in Hollywood, Florida, and had many wonderful friends, but were especially close to one couple: Norman and Mercedes Dubin. Dad and Norman were best buddies and both heavy smokers until Norman became ill with emphysema and died a very painful death. My father was so affected by his close friend's passing that he never picked up a cigarette again.

At seventy-one, my mother was diagnosed with precancerous cells in her remaining breast, and the oncologist felt the safest route was a second total mastectomy. After so many years since she'd lost her first breast, the surgeons now told Mom they could rebuild both breasts if she wanted, but at 71, she explained she just wanted to be healthy.

I took my mom for her pre-op appointment the week before her surgery was scheduled. Everything looked like a "go," though the doctor noted a small shadow on the X-ray, which he attributed to the needle biopsy having left a little blood behind. My sisters and my brother flew into town to offer their support, and it was nice to see everyone together, laughing and happy following the successful surgery.

Two weeks went by quickly, and I brought my folks to my mother's post-op appointment with the oncologist. He told us that her breast looked great, and they had "gotten it all," so she was free to go home and enjoy the rest of her life. Overjoyed, I got up with my parents to leave. As an afterthought, I asked about the small shadow the doctor had mentioned during the pre-op. He admitted he had totally forgotten about it.

"If you want," he said, "we can run a scan just to make sure it was nothing, but I'm not worried."

The next day, I took my mom for the scan. Several days later we were called into the oncologist's office for the results. He sat across from my mom and dad while I stood as he read off the radiologist's findings as if he were reading the weather report.

"Jean, you have non-small cell lung cancer that is in stage four and has metastasized to your lymph and bones. I would say that you have approximately three months to live."

What the fuck? I had aunts and uncles on my dad's side of the family who were smokers, like him, who had died of lung cancer, but my mom had never smoked a day in her life.

I got my emotions under control, and then told the doctor in no uncertain terms that his answer was the wrong answer and he was fired. I led my shocked parents out of the office and told them we would go back to MD Anderson, a leading cancer research and treatment hospital in Texas where my dad had undergone successful aortic aneurysm surgery a few years earlier. I booked an appointment with their leading oncologist two weeks later and set about learning as much as I could about non-small cell lung cancer. My mother was everything to me. Being the baby of the family and her gay son meant somehow that we shared an indescribable bond.

While looking online for the most cutting-edge therapies, I ran across a drug called IRESSA®. It was not conventional chemotherapy and had only been found to be effective in a small percentage of the population. But the thing was, it had proven helpful in about ten percent of those who were administered it, and all of that ten percent were ethnic women. Well, my mom, female and Jewish, met both those criteria.

The first miracle that followed was that when I told my friend Clark what my family was going through, he informed me his mother was actually a scientist working at AstraZeneca, the company that created IRESSA. At my request, he called her up, and with her help and after seeing the specialist at MD Anderson, my mother started on this experimental, once-a-day pill. Less than six months later, not only was she in full remission, the cancer that had spread to her bones had died off and was being filled in by new healthy bone! We did not know how much time she would have before the drug was no longer helpful, but we were ecstatic nonetheless.

Then there was my dad. During one of our trips to Texas, my sisters were the first to leave MD Anderson for the airport to fly back to Austin, where they both lived, not far from each other. As the rest of us began loading bags into another taxi, Dad asked where the girls were.

"Aren't they coming with us?" he said.

I told him his daughters had left an hour ago. I reminded him they had kissed him goodbye. My dad shook it off and got in the car. But that was the beginning of the long and extremely sad end that is called "Alzheimer's."

At first, it was little things, forgetting he had asked a question or told a story. At seventy-five, forgetting things seemed sort of normal, though, so we did not think anything of it. But as my mom began to feel stronger, she also realized that my dad's problems were more serious. She was the one who told me we needed to take Dad to his doctor. My father had seen the same family physician for many years and had great faith in him, so we went there first. The doctor spoke with my dad for about fifteen minutes and did a basic cognitive exam, then reported that he did not think there was much to worry about. Sadly, over the next few months, things continued to worsen, and finally we took my father to a specialist, who confirmed the beginning of Alzheimer's and put Dad on a couple of medications known to slow the process. The good news was that he did not have what is called Early-Onset Alzheimer's, which progresses much more quickly, killing off brain cells and robbing people of their memory until they no longer know how to do the most simple things—even swallow. This horrible form of the disease can be terminal within three to five years. My dad's disease advanced far more slowly, and it wouldn't be until later, when he was about eighty, that we determined it was time to take away his car keys.

Those first months after my mom's diagnosis and my dad's gradual mental decline, I began to mourn, even though they were still with me. I mourned as I had when I lost Jonathan, my favorite horse from my younger years, and as I had with the decline of my two beloved Jack Russell Terriers, Half-Halt and Pirouette, both of whom lived to be nineteen years old.

Half-Halt was a very tough little guy who was prone to attack anything five times his size and had almost been killed several times when he did. Still, he managed to grow old, outlasting several of my boyfriends and finally loving Robert almost as much as he did me. For many years, my prayers were answered that he would stay healthy and well. (I am not very religious but have always prayed to the universe to keep my loved ones, two- and four-legged, healthy and well. In return, I promise that I will do my very best to make the universe and my loved ones proud of me every day by doing good deeds and spreading LOVE! I continue this prayer today.) But eventually, age caught up with him.

I called my veterinary specialist and asked if there might be one more miracle in the cards for Half-Halt. After a pause, he said, "Robert, Half-Halt is nineteen years old! That already is a miracle!"

I walked into the vet clinic with Half-Halt, no longer able to walk or stand on his own, in my arms. My vet looked at me, my face no doubt telling him of a sorrow he had seen countless times before.

"Robert," he said. "Give me Half-Halt."

I hesitated but held my dog out for him to take. As he lifted Half-Halt from my arms, he told me to turn around and walk out of the office. He knew I could not stand to watch what was going to happen next.

Until that moment, with the people I had lost and my horse who had passed away, tragedy happened "to me." This was something so different. I was making the decision to end my dog's life. I was crushed by the weight of this choice and sobbing as I got back to my house where Robert and Pirouette waited, knowing I was inconsolable.

I will never forget that night, as I was trying to stop crying long enough to fall asleep. I prayed to the universe for a sign that Half-Halt was okay, and at that very instant, Pirouette, curled on the bed near my feet, began barking in her sleep, her paws moving as if she were running and playing. Her dream lasted a few minutes and soothed my sadness, actually putting a smile on my face and making me feel I would be all right after all.

Five years later, we were living in Wellington, Florida, and Pirouette had reached the age of nineteen herself—no less a miracle than Half-Halt, having had two hip surgeries and lost her hearing and sight. One day she was standing near me when her hind legs seemed to slip out from under her and she fell on her side. Just as quickly, she was back up on her feet, but I knew something was seriously wrong, and off we went to our vet, the incomparable Dr. Richard Ringler. "Doc" Ringler was famous in Wellington for a lot of reasons, most importantly that he had kept more dogs alive than any other vet anywhere. He was also built like a beanstalk, standing well over six feet, and had the greatest personality anyone could hope for. He truly loved every single pet that came in his door and would go to any length to keep them happy and healthy. He was also a radical Democrat, and he and I would go crazy together, working over the politics of the day.

Doc looked at Pirouette and could not find anything in particular wrong. He took X-rays and blood and did an ultrasound but nothing unusual popped up. Hours later, the clinic was about to close and my dog and I were about to head home without answers when suddenly, she did it again—Pirouette's hind legs slipped away from her, and she was on her side and right back up a second later. Luckily, Doc saw it happen.

"Oh my god!" he said. "Hold on while I get the EKG machine. I think I know what's going on."

Doc determined that Pirouette was having heart arrhythmia. He got on the phone with the same specialist who had replaced her hips, Dr. Rob Roy, and after what seemed like hours but was only a few minutes, he ended the call and turned to me.

"We have one option," he said. "Dr. Roy can operate in the morning and put a human pacemaker in her to regulate her heart beats."

I was told this was the first time in Florida, and actually one of the first times in all of America, that such a procedure would be tried on a dog. Interestingly, once a pacemaker has been used in a person, that particular device can never be used again on other people, and so, in rare cases, used pacemakers find their ways to veterinary clinics. And sure enough, the next morning Pirouette was given a new lease on life, her heart soon ticking away again in perfect rhythm.

I thought about how much she'd enjoyed the pram I'd bought to get her and my bags to our place on Fire Island, New York, the summer before. It had just been too hard for her to walk on the boardwalks, what with the cracks she would constantly get her paws stuck in. I didn't care that Robert and my friends acted like they didn't know me as we got off the ferry in The Pines. There were plenty of boys who, thinking I was a daddy with a baby (very hot!), came up and asked to see the infant within. I smiled, pulling back the hood on the pram, and there was my canine child, asleep on her back with all four legs up on the air.

Thanksgiving Day in Wellington, we were going to celebrate at our home with a big group of family and friends. Pirouette was by the kitchen door, asking to be let out into our large yard, and I let her out as I always did. She never roamed farther than the grass that ran a few feet along the side of the house. At that moment, the doorbell rang. I looked at my dog, standing there next to the house, and then ran to see who it was. There was a package delivery that I quickly signed for and carried with me back to the kitchen, only to find that Pirouette was not where I had left her outside the door.

I was filled with terror as I yelled her name, knowing perfectly well she could not hear me, and went running around the side of the house, my eyes scanning frantically for any movement that might be her. Then...I saw her body through the water...at the bottom of our pool.

Without thinking, I dove in, grasping her lifeless body and carrying her to the surface. I desperately began giving her CPR, but at nineteen, Pirouette was never coming back.

The guilt I felt for allowing my beloved pet, deaf and blind and utterly reliant on me, to drown was more than I could bear. I wrapped her carefully in a blanket and found a box that I laid her into. Then I dug a grave under a pine tree in the backyard and buried her there.

Numb and sick inside, I went into my home, packed some clothes in a bag, and left before anyone arrived for our Thanksgiving celebration.

As my family and closest friends heard about what had happened, my phone began ringing nonstop. My mother pleaded with me, as did the others, to come be with them, but I simply could not cope with speaking to anyone, much less joining them in my home for Thanksgiving. I had never felt, even from the other losses I had experienced, the kind of incredible guilt I was experiencing. I did not feel that I deserved their love or condolences that day.

Over time, I came to recognize that Pirouette had been on borrowed time; she was most probably only days away from passing naturally when I lost her. Still, the scar on my heart from that day will be with me for the rest of my life.

Robert's father, Aaron, had survived a heart attack in his forties, not long before divorcing Robert's mom. At the time, Robert and his half-brother, David (they have different fathers), were in their early teens. (Robert also has a half-sister from a different mother who is slightly older than both boys.) Upon his parents' divorce when he was ten, Robert had to grow up quickly and assume many of the responsibilities of an adult. He took the California High School Proficiency Exam when he was sixteen and went right to college. When he had completed three semesters, Robert moved to New York with his boyfriend Randy to run a large printing and advertising company. Randy was a professional ice skater in a successful touring company, and the two of them went to Seoul, South Korea, for a six-month stint. There, Robert became the company manager of the ice show.

Coming out as gay caused a rift between Robert and his father, who did not understand it at the time. I was with them when they met again for the first time: We were in Los Angeles for what I was worried would be a disastrous lunch. But when the two of them sat across from each other, the first thing I thought was, "Oh my god!" They shared so many similarities—good looks and strong bodies and tiny nervous tics, right down to the way they sometimes tripped over their own feet as they walked.

This first step happily led to their mended relationship. Aaron became our biggest fan, coming for visits and even going to the Olympics to be with us and be part of the fun and excitement. Aaron was focused on bettering himself. He attended AA meetings and searched for happiness and better mental, emotional, and physical health. Seeing how fit Robert was, he went on a drastic diet and began working out vigorously at the gym. He was so proud of his weight loss that he sent photos of himself, showing off his new and improved physique.

It was particularly tragical, then, when one morning as he was on the treadmill, Aaron suffered a major heart attack. He was taken to the hospital and put on life support. Robert immediately flew to Los Angeles to be with his family, but there was nothing anyone could do for Aaron. His brain was dead. After many days, it was Robert who finally had to sign the paper to have his father taken off life support to allow him to peacefully pass away.

Robert returned home, seemingly calm and almost unscathed by an incredibly heartbreaking two weeks. I was concerned that he was just putting on a brave face and all was not well, but he assured me he was fine. I was inspired by his strength, and we went about our lives again.

Then, a few years later, Robert's fifteen-year-old niece, David's daughter, went in for a routine surgery to remove a small, benign tumor in the back of her neck. During the procedure, the surgeon accidentally hit an artery and the young woman with so much life still ahead of her sustained a massive brain hemorrhage. Once again, Robert had to fly to California to be the strong brother. David and his wife were understandably in shock but waited until Robert could get there and say goodbye to his niece before the machines were unplugged and she was allowed to pass away.

I could not believe that my husband's family was going through a second funeral in such a short time.

I had never been to a funeral until Robert's dad's, much less one with an open casket and viewing. I flew out immediately to support Robert as the preparations were being made for his niece's memorial service. It could not have been more sad, with classmates from her school, as well as family and friends, mourning the loss of this beautiful little girl, who had left us far too early.

Looking at her, like a porcelain doll, so peaceful in her casket, I wondered, as I still do, for what purpose is this ritual? I understand that humans, of all different religions and for thousands of years, have shown respect and honor for their dead with some form of viewing and praying over the corpse before the coffin is laid to rest in the ground. A piece of me, though, thinks the acres of land that house our dead could be far better used for farming...or perhaps for our horses to graze on. I believe, if there is such a thing as a soul, when we die it has zero attachment to the vessel it inhabited and would most probably rather have those grieving be happy—happy for the soul's new freedom as it moves on to wherever its next adventure might take it. I would rather look at old pictures of those I have loved and lost, and send my adoring thoughts out into the universe in their memory, than go speak to a stone where their bodies were buried. But that's just me. Everyone must find their own way to mourn their losses.

Amazingly—actually, *miraculously*—my mom went from her diagnosis of terminal cancer that was supposed to end her life inside of three months to five years in total remission, all because of that little pill, IRESSA®. Although the signs of short-term memory loss were slowly getting more obvious in my dad's behavior, he and Mom took trips to visit all their kids and grandkids around the country. Much of the time, they would bring Mercedes, my mom's best friend, with them. Mercedes was like a second mother to me since I lived nearby, and we were all very close, celebrating birthdays and holidays together. We had huge parties for my mom's seventieth and seventy-fifth, as well as my dad's eightieth birthdays, inviting family and friends from all over to come celebrate their lives and their being survivors!

These good times came to an end when the doctors found a new tumor in my mother's hip. After over five years of remission, she was facing a new round of chemotherapy. This one made her very sick and tired, and it resulted in the loss of her hair.

Around this time, my older sister Margo found out that she was BRCA1 positive, meaning she had a gene that drastically increased her chances of getting breast cancer during her lifetime. My other sister, Dale, had already been diagnosed with breast cancer and had a lumpectomy, followed by a chemotherapy that worked to eliminate the probability of hormone-driven cancer but also threw her directly into menopause, something that was physically and emotionally beyond traumatic for her. With all they were going through, it was remarkable how my sisters and brother were one hundred percent there for our parents as they went through the next years.

My mother's doctors began changing her chemotherapy from one drug to another, depending upon how she was dealing with the side effects. She was more than just a tough lady—my mom was the proud matriarch of our family, adored by all of her posse. I used to joke that Mom would not go down to the end of her driveway to get the mail unless she was perfectly dressed with her makeup in place. But four years of sickness and lack of quality of life took its toll, and she finally said she was done with the drugs.

Unlike my father, my mother had always made it clear she was in charge of her life and would be in charge of her death. She spoke to me and my siblings about her wishes and made arrangements to have the pills she would need when the time came to end her life...*before* she was in the kind of pain she had no intention of dealing with. We all respected her decisions, including that her cremated ashes be sprinkled into the small lake behind my parents' home in Hollywood, Florida.

This, however, was not to be. Mom became so ill that she needed more care than was possible in her own home. It was decided she would fly to Austin and live out her time with my sister, Margo, and her husband, Bob (who is not only a wonderful brother-in-law but also a doctor himself). The move would allow my mom to see my other sister, Dale, and her children (my nieces), who also lived in Austin. Of course, my brother Al and I would make as many trips to see her as possible.

The question of what to do with my dad was an issue, as by this time, he had gone through all of the classic chronological symptoms of Alzheimer's. At one of our family reunions, which we had begun having just after my mother's diagnosis, we were all staying in a rental home and were getting ready for breakfast for the whole crowd when my dad came out of the bedroom wearing my mother's robe. Now, my mother was about five feet tall while my dad was about five feet nine inches.

As you can imagine, our whole family got to see my dad...really way too much of him, and in a totally new light! I told him to take a look in the large mirror on the family-room wall and see if he noticed anything "not right" about the picture. Having done so and without saying a word, he proceeded back into the bedroom and shut the door behind him.

Worried that he was angry or embarrassed, I went to his door and knocked. It was locked and no sound was coming from the room. We all looked at my mom, who simply shrugged her shoulders and told us to leave him be.

Less than five minutes later the door opened and out pranced my father, now in his *proper* robe but sporting my mother's fabulous wig. Without missing a beat, he said, "I don't have any idea why you would think something is wrong with me!"

We all broke out in laughter, but running underneath was the distinct feeling that our journey as a family was about to become one of great sorrow, perhaps sooner rather than later. How much time we had left with our beloved parents, my siblings and I had no clue. We simply made a pact that we would have annual or even biannual reunions from that time forward, all of us together in one place, each time to be determined, while we had the family intact.

The year 2012 was the hardest I can remember. My mother's life was coming to an end, and in mid-June, Margo explained that she would very soon need hospice care for her. As I fought back my sadness, I asked my sister, "When is she planning her demise with the medication she keeps by her bed?"

As I've mentioned, Mom, the ultimate "decider," had always been firm that she would not wither away but instead end her life exactly as her own mother had—dressed in her finest nightgown, hair and makeup perfect, just the right amount of her most expensive and elegant perfume, wig perfectly placed, looking gorgeous, like the star she had been throughout her lifetime. She believed, as I do, that details are everything. Or so I thought.

July Fourth weekend was, as always, a big party weekend on Fire Island, where Robert and I had our summer home. If you don't know Fire Island, it is a long barrier island off the coast of Long Island that gets skinnier as it stretches away from New York City. Of the seventeen communities on the Island, two of them, The Pines and Cherry Grove (which neighbor each other), are "gay towns." They are both only two city blocks wide between the ocean and the bay and are amazingly beautiful with homes built on stilts and no cars.

With all that was going on—my mom's and dad's health failing, and I had committed to coach the riders from the Canadian Dressage Team at the upcoming Olympic Games in London—Robert and I were doing our best to have a lot of fun. We went to a big Friday-night party in Cherry Grove that went until three in the morning. Normally, we would have left early enough to catch the last water taxi heading back to The Pines, but we were having such a good time and had imbibed more than enough when we realized it was past the last boat, and we would have to walk back to our home. On a beautiful, star-filled night, the trek from Cherry Grove to The Pines is a lovely walk, either on the beach or through the small dune forest, appropriately called, "The Meat Rack." About five of us headed out together, walking along the boardwalk, when suddenly we came to the abrupt end of our pathway, which had obviously fallen victim to the hurricane that had hit Fire Island the year before. Though warm, it was pitch black out, and we peered cautiously over the edge of the end of the boardwalk, staring down perhaps five feet to the ground where we could see collected water for a good three feet across before we would be back on solid ground.

We decided to jump down, one at a time. The first guy jumped off to the right and fell, rolling a bit upon landing, but said he was fine. I went next, thinking I would jump in the other direction, hopefully onto more even ground. I leapt a little to the left and came down directly on a log no one had noticed and right on my left knee. There was an audible crack.

"Are you okay?" Robert called from above.

Before I even responded, the boys sensed it was not good, and they each jumped off the shattered end of the boardwalk quickly to see what had happened to me. I sat there a few minutes, trying to decide if I had broken my leg or just sprained and bruised it. I determined, having broken my leg when I was fourteen, that this was not nearly as painful, for sure, and I motioned for Robert and a friend to try and pull me up. I seemed to be good to walk home—that is, until I stretched my left foot out and stepped down, putting weight on it. I immediately collapsed to the ground, got back up, and tried again...and down I went.

But the show must go on.

With a friend on each side, I hobbled the one and a half miles home.

Later that day, our friend Allan Gandolfi, an emergency room doctor, got me some crutches and told me to ice my knee and get to a specialist to diagnose my injury as soon as possible. He thought it could be a tear of the anterior cruciate ligament (ACL).

Doctors' visits were simply not an option, as I received a message from Margo that Mom was weakening and probably only had days left. Robert packed our bags for Austin, as well as helping me choose what I would need for London, as I would have to leave from there to get to the Olympics on time. We were just a few days from the Opening Ceremony.

Margo picked Robert and me up at the airport, and we tried not to get too emotional together as we drove to her home. Upon arrival, my sister Dale and Margo's husband Bob embraced us. Before I limped down the hall to see my mom, I asked the others, "So, what happened to, 'I am not withering away or feeling pain when I die. I have my pills for when I am ready!'"

Margo just shrugged her shoulders and said, "She obviously changed her mind."

Robert Dover

As I hobbled to her bedside, naturally, my dying mother immediately asked what had happened. Was I all right?

"Mom, I'm fine."

As I told the story of the three-in-the-morning boardwalk she did not laugh at all, saying, "You could have killed yourself!"

"Yes, Mother, but I will be fine."

"What about the Olympics? How are you going to get around on those?" she demanded, pointing to my crutches, leaning by the bed.

"Robert will help me," I lied, in order to put a stop to *that* conversation. "Mom…" I hesitated. "Are you in a lot of pain?"

"No, I'm just tired all the time now, and your poor sister and Bob have to take care of me," she replied. Then, with a smile, she went on, "They've been wonderful, and the nurse comes once or twice a day to keep my pain and coughing to a minimum. It's actually been a happy time with the girls and Bob and the two little dogs…they jump up and down as they please."

I started to cry and moved closer on the bed next to her as she leaned to hug me.

"No one's getting out of this alive," she reminded me.

The way she said it made me laugh and get ahold of myself.

Mom asked how long Robert and I were visiting, and I told her I had no plans to leave, at which point she reminded me of the Olympics. I explained that I would postpone or cancel my trip to London. I wanted to stay with her.

A stern look came over her face.

"The Canadian riders are counting on you. You have to be there for them," she said. "And anyway, I am going to be here when you get back."

"In two weeks?" I asked.

"Robert, I am going to be here for my birthday."

Assuming her drugs were kicking in, I said gently, "Mom, your birthday is December thirty-first and we are in July now."

My mother just gave me one more tough look, and I promised her I would fulfill my duties.

The next day, I flew to London while Robert headed back to Florida. We had planned for him to come when competition began, and that was still a week away. But two days after I arrived, while I was still learning how to get around the venue and back and forth to the hotel, Margo called to tell me Mom had passed away.

The day after I left, Margo said, our mom had seemed much better, feeling good enough to get herself up and stay up, cooking all three meals for everyone in the household. I later learned that many dying patients undergo a thing called a "surge," in which the person will, for no reason doctors completely understand, seem to be doing much better than their actual health would suggest possible. There have been instances of individuals actually coming out of a coma and telling their loved ones goodbye...that they love them. Anecdotally, the surge is almost always the day before the patient passes away.

And so it was for my mom.

Crying, I thanked Margo for all she'd done and hung up. I looked down at my knee, now about the size of New Jersey, as even with my crutches and the brace our friend George had given me to wear, I kept falling down when I put even the slightest weight on that foot. I was a wreck!

I immediately called Robert to let him know about Mom, and he could instantly tell I was in both physical and emotional distress.

"What can I do?" he asked.

Sobbing, I told him I just could not get through this without him, and he was on a plane to London that night.

Upon Robert's arrival, he took one look at me and called our friend, Sonny Tanna, who lived in London, to find help us find a top knee specialist that we could get in to see that day. Within minutes he came through for me, and Robert helped me into a taxi to head to downtown London.

The doctor, an African American man who had moved to London to work with a prominent group of orthopedic specialists, inspected my knee.

"There's good news and bad news," he said after a number of fairly routine-seeming tests. "The bad news is that it appears you have completely ruptured your ACL and possibly done more damage, so we will take you down for an MRI in a few minutes so we can see exactly what the story is in there.

"The good news is that you have to wait three weeks no matter what—the surgery can't happen until the swelling goes down. In the meantime, I am going to have someone come to your hotel later tonight to fit you with a proper brace for that leg. Just so you know, the brace you have been using is not only probably one of the very first of its kind and a museum piece, it is also for the other leg. That's why every time you put weight down on it, you fall down—there is no support on the correct side!"

The things we learn.

My MRI showed that I had indeed ruptured my ACL, both menisci (two other neighboring ligaments) were blown out, and I had a small fracture to the back of my knee. But the next day I set out to coach, now outfitted with a much smaller, more sophisticated brace, and a nice, red "mobility carrier" that would take me from the hotel room all the way into the venue to my Team. Appropriate Canadian flags adorned it! I was set to go and was just so fortunate to have my loving husband there to help me see it through.

I had taken on Canadian Team member David Marcus as a student the fall before to help bring his horse to Grand Prix. The next week, as David was warming up, the skies just opened up. The downpour was so bad during his test that, as he came around toward C, his horse just stopped and turned his tail toward the rain. There was no way David could recover from it. With him out, the Canadians couldn't complete a Team score, but the riders did their best, as did the Americans, who were staying in our hotel as well, and for whom I was also secretly cheering.

And then it was over. Robert and I flew to New York, having made all the plans to do my surgery at the Hospital for Special Surgery, number one for knee reconstruction in the world. I spent a few weeks on Fire Island after that, recovering and beginning a grueling year of physical therapy. Having been on crutches for weeks, my injured leg had atrophied to half its normal size. Other than my swollen knee, it looked like I was standing on a toothpick. I had to slowly relearn how to walk on it and climb up and down a stair with confidence that my leg would hold me. It was real and painful work, and sometimes I would suddenly think of my mother and break down. So strong was our bond that I would clearly hear her in my head. This still happens, usually when I have done something stupid (which is all the time) and she wants to straighten me out.

Dad was failing. Close to my sisters in Austin, we found a facility that specialized in Alzheimer's patients. On one of the most difficult days of my life, I flew my father from Fort Lauderdale to Austin. Getting him to the airport and onto the plane in a wheelchair was no small feat. Then, during the flight, he had to go to the bathroom, and as we were walking down the plane aisle to the lavatory, his pants fell down around his ankles. There I was, trying to get his pants up, trying to get him to the bathroom—just trying to survive.

My sisters met us and we all took him together to the facility, which we hoped would be a safe and good environment. But it was so sad.

Winter came, and I went to Texas to visit him and my family. By this time, Dad was not sure who we all were but could still reminisce about things, people, and events from decades before with pretty decent accuracy. Now, my father would give the shirt off his back to anyone, but he was never someone who would socialize with just anyone, and I walked in to find him standing in a circle of people, holding hands and singing

Christmas carols...I didn't even know he knew any Christmas Carols! I had to laugh and cry at same time.

I was pretty shocked on another visit when I walked in and found him in a wheelchair, covered in cuts and Band-aids, with no shoes on. In my usual, shy way (NOT!), I called for the nurses and demanded to know what happened. Where were his shoes?

Apparently, Dad had gone into a female resident's room and begun trying on *her* shoes...until she showed up and they got into a fistfight. Thus, no shoes.

Oh my god!

I wheeled my father into his room and tried to ask him what had happened, but he was no longer speaking in anything but gibberish and clearly had no idea what I was talking about. He would get a look on his face as though he was about to relate something of importance to me, but then only a series of unintelligible mumbles would come out of his mouth. I found him another pair of shoes, slipped them on his bare feet, and proceeded to wheel him toward the clear glass door that opened up to a small yard. The door had a code to unlock it as a safety measure to keep the residents—many of them suffering from dementia or other issues—from wandering. Just as I began entering the code to go out, a nice-looking elderly lady walked up, asking if I could help her.

"I have a baby girl and they've taken her," she announced. "I must get my baby back! Will you help me find my baby?"

I shook my head as I opened the door, moving to push my father's chair out into the afternoon sun. The woman grabbed hold of my arm, and I brushed it quickly away as I turned to close the door behind me. The lady was pulling on the handle on the other side—and was pretty strong for her age! Finally the door clicked shut, and the woman pressed her face against the glass.

"I'll remember this!" I saw her say as she stared at me.

A month later, my father stopped eating and was sleeping almost all day and night. I asked Margo if I should go see him, and she said no, I should stay home, he had no idea who I or anyone else was now. He had forgotten everything and everyone, even how to swallow.

Dad passed away in his sleep, and I was honestly more relieved than upset. Unlike my mom, who was sharp and in control to the end, I had begun accepting the loss of my dad the day he was diagnosed with Alzheimer's. It was a release to be finished with feeling the sadness of watching a person you know and love lose every memory and basic skill he ever had.

I live with one major regret about my father. He had, though I was not aware of it when he was alive, a plot in Chicago where he wished to be buried next to his parents, brothers, and sisters. I don't know if it was because I was overwhelmed by death or funerals, or if it was the idea that gravestones take up valuable space for horses to graze on or homes to be built, but I chose not to meet up with my family for his service. I know they were disappointed in me for not coming. I am as well. I should have been there for them and to celebrate the life of my father.

For that...I am very sorry.

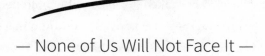

— None of Us Will Not Face It —

In the years following my father's death, the world lost numerous people in what felt like quick succession—Whitney Houston, Michael Jackson, Prince, and others. Each brought up deep sorrow in me, as they felt so tragic and unnecessary.

I cherish every single day in my life. I know we are all "getting off this bus," some sooner and others later, but I pray in my own way to keep my good health and that of my two- and four-legged loved ones, as long as possible, and to keep this grand adventure going. As I like to remind people, "This is my movie and nobody's going anywhere until I say!"

None of us will not face loss, and mourning is not something we just "go through" and come out the other side. It is more like a gaping wound that slowly turns into a nasty and sometimes outright uncomfortable scar. The severe pain does diminish over time, but your scar will remind you, time and again, of the loss it represents, and bring you to tears. A photo, a place, even a smell, can bring you right back to a time when the one you lost was still with you and that feeling wells up, taking you into the darkness. Gradually, though, we learn to recognize that the time we spend obsessed with the past is time we could be productive and joyful. And so we live on and hopefully learn to cope better with our losses and come to terms with mortality, especially our own, for therein must be where we truly find grace.

I am still searching, perhaps like you, for this wisdom. To be honest, I am still not there. I walk my dog Simon every night, and each time I look up into the stars and listen to my mom as she speaks to me, chastising me for something ridiculous I did that day (which happens practically every day!) or reminding me to help my sisters more than I do. As it turns out, Jewish guilt has a much longer shelf life than our loved ones. That being said, I would not trade my starry-night conversations with my mom for anything. They remind me of how she looked, sounded, and smelled, and that makes me feel loved in the way only a mother can love her children—unconditionally and forever. ●

1. You know you have the right mother when the quote next to your first baby picture is, "A star is born"! I felt special and adored by my mom throughout her life—and still now every single day! ●

PREVUE by Toloff
OAK PARK·ILLINOIS

2. Teachers, from first grade on, commented on how mature I was for my age. Perhaps that is why I look like I am off to university or my first day of work here. ●

3. My mom Jean and her young family: My brother Al, eight years older than me, who was off to university before I could ever get to know him, and my sisters Margo and Dale. ●

4–5. My dad, Herb Dover, felt he had to sell his lovely horse Tex when my mom and he started having kids. He auctioned Tex off in a cancer fundraiser in Chicago. ●

6. Skeeter was not my very first dog but the first one I considered my own, even if my siblings made me run from them only to have Skeeter chase me and bite me in the butt, sometimes pulling my pants right down and making me cry. ●

"SKEETER" Dover lives in a highrise on Golden Isle. Newly arrived from Freeport, Bahamas, "Skeeter" has lived in Toronto, Canada and Chicago. This much travelled 8 year old wire-hair terrier is the highrise "pet-of-the-week." Says Mrs. Dover, "In the Bahamas, Skeeter had the run of the neighborhood. But now he is walked on a leash, I am getting all the exercise."

7. As a kid, one of my nicknames was "Runt" as I was very small and weighed far less than most kids my age. Here I am at Camp Timberland where I and my guinea pig spent several great summers before I caught the "horse bug." ●

8. My Bar Mitzvah in Freeport, Grand Bahama Island, was the very first one performed in the Bahamas. Since there was no synagogue, one was created in the ballroom of the King's Inn Hotel, and the rabbi was flown in for both weekly education in Hebrew and to conduct the ceremony. ●

9. The traditional lighting of the candles by my family and relatives went well until I ran out of candles, and my relatives from all around the world were still coming up to light one! I almost panicked, then simply blew them out and started lighting the same ones again as everyone cheered me on. A truly special occasion for any Jewish thirteen-year-old! ●

...sh' Finds New Home

"IT WAS MY BEST DAY," SAYS ROBERT DOVER
... when Ebony Cash arrived in Freeport Monday

the je zy '

Eb , m... ...ip in a cra' nd under sedation. The hor stands 16 hands high, pr ty large as horses go, nch indicates the size of the te. No suitable ramp was ailable, but a fork lift was astily summoned.

Inside the plane, Ebony's handlers took the crate apart, reassembled it on the fork lift, and led Ebony back into the crate. This was the part Robert couldn't watch — Ebony's descent to the ground, in the crate and aboard the lift, was slow and shaky.

"Ebony was pretty good," said Robert's friends.

The rest was easy — Robert led Ebony into the trailer, and they were off to the horse's new home at Pinetree Stables.

Ebony, an unusually handsome horse, is black with white star, race and snip on the face, plus white socks on his back legs. He is a trained hunter, born in Kentucky, half thoroughbred and half American saddle bred. He is six years old and weighs around 1,500 pounds.

of low tree watch loaded cargo made

sion of his coming Bar Mitzvah, June 14. Robert will be 13 and, according to custom, will read the Maftere at Services for the first time.

Robert has lived in Freeport since last August and came to the Pony Club his first day here. He is in the advanced class in equitation. and has been riding "seriously" for two years. He is a student at St. Paul's Senior School.

10–13. My Bar Mitzvah present was my very first horse, Ebony Cash. We flew to Miami and bought him from Phil DeVida, Sr., for $1,500. The story of his arrival in this article from the local newspaper shows how multi-talented he was, besides becoming my best friend. ●

14–16. No kid could have gotten a better first horse than I did with Cash. He was everything to me as well as being a beautiful show horse. We did it all: dressage, jumping, endurance, foxhunting, polo, and so much more. ●

17. At fifteen I bought Somerset Son (Sonny) as my Pony Club and eventing horse. We had a rather tumultuous relationship, but I learned huge lessons from him. ●

18-19. When living in Atlanta and training with Elizabeth Lewis, I bought Jonathan Livingston Seagull. (I also had this haircut and was a huge geek!) Jonathan and I performed exhibitions when not competing. In order to advance my dressage education, I took him up to Virginia and Maryland where Colonel Bengt Ljungquist, the US Olympic Coach, was training. Later, Jonathan would help me make my very first "long list" with the US Equestrian Team. ●

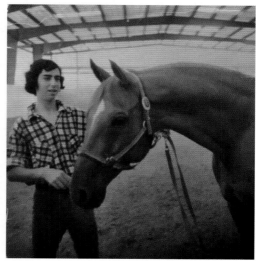

20–21. Anne Reiley, shown to
the right, her husband
Bob, and their daughter,
Beth, pictured with me
above, became my second
family. They took me in
so I could train in Virginia
and Maryland with Colonel
Ljungquist while also
advancing to the Pony
Club "A" level. ●

22. Two important people in my life (shown here together, although they eventually divorced) were Ruth and Sam Barish. Ruth, one of the smartest people I have ever known, did more for me as my student than I ever did for her and pushed me to figure out a way to purchase Federleicht, the horse that would ultimately change my life. Sam, though not a horseman himself, got involved with the US Dressage Federation because of Ruth and would eventually serve as the organization's president for many years. ●

23. With the urging of student and friend Ruth Barish and financial aid from the wonderful Caroline Muldoon, I bought three-year-old Federleicht from Gerd Zuther and November Hill Farm. This amazing horse would go on to change my life time and again for the better! ●

24. Thank you seventies for this unforgettable image! I definitely was trying to look like the famous Olympic swimmer Mark Spitz. ●

25. In 1980 I trained Patience Priest and others at her Sugarland Farm in Poolesville, Maryland, where we built a business together. At the time I was just figuring out I was gay. I came to realize Patience cared for me more than as a friend when she bought me a beautiful ring, which I still wear, and actually made a twin for Robert as our wedding bands—go figure! ●

26. Patience and I procured Lago Maggiore, a wonderful horse trained by Willi Schultheis. I would later take a clinic with him in Kentucky at the farm of Liz and Dieter Felgendreher where I would tell Herr Schultheis I thought Lago was thirteen and he would explain the gelding was closer to twenty! ●

27. Herr Schultheis teaching me with Dieter Laugks translating. I went on to live in Germany and learn the language. ●

28. Sitting at a clinic watching with Simon Barber, a wonderful friend who later passed away from AIDS. Simon was one of the reasons I became an AIDS activist, and along with my husband Robert Ross and friends, founded the Equestrian AIDS (now Aid) Foundation, dedicated to helping people in the horse world fighting AIDS and other life-threatening illnesses and catastrophic injuries. ●

29. In 1982, I was hired by Performance Sales International and moved to Virginia to work at Chestnut Lawn Farm, their North American headquarters. As a perk for my job they bought me PSI Romantico, a horse I went on to sell to a very kind syndicate and who helped me make my first Olympic Team in 1984. ●

30. Romance Farm Inc. became one of the largest dressage operations in the country, and I was catch-riding horses right and left, often asked by people who wanted me to show their horses at the last minute. (If you recognize this horse and want to let me in on who it is I was showing here, I'd really appreciate it!). ●

31. Romantico was a young Grand Prix horse when he came to me with a lovely temperament but not the most correct paces. He had a super trot for that time and good piaffe and passage, but everything in walk and canter was not easy. ●

32. With Romantico at the Palm Beach Dressage Derby in 1983. ●

33. Danish-born American dressage rider and benefactor Janne Jansen Rumbough helped put on the first Palm Beach Dressage Derby in 1983. I was lucky to have Romantico that year and won it. Janne still competes at Grand Prix and also sponsors top US rider Mikala Münter. ●

34. Romantico and I, lucky winners are proudly standing next to the founders and organizers of the Palm Beach Dressage Derby, my great friends Gisela and Howald Pferdekaemper. ●

35–36. 1984 was a banner year for me. I made my first Olympic Team and with Romantico, Federleicht, and other horses (including Mosquito below, owned by Angelica Duda, and Amor, right, owned by her best friend) owned by clients, swept all divisions at Dressage at Devon, from Fourth Level through Grand Prix! ●

37. My folks always loved bringing friends and relatives to the Palm Beach Dressage Derby when I was competing. Here they are with me and my dog Half-Halt, and my cousins Ray and Izzie. ●

38. Federleicht won the Grand Prix in Lausanne, Switzerland. ●

39. In 1985, the US Team won the gold at the North American Championships. Hilda Gurney on her fabulous Keen is to my right. Next to her is Diana Rankin with Lady Killer and to my left is Debbie Bowman on Falstaff. ●

40. Juvel, owned by Gwen Blake, was as headstrong as any stallion could be. One minute he would be quietly warming up and the next he would have jumped into the bushes. We would wrestle around for a few minutes and come out with twigs in our hair, scratched up a bit, and then would (most of the time) go into the arena and win the class. ●
Photo by Karl Leck

41. In the 1980s, one of our top international judges, Edgar Hotz, used to come to my farm week after week and score my Grand Prix test and tell me how to improve it to earn more points. He sadly passed away in 2001, far too soon, but had a huge impact on my career for which I am very thankful. ●

42–43. Robert Ross came into my life Fourth of July weekend in 1988. Our first real date was not until March, 1989, but it was definitely love at first sight for me! Here we are going on our very first cruise together to the Bahamas. ●

44. Turnabout is fair play. I got to follow Robert around and hold his Grand Prix jumper Bohemian by the arena for him. I'd be really relaxed until he would begin his course, and then I would look crazy, lifting one leg up every time his horse would leave the ground to jump, as if that would somehow help! ●

45. I am with Robert, my mom Jean, and her best friend (my "other mother") Mercedes Dubin (who was also our interior decorator), and Robert's mom Julie. This was at our first Wellington home, which we spent more on decorating than the home cost. A lesson learned! ●

46. Robert not only married me, he also inherited my two dogs, Half-Halt and Pirouette. ●

47. Robert worked very hard to achieve his goal of becoming a successful hunter-jumper rider and trainer. ●

48. Half-Halt did not like very many people but loved Robert, with whom he shared many a Sunday football game on the couch! ●

49–50. I was a workaholic until Robert began to make me take short vacations at the end of every competition tour in Europe. Below I am in Mykonos for our first of many trips there. ●

51. A true horseman, Robert did everything with his horses during our first years together, from the riding and training to the grooming and bathing. ●

52. Robert trained with the great team of Joe Fargis and Conrad Homfeld, both Olympic gold medalists. The lovely mare Galiana was a wonderful gift to him from my sponsor and our friend Jane Forbes Clark. ●

53. Joe Fargis took over the ride on our young stallion, Cor d'Alme Z, who was an amazing jumper and later went on as a seven-year-old with Joe to win his first three Grands Prix. He was sold to Norway shortly after for what would be a life-changing amount of money! ●

54. The World Equestrian Games in 1990 in Stockholm did not go as I'd hoped with Waltzertakt, owned by Walter and Mary Anne McPhail. He had strained a tendon on the long trip from Germany, and I could only walk him until the day of the jog, one day before the Grand Prix. Just getting the horse, who we sometimes called "Crazy Walter," to enter the stadium as the orchestra was finishing up its final program at the far end of the arena was close to impossible. He was beautiful but for sure the most challenging horse of my career. ● *Photo by Karl Leck*

Beauty, Death, and OCD

Facing Down Fear

6

CHAPTER

Have you ever feared someone was saying or thinking something very negative about you, only to come to find out it was the exact opposite case and the person really admired you? Maybe you mistook shyness for dislike? That was the story of my life growing up. Before she passed, my mom related to me that she had been exactly the same way in her youth—always afraid that others would not love or appreciate her. She was actually universally loved by every person I ever spoke to. Nevertheless, she, like me, would go to extreme lengths to please others so they would love and accept her.

Fear of disappointing others and failing to succeed have been the central themes of my life. Whether in school, business, or in sports, I have been driven to achieve successful outcomes to the point of obsession. In this, I do not believe myself to be the exception. To some degree, we all work in this way.

As a kid, I was so afraid of failing others or myself that I would punish myself if I thought I had done something wrong. I would go without food and put myself in a "time out," either under my bed or in my closet, usually falling asleep only to wake up to my mom calling out my name for dinner. Later in life, I would go to great lengths to make others like me and would obsess over the thought of anyone who did not, even if I did not find that person particularly interesting. It was a compulsion for me to seek admiration and personal perfection. I was always confident in what I could do, both as a student and as a horseman; however, I had a great deal of fear that I was not attractive enough to others, based on my understanding of what "handsome," "pretty," and "good-looking" meant. Classic good looks, whether in an animal like a horse or in a person, seemed totally objective to me. Symmetry and beautiful and harmonious features devoid of blemishes were obviously the qualities that were desired—you only needed to open up a copy of GQ to grade yourself against the gold standard. And there I was, a skinny kid with bad teeth, a big nose, and a Jewfro. When I would go out with my friends, I would inevitably end up standing against a wall, watching beautiful people walking by and seeing how easily my friends would begin chatting with them and, more times than not, getting a date. I was just too afraid of being rejected to put myself out there and try. Naturally, I often ended up alone and lonely.

What changed? I began to become more successful in my riding career, and my self-confidence, which was already strong in the equestrian side of my life, began to bleed into the social side. People who I found interesting began to reciprocate, and my circle of friends began to grow, both in- and outside the equestrian community. Still, my constant concerns that I was not good-looking enough, based on my own judgment, precipitated many changes to my looks over the years, some which were good and healthy choices and others which, given the chance, I would take back.

I was ashamed of my teeth—the big gap between my two front top ones and my crooked and overcrowded bottoms. I decided, during the 1988 Olympics in Seoul, that I'd had enough of being a skinny rail, even if that look was appropriate for a dressage rider. I wanted to be muscular and super toned, so I set out daily to the gym in the Olympic Village to begin the process (and as of today, I have never stopped).

However...my fear of not being physically admired led me to making other choices as well, some of which had less than optimal results.

In my teens and early twenties, I struggled with how to wear my hair so as to minimize my nose, which I thought was the size of New Jersey, and what I called my "Jewish bump." I tried straightening my hair, coloring it, and letting it grow really long, but my nose was not going away. I also had the "Dover chin," which was too small and undefined.

In my late thirties, I finally persuaded Robert that I had found a doctor who would do a fantastic job, and though expensive, it was worth my happiness. We went for my interview, and the doctor showed me what he would do to my nose and chin and said that he would even "do my eyelids" for a tiny bit more money. The first floor of the building housed the doctor's consultation office. The second floor held his operating theater and the convalescent rooms that looked out over the ocean. It all appeared to be top class, and I was excited to be getting my new nose and chin the following week.

All seemed to go well with my procedure, and I had very little discomfort the night after and round-the-clock nursing care. The doctor came and changed my dressing and showed me how I looked. With the cotton in my nostrils and my eyes bruised, I pretty much looked like I had been hit by a truck, but he said that it was totally normal, and I would look perfect in about a week.

Over the next few days, the bruising did indeed subside. The problem was that, in breaking my nose and taking my "bump" away, not only did the doctor not do anything about my deviated septum (a problem that had always impaired my breathing), I now looked nothing like myself with a nicer nose. I looked so much like someone I didn't know that I shocked myself every time I looked in a mirror. Even my mother, who would *never* say she did not like the way I looked, had a hard time looking me in the face and only said that time would make things look better.

"HOW MUCH TIME?"

In the end, it took three years and gravity doing its work for me to finally resemble my old self and finally feel happy with how I looked.

Still, my fear of aging and dislike of my looks meant I did not stop with one botched procedure. I did not like my neck and once again talked Robert into letting me have a neck lift. How complicated could it be? I had already tried lots of non-surgical methods of reducing my double chin. The chin implant had helped, but it was not enough. Again, the procedure seemed to go well, and for a day after, I thought I was in the clear. But two days later, I started to get a nasty lump that looked like an infected abscess under the left side of my chin. It got worse and worse, and I ended up back in the doctor's clinic to have it excised and drained. It was a mess, the likes of which the doctor said he had never experienced before with any of his patients.

Well, a year later, the result was still so ugly the doctor redid the entire procedure for free. I must say it was kind of him to feel responsible for my satisfaction with the outcome, and the second neck lift worked much better. Though I would probably advise against others following in my footsteps, I have been much happier with my looks as I have aged—even if I found that happiness not so gracefully!

Fear of coming out as gay occupied another part of my life. It's funny that I was least afraid of coming out to my family, and in fact, never really did have "the talk" with my parents at all. They, as well as my siblings, acted as if they had always known I was gay and were just waiting to see when I was going to be let in on the secret.

Where it was harder was at school and at work. I had always kind of had a girlfriend as I grew up, so coming to the realization that I was gay was an enormous shock to me. I was unsure how to tell my roommate, as well as my close friends, and feared losing them and being ostracized—or worse. For days after my first time sleeping with a guy, I remember slumping down against the wall in the trailer I shared with my college roommate, Gene, and crying for hours and hours. I hid my inner turmoil from Gene and everyone else, including my family. What would I say to them? To him? To my other friends who thought they knew me? As I sat there sobbing one day, Gene came in and knelt beside me, putting his arm around my shoulders. I struggled and finally uttered the words, "I am so sorry...but I think I am gay." Gene's arm did not move, even an inch, and he told me it did not matter at all to him and anyone worth having as a friend would accept me just as I was.

INCREDIBLE!

In the end, not only was I accepted by the group of friends I was afraid of losing, I actually found an entirely new group of friends within the gay community.

Still, my fear of being ostracized by my equestrian and Olympic communities was still very debilitating to me. Many did not recognize back then (and too many still do not) how emotionally and physically detrimental it is for people to believe they will never be accepted for who they are. Consider the stress athletes live with every day in trying to be the very best in order to "make" teams and represent their countries. Now add to that a fear that their sporting community, as well as the Olympic family, will not accept them because of their sexuality. This is the reason we still see so few openly gay members on professional sports teams or out-and-proud Olympians. Trust me, they are there on most teams in the vast majority of sports. Those, like myself, who make the decision to come out, generally have two results: First, they relate to others how they are so much happier with the weight of the secret off their shoulders and the ability to finally be their authentic selves. For the most part, the reactions of their teammates are extremely positive, showing how far mankind has come in recognizing we are all the same and love is love! Second, something I have experienced over the years, is the effect an out athlete can have on young people who see the athlete's story. It can give them the courage to be true to themselves.

Nothing could make me happier than that!

Obsessive Compulsive Disorder (OCD) has plagued me my entire life. I was supposed to be left-handed like my mother, but as a small child, pencils were forced into my right hand by teachers. Today, while I write awkwardly, holding my pen rather like an ice pick, I do many other things as a lefty. It still bothers me that I do not have good penmanship, and that is just the tip of the iceberg when it comes to my OCD.

I am not comfortable with asymmetry or blemishes. If I am at a party at someone else's home and there is a picture hanging crookedly on a wall, there could be a hundred people between me and the picture, but I will slowly but surely make my way over to straighten it. I am the same with hygiene, conformation, colors, singing...pretty much everything.

Once, Robert and I had friends over and one of them tracked dirt into our living room. I could not take my eye off the spot near our friend's feet on our sisal rug, knowing any second our friend's shoe might grind the loose dirt further into it. Finally, I got out my electric vacuum cleaner and asked everyone sitting on the couch to lift their feet. *Voila!* The pending disaster was prevented, and I could once again concentrate on what people were saying.

Having OCD has been both a positive and a negative in my career. One of the most important qualities a dressage rider must have is a strong attention to detail, since we are judged by how perfectly we, together with our horses, execute all the beautiful movements that are exhibited in our tests. Day after day, month after month, and year after year, we repeat these exact same movements as Grand Prix riders, hoping to get as close as possible with each one to that magic "10." Interestingly, "10" in most sports does not truly represent "perfection" but rather stands for "excellent." One would think that the top fifty athletes in the world in any sport would be getting mostly "10s" by the time they are competing at the Olympics. But this is far from true, for whatever reason, and those like me who are obsessed with achieving perfection find it difficult, and even frustrating, when it constantly eludes them.

If I get on a horse and one of the straps on the bridle is not tucked into the little leather keeper and is therefore flapping as the horse moves, I am unable to keep training until I have stopped and fixed the problem. The same goes for a bit of shavings stuck in the horse's mane or tail, or when a student comes to the arena with dirty boots or an unkempt-looking shirt or hair. Everything must look and feel exactly right to me before I will begin a lesson. Understanding my OCD behavior has enabled me to talk about it and try to control it in order to prevent negative repercussions.

It was 2005 when I learned for the first time that I had to let go of my need for things to be perfect.

Robert and I had built a beautiful house in Bridgehampton, New York. It stood on the highest parcel of land at the top of a ridge that looked down over farms, including one previously owned by Kelly Klein and now owned by Madonna, all the way to the ocean. Every room had this lovely view, and behind our backyard—which held a fabulous, fifty-foot, gray-bottom pool and spa—was a large preserve, affording us super privacy. Our house was based on the plans from George Washington's famous Mount Vernon estate, although we'd blown out the walls that, in Washington's home, created many small rooms that were easier to heat in winter. We adhered to the original design's attached wings on each side of the main house—one for a large kitchen and housing for Washington's slaves, and the other for his horses and carriages. One of our wings was a guest apartment, and the other was a large den with a sleeping loft above. The house was, like others we've built before and after, a product of many months of painstaking work and a labor of love. It was a great place to entertain friends and guests, and we were very proud of it.

Two of our friends, Sean and Randy, came out for a nice August weekend. They are awesome, successful people, as well as trailblazers in the gay adoption movement. They brought along their three kids: twelve-year-old Jesus, two-and-a-half-year-old Daley, and six-month-old Essie. Another friend, Scott, had also come out for the long weekend—so we put the family in the guest wing and Scott in another guest bedroom in the main house. I knew the kids were having fun by the laughter coming from that side of the house as we all got into our bathing suits and headed out to the pool.

It was a great afternoon with gorgeous weather, and everyone was enjoying the pool and the sun. We decided to barbecue, and I left for the outdoor market at the bottom of our road to pick up fresh sweet corn and tomatoes to go with our meals. When I returned, it became apparent that there had been a mishap in the spa with the baby, who did not realize it was not a toilet. Fortunately, the boys were on the problem, immediately draining the spa and refilling it with sanitary water.

With no pool time for a bit and the kids loaded with energy, they spent the next hour playing games and drawing, sometimes on paper... and other times on the walls, doors, and floors.

I was absolutely horrified to see the carnage in our home, but it got to the point where I finally looked around and remembered that what I was worried about were just "things," all of which could be cleaned, fixed, or replaced. What could not be replaced was the laughter from the kids and our amazing friendships. Once I came to that realization, I said to myself, "Fuck it! Let them tear the place apart!" It was at that moment that I let go of my OCD and began to have fun with the group.

On Sunday afternoon, Sean and Randy wanted to attend a party, so Robert, Scott, and I took the kids to the annual country fair in Bridge-hampton. As soon as we got there, Jesus wanted to go on a ride. Not just any ride—this was a kind of Ferris wheel with cages that turned over in circles and spun round and round as they circled the wheel. Naturally, I was the only willing adult, and off we went, while the others watched.

Only a few seconds into a spin, both of us realized the Ferris wheel had been a mistake. We were dizzy and beginning to feel sick to our stomachs, enough that Jesus asked if we could get the guy to stop the ride. I told him to shut his eyes and try to relax—I was sure we were almost done, and thankfully, I was right. As we got off, Jesus said he didn't want to go on any more rides, for which I was extremely thankful!

We played the entire arcade and won some big stuffed animals that delighted the little ones, as well as eating all kinds of food and candy that was most certainly not healthy. We were about to leave the fair when Jesus spied another ride and was emphatic about getting on it. Everyone looked at me, so I obediently followed him to the entrance of the infamous "Rotor," the ride where you stand against the curved wall of a disk that begins to spin until it is going so fast that you are literally pinned against the side as the floor is dropped from under you.

Sounds like fun, right?

Jesus stood next to the exit door with me next to him, and all the others on the ride lined up around the disk, so naturally some of us were looking directly across at each other as we began to rotate. Jesus and I were laughing and yelling as the world spun round, until Jesus got my attention. I turned to look at him and saw he was turning sort of a green color.

"I think I'm going to be sick!" he yelled over the ride.

Before I could get any words out (which were going to be, "Jesus, turn your head the other w-a-y-y-y!"), he threw up all over me, the centrifugal force of the ride ensuring I was covered from head to toe with vomit.

As you can imagine, most of the folks on the ride looked horrified—all except for the kids, who were all laughing hysterically! Jesus was totally clean—not a drop on him. I didn't know whether to laugh, throw up myself from the smell, or cry! The Rotor came to a stop, and you have never seen people run off a ride faster than those on this one, with looks of both pity and disgust. As Jesus and I walked down the ramp, I asked the attendant if he knew where there might be a hose.

"Sorry," he answered with a shake of his head and no acknowledgment whatsoever of the vomit on my shirt. With that, I told Jesus to walk quickly to my SUV, put the windows all down, and open the moonroof—we would spray me down at home.

And yes, I made Jesus hold the hose!

— Little Secrets —

The summer weekend with my friends' children was evolutionary for me with regard to learning how to let go of needing everything in my life to look and be perfect. I still have issues with messiness, things being out of place or crooked on walls, and blemishes or lack of symmetry, but I try to let that go and just have fun, more and more. I do have high regard for those who pay attention to detail and are strict about their cleanliness and that of their surroundings—and perhaps that is not such a terrible thing in this day and age.

Fear, for whatever reason, is an emotion that rarely produces a positive outcome. Much of the time it is caused by irrational thoughts with zero basis in reality. The key is figuring out how, in the face of any kind of fear, to create a life in which it does not take over and wreck your day-to-day existence. Over the years, I have learned not to try to sweep my fears under the rug. Doing so creates a "little secret" and begins a narrative where others are misled, sometimes very subtly, by your reluctance to discuss your fear. We all have these little secrets, and most of the time they go unnoticed and without repercussions; however, in some cases the little secrets grow, layer by layer, in our most important relationships. The fear of uncovering the truth and putting it on the table for all to see mounts as more little secrets are added.

It is not easy to reveal your innermost fears, especially when you think you may be judged and possibly even rejected by those whom you love the most. This is exactly the time to seek outside therapeutic help and advice. A great therapist will ask you, "What is the worst thing that could happen from your unveiling the truth to someone else?" You might say you are afraid you will lose someone. Perhaps you will...but just imagine that person was going to tell you exactly the same little secret. Would you reject the person and choose to never see the person again?

Ultimately, LOVE wins, and those who are meant to be in your life will overcome the hurt from learning the secret and will not eject you from their lives. It took me decades to come to this realization.

When it comes to fear, it is one thing to recognize that putting your hand on a hot stove is going to hurt. That kind of fear is "intelligent."

It is fear of the unknown that paralyzes your emotional or psychological growth and stifles your evolution toward self-awareness and self-actualization, and it is this fear that it should be our goal to supersede. I guess it is all about finding a balance in one's life, as it is with most things. That which brings us joy and happiness each and every day while doing the same for others is a great goal to seek.

As I wrote this book, Robert and I were self-quarantined due to the COVID-19 pandemic. It is quite possible that there has never been a time when so many people around the globe shared the same fear. World Wars did not affect as many countries as the coronavirus. While plagues of the past certainly killed many millions of people, there was no Internet to spread the alarm like the pandemic that overtook us in 2020. It was a new dread: How many of us will be killed? Will we be the lucky ones and be spared?

I have always had a very healthy (or perhaps unhealthy) fear of death. I remember as a child, lying in bed in the middle of the night, feeling terrified that I might go to sleep and never wake up. I would obsess over the inescapable truth that, no matter what I did, someday I would die. I would consider facts like everyone dies and most believe in an afterlife... but as much as I wanted the afterlife to be true, my gut said I shouldn't bank on it. I remembered reading somewhere that "energy, which is what we are made of, never ceases to exist; it merely changes or moves out of our bodies, and this is the part that is our soul." Or the energy might just dissolve into the atmosphere and then "swish"—nothing. Finally, I would tell myself, "Look, Robert, you go to sleep every night and are basically 'gone' until you wake up again. Yes, you are pretty confident you will wake back up, but the time away where there is 'nothing' is not scary at all, when you think about it."

Still, if that is what it is, then...can I put it off another a hundred and fifty or so years?

I like to imagine the life of one of those huge sea turtles, swimming around the ocean for over a hundred and fifty years, seeing beautiful underwater places, then perhaps heading back to my birthplace each year to leave my legacy of eggs on the beach. I'd wave my flipper as I headed back to the sea, calling: "Good luck, kids! I hope you all make it, but it's a tough world out there and not all of us can live as long as I have!" ●

Robert Dover

Going Off Course

The Art of Failure

7
CHAPTER

When I moved to Germany in 1986, it was in the dead of winter after what for me was an enormous failure—placing thirty-seventh that summer at the World Championships in Toronto. I had received an incredible invitation that seemed too good to be true from Olympic Gold medalist Gabriela Grillo, to come to her farm with my horse Federleicht. Gabby had extended the invitation to David, my boyfriend at that time, and also a dressage rider. We could live for practically nothing in one of the two gatehouses on her estate, and she helped us secure stalls for the five other horses, owned by clients, who came with me on this great adventure. It seemed fortuitous that I had just won the spot to compete in the upcoming World Cup Finals in Essen, Germany, which was to take place a couple of weeks after our arrival. With such a perfect plan and such goodwill behind me, how could I not succeed?

After a very long day, flying with seven horses and our two Jack Russell Terriers, Half-Halt and Pirouette, overseas, we arrived in the town of Mülheim an der Ruhr, about an hour outside of Düsseldorf, in the middle of the night. Unfortunately, the van driver could not find the Grillo farm. (In 1986, there were no cell phones with GPS.) We rode up a number of long and winding driveways that ended up being the wrong address before finally stopping at the entrance of the Red Cross, where the driver asked for the directions to Stal (Stables) Grillo.

David and I were exhausted as we unloaded the equally tired animals, along with equipment, feed, hay, and basically all of our belongings, into the barn aisle. We did as we were directed through our interpreter (the driver) and at the command of Stallmeister (Stable Master) Luke, who we had not-so-gently awakened with our late arrival. Once the horses were set for the night, Meister Luke sent us with our driver and personal belongings back to one of the two identical gatehouses near the front entrance of the farm. However, unlike the perfectly furnished and appointed home across the driveway—which Gabby used for her trainer, General Paul Stecken, when he came each week to teach her—our apartment was almost completely devoid of furniture, save for a mattress on the floor in one bedroom and a small television with antenna "ears" to catch the three channels available in Germany at that time. Still, it was warm, had cold and hot running water, and was to be our home for the foreseeable future. I was determined to learn how to be a "winner" in the biggest arenas of the world and had made a commitment to myself that I would not return to America until I had succeeded in doing so. I did not care how long it might take or how much I would have to sacrifice; I was determined.

The morning after our arrival, having fed and taken care of our horses, we met up with Gabby, who greeted us with a hug and took us to her home, otherwise known as "Landhaus Grillo," to meet her mother. The house reminded me of a set from the prime-time soap opera *Dynasty*—sort of a less-antiquated version of a castle. Frau Grillo was sitting in a beautiful, wing-backed chair, her hair silver-blue and pulled back in a knot. She welcomed us, said she hoped we would enjoy our time in her country, and announced that this would be the last time we heard English, so if we wished to keep eating, we would need to learn German.

Over the next ten days, I prepared for the World Cup Finals with the help of Gabby and General Stecken. To be honest, I probably gained the most information from Stallmeister Luke, who had spent decades grooming and being the eyes on the ground for Gabby and others before her. For sure, Gabby and the General watched Federleicht and me and had valuable pointers, but Meister Luke would do his best to convey in *slow* German and hand signals that my horse needed to be more through and on the aids and forward-thinking through my tests. As much as I was trying to make my horse more electric, he just felt listless and unlike himself, and I was alarmed when I came into the barn and saw that Feder's legs were all very swollen from the knees and hocks down to his feet. I immediately asked the number for the vet, but again, Meister Luke came to the rescue, explaining that he saw such behavioral and physical changes all the time when horses came in from a different climate and their grain and hay was changed.

Sure enough, Feder was back to normal a couple of days later. Normal...but still not forward-thinking or electric enough to be brilliant. When we competed in the World Cup Finals, we landed in eleventh place out of the thirteen riders entered.

Failure!

The following week, General Stecken took me aside, with Gabby standing by, and told me that I would never be able to do my horse justice, and that the best thing I could do for Federleicht was to sell him to Gabby so that she could bring him to his potential. I was devastated to stand before this great trainer and hear him say that I was not good enough for the horse I had trained since he was three years old and on whom I'd represented my country. Holding back tears, I told the General that I had already entered several spring shows, in which I and my student, Hector Rodriguez of Colombia, were planning to compete.

"If I don't do any better by the end of our spring tour," I said, struggling to compose myself, "I will sell Federleicht to Gabby."

With that, General Stecken and Gabby walked away, and I finally broke down and quietly cried in a way I thought would go unnoticed, but Meister Luke had been listening around the corner and gave me a look that said, "Pull yourself together. It's going to be all right."

Over the next few days, I trained with Meister Luke on the side, saying, "Good!" or "Again!" and after a week, things really felt better. I also had the great fortune to meet a young lady named Petra Kasseberg (later, Hofmann), who rode at Gestut Eschenbruek, where I kept the other horses I had brought to Europe. She had heard I was looking for help to take with me on my "European tour" (the series of competitions I'd entered with the intent of gaining international experience and recognition) and was very enthusiastic about coming with me. I explained that I was pretty poor, even though people who did not know me thought that my being in Europe with seven horses must be evidence that I was born into great wealth like so many others in my sport. Petra didn't care—she bubbled with enthusiasm and said she would help me with everything and anything I needed. She began grooming for me the next day and quickly became my "Number One": She was a super ground person and trainer, seeing as she was a *Bereiter*—a certified horse trainer and riding instructor in Germany. In other words, Petra was *way* overqualified for the job, but it seemed she liked me right away, just as I liked her, and was determined to go on this adventure with me.

I was gaining confidence daily as my student Hector Rodriguez, his wife Diana, and I set off on my first major European tour. Petra rode in the van with the horses to ensure all were safe and taken care of on the road. We had chosen three shows that would start in Lipica, which was in the former Yugoslavia (now Slovenia) and where the famous Lipizzaner stallions truly came from (a fact I had not known). The show was actually held at the Lipizzaner Stud Farm, which dated back to the fifteenth century and still bred pure Lipizzaners and trained their riders to perform for the public, just like the Spanish Riding School in Vienna.

Federleicht and I placed third in the Grand Prix in Lipica, which was a major boost to my confidence. I had been working very hard on the basics with him and it carried over into the show arena, as it should. The following day, in the Special, we placed third again, out of thirty-two combinations! The class was won by Christine Stückelberger, the famous Swiss rider who had won Olympic Gold and many medals since the early seventies. Suddenly, I began to feel a sense of assuredness flooding through me, and with it came both relaxation and increased drive to be not second, but the winner!

Christine, however, had been a great champion for over a decade, and there was no way the next day that anything would stop her. Federleicht and I ended in second place in the Freestyle (the test to music). I was so proud, not only for proving to myself and others that I was, in fact, an international rider on my way up, but that I was also a promising coach, having trained Hector, who placed a very respectable ninth in the class.

My happiness grew as I made new friends from various countries, who now no longer looked down on me as "that stupid American rider" but rather showed admiration for my skills and harmonious connection with my beloved Feder.

On the last day of the show, the head judge, Wolfang Niggli of Switzerland, strolled up to me as I was standing on the hill overlooking the arena one last time and said, "Robert, I have to compliment you on your new Freestyle. Everything about it, from the choreography to the music, is so much better than what you did a month ago at the World Cup Finals! Well done!"

I was quiet for a second before replying, "Thank you very much, Mr. Niggli."

As I walked back to the barn to pack up in preparation for our next competition, I smiled. You see, I had not made one single change to my Freestyle since the World Cup, *including* the music and choreography! I had made so much real headway in the last few weeks that Feder's fluid and mistake-free ride to the exact same music was unrecognizable.

What happened after my Lipica results led me to two observations: First, being technically correct and showing the confidence that stems from having really done your homework makes others gravitate toward you in very positive and sometimes rather remarkable ways. Second, music, dressage, and art in general, being subjective, can create a situation in which being "in sync" with the rhythm and "harmonious-looking" is all you need to earn high scores. I used to say that I could take a trash can lid and a stick to beat out a rhythm, and as long as I hummed a few notes while riding a clean test exactly to the rhythm of my pounding, the judges would say they loved my music. That has changed to a degree over time as more judges have become better educated, but it is still up to each to decide if he likes one piece of music over another and if he feels it fits the horse and rider being judged.

———————————

After my early successes, I built up a large clientele of great students and friends, and at one point, had seventy horses in my barn. One of those clients was the McPhail family: Mary Anne, Walter, and their daughter Melinda. I loved all three of them (and still do!) and taught mother and daughter on their horses, including a nine-year-old gelding named Waltzertakt, nicknamed "Walter" and sometimes not-so-lovingly referred to by his alter ego, "Crazy Walter." He was a beautiful horse and actually quite talented, which I found out the first time I tried him. He also had a very short fuse that, once lit, could go off and bring out an animal that not only could do things to hurt you, but lacking any sense of self-preservation, could kill himself in the process!

Walter could be really very sweet and began learning the Grand Prix quite quickly. He even started to show signs of becoming an international winner—of sorts. The problem was that at any moment, almost anything could set him off, and the kind of rampage that might ensue was anyone's guess. (He would go on to win not one but two Grand Prix National Championships at Gladstone and was nominated to our World Championships Team in Stockholm in 1990. On the way to that, however, were shows that I will never forget, even if I tried—and believe me, I have tried!)

Walter was one of the seven horses I took to Germany in the winter of 1986. The McPhails had placed great deal of trust in me to allow me to take their horse, and of course I did my best to keep expenses for them, and for all my clients, as low as possible. One way to do that was to fly the horses in single-stall containers, three abreast, to Frankfurt, Germany, on Lufthansa airline. Not having flown with horses before, I had no idea as to whether this arrangement was more or less safe than the usual double stall containers, but I knew it was a hell of a lot cheaper. I put Walter between two other horses, one traveling with me and one who was with someone else but made up the third spot in our container. David and I were on the flight with my dogs, Half-Halt and Pirouette, and all was quiet.

After landing we had to wait what seemed like an eternity before airline staff began to unload the containers on their pallets, using forklifts to lower them to the ground. I remained in the sectioned-off front of the container to comfort my two horses as we were moved, to little effect—something about the way the container began to shake during the process set "Crazy Walter" off and calm turned quickly into a nightmare. He pulled back, almost to the point of lying down, but feeling the pull from the two lines connecting his halter to the bars at the front of the stall, he then leapt forward, practically jumping into the front of the container with me. Again and again he went backward and then flung himself forward, hitting his head on the top of the container and striking me with his hooves as he got his legs over the front of the divider where I cowered. It took several minutes before we were finally on the ground. Both the horse and I were bleeding, and there was no doubt that Walter needed immediate medical care. A horse ambulance was summoned, and off he went with a handler to the closest equine hospital. Luckily, I only had a few bad scrapes, but I was badly shaken, nevertheless.

Walter recovered and went back to work, but not without drama. There was a brown sliding door at the far end of the indoor arena, through which the tractor could come to rake the footing. It rained practically every day in our area of Germany, and for some reason, the inside of that sliding door would get a dark splotch in the middle from moisture condensation. Well, that was enough for "Crazy Walter." He would stop halfway down the arena and refuse to go anywhere near it. It became so bad that one day when the vet was there to inoculate horses, I dismounted while schooling the gelding and asked the vet to take a look at his eyes. I wondered if perhaps he had cataracts or some other partial blindness and felt terrible that it was a possibility, given the trauma that he had endured. After a careful look, however, and with a sort of a chuckle that made me know he was partly joking, the vet handed me back the reins and declared Walter had nothing wrong with his eyes that a good spanking could not cure!

Rats!

In the spring of 1988, I had a nice show scheduled in Paris, in the famous Bois de Boulogne park. The stables had been set on the other side of a very busy downtown street. The local *gendarmes* were there all day and evening to assure riders, grooms, and horses could cross without issues from ongoing traffic.

Or so I thought.

That afternoon, I rode Walter up to the intersection where the police were stationed and ready to stop traffic. The horse took one look at the white painted stripes of the crosswalk and reared up, then bolted back toward the barn. I managed to stop him after several strides and turned back around toward the crosswalk as Petra came running to help. We both thought she could take the reins and lead us across the street to the park, but Crazy Walter would have none of it, rearing up and whirling around again, literally picking Petra up off the ground as the three of us went sailing back toward the stables again.

Collecting myself, the horse, and my nerves, once more I made my way to the crosswalk and the policeman who now was looking at us with justified trepidation. But this time, just as Walter was getting to that point of making a bid for home, I turned him around and began backing him up. Not seeing where I was directing him, he proceeded to back right up, across the road, and up onto the sidewalk on the opposite side. There I turned him around to face the nice green park, toward which he gladly resumed marching. We actually had quite a good show, placing well in both his classes.

Walter progressed to the highest level, the Grand Prix, and we had a number of successes: back-to-back National Championships, wins in Stockholm, Rotterdam, and Münster, and a fun exhibition under the lights at the Washington International Horse Show. But there were also failures—dramatic ones—a World Championship Qualifier in Neumünster, Germany. Our US squad of Marie Meyers, Betsy Steiner, Shelly Francis, and Kathleen Raine were all riding, coached by the famous Herbert Rehbein, one of the greatest trainers of the twentieth century. The show took place in an indoor stadium with a warm-up arena about three hundred feet away. Training the day before the competition went very well, and I was hopeful that Walter might be really good.

The next evening as the class began, it was cold and rainy. The steward told me it was time for me to make the trek from the warm-up to the show arena, and as we headed over, I could tell that Walter was not in the mood to play along. We had almost reached the entrance to the main hall that led to the ring where the judges and spectators were anxiously waiting when up he reared and then bolted back toward the comfort of his friends in the warm-up area. Herbert, seeing my situation, came running to my aid, took hold of the reins, and marched us back toward the entrance to the hall again. Before I could say, "I think this is a bad idea," up and around went Crazy Walter again, this time dragging Herbert along with us, practically all the way back to the other arena.

Shaken, it occurred to me that I knew exactly what to do. I told Herbert to leave it to me, and Walter and I proceeded back toward our goal. Just before that dreaded spot where my horse refused to go forward, I stopped, turned him around, and began to back him up, just as I had done to cross the street in Paris several years before. In we went, down the hall to the entrance doors to the main arena. As I backed him through the doorway, I told the two men in charge of the entrance to close the doors as fast as they could and not to open them up again, no matter what they heard, until they knew my test was done!

As soon as the attendants shut the doors, I wheeled Walter around so he was facing the head judge at the opposite end of the arena. My horse stared—at the judges, the tables they were sitting at, and at the packed audience, which was now chuckling as they had never seen an entrance like this. This amount of stimuli was actually so much that Walter could not decide what to think, so we began our Grand Prix pretty well. Going very forward was working until we got to the far end of the arena where we had to do two walk pirouettes, similar to a dancer doing a twirl. We completed the first one nicely, and as we were about to do the second one, a spectator got up from a seat in the stands and allowed the base of the chair to fly up and hit the seat back, making a noise that caught Walter's attention. He stared up into the crowd and began backing up in the direction of the judge and scribe sitting in the corner by "H." The scribe went running toward the other end of the arena while the judge stood his ground for a few seconds until he saw my horse was *definitely* not in his right mind. With that, the look on the judge's face changed, and I watched him try to scale the seven-foot wall up into the spectator's bleachers. Just as a few people in the first row began to pull the judge from "H" over to safety, Walter's hind legs hit the white PVC railing of the dressage arena, and we went flying forward, ending back in the middle of the ring, staring at the judge at "C." Acutely embarrassed, I saluted the head judge and turned to leave as I heard the announcer say something kind about how I treated my horse so nicely under the circumstances. I listened as the crowds applauded my horsemanship.

Walter taught me patience and humility.

Once, while working on the piaffe with Herbert Rehbein at his farm in Germany, Herbert came up behind us and said, "Hold on!" as he whacked Walter on the butt with his whip. Off we galloped toward the far wall, a seven-foot, slanted kickboard with a four-foot by four-foot window above it. Before I could even think, Crazy Walter was trying to scale the wall to and somehow jump out the window with me still aboard. Fortunately, the wall was too high and slippery, and we finally came back to earth.

Another time, I left Walter with Gabby Grillo's assistant trainer for a week while I went to watch the European Championships in England. I explained the gelding had a "short fuse," but of course, the German trainer waved me away, saying all would be fine. When I came home and asked about the horses, the look in the trainer's face was completely changed.

Apparently he had been riding Walter, and the gelding was not responding well enough to his leg. He had picked up a whip and smacked Walter on the side, at which point the horse immediately leaned up against the arena wall and proceeded to slide his body down the kickboard until he was lying on his side in the dirt. Fortunately, it all happened sort of like a slow-moving train wreck. The trainer was able to step quickly away as the horse hit the ground, having a good-old-fashioned tantrum, thrashing his head and legs back and forth in the dirt. After a minute, he simply stopped, got back up, and shook the dust from his body all over his rider.

The lesson I learned here? Respect the power of the horse and try to understand his thoughts better. We need to think like them instead of trying to make them think like us. The same rule can also apply to our relationships with more than a few people in our lives.

Prior to the 1992 Olympics, I was riding Lectron, a beautiful, black stallion, also owned by Walter and Mary Anne McPhail and formerly ridden by their daughter, Melinda. Lectron had been hard for her to bring along to the Grand Prix, so it was decided that I would train and compete him for a year or two, then give him back to her so she could try out for the next US Dressage Team.

Lectron began to bloom in his physique and became highly competitive, making our European squad and then placing well in the international competitions leading up to the Olympics in Barcelona. We were actually a top-ten favorite as we came to the first day of the Games! Back then, each horse-and-rider combination had to go into the "Ten-Minute Ring" before going to the main stadium. In that small space, no one but the rider, not even the horse's groom, was allowed to touch the horse.

With only a minute left before we were due in the Olympic stadium, I remembered we had not tightened Lectron's noseband after warm-up, a thing we traditionally did prior to riding a test because he tended to stretch the leather with his strong jaws. The stallion had a nervous twitch that only showed itself when he flexed his head and neck in just a certain way, which made him look the most beautiful from the ground but caused him to feel anxious. I yelled up the hill to where our coach Herbert Rehbein stood, and asked if I should quickly get off and tighten the noseband myself. Herbert waved and called back that he thought we looked fine as we were, and so off we went to the stadium.

Lectron felt great as we trotted around the outside of the arena, greeting the judges as I confidently passed by their boxes. The announcer told the huge audience of eighteen thousand spectators from around the world about my horse and my past accomplishments. The bell rang, indicating I should begin my test, and I made a small circle in front of the stands before entering the arena at "A."

Just then, Lectron twitched his head, and as he did, his tongue went up and over the two bits of the double bridle, something that he had never done before and could not have happened had I tightened his noseband just one hole more snug. This was the veritable rider's nightmare!

My thoughts came rapid-fire:

- *"Should I get off and try quickly to put his tongue back under the bits?"*
- *"Should I stop and give him rein and hope he does it himself?"*
- *"Should I excuse myself and walk out of the stadium in disgrace?"*
- *"Should I just forge on and hope for the best?"*

I chose to hope for the best and rode straight down the centerline with Lectron's tongue hanging out the right side of his mouth like a flag waving at the crowd. But Michael Poulin had already gone on his horse, Graf George, and received a 62%, not good enough to help the United States to a medal. I had to try my best to navigate my horse through the test without mistakes to gain as many points for the team as I possibly could. The problem was that taking pressure on the reins would have forced the bits upward. Usually this would have contacted the roof of the horse's mouth, but in this case, it would have pinched the underside of Lectron's tongue, with unknown consequences. My only chance was to push my hands forward and try not to touch his mouth at all while guiding him through the test we had done so many times using only my legs and seat.

Lectron was a kind and gentle stallion, and he tried his best to listen to my cues. Other than his tongue being out, which brought down the scores from those judges who could see it as we went around the arena, he proceeded to do quite a good test. Of course, in our sport, seeing the tongue clearly outside of the horse's mouth earns no higher than a "5" to a "6" (out of "10") for those movements, regardless of how beautiful the movements are otherwise. At the end of the test I left the arena with a heavy heart, feeling I had let down my team, the owners, my horse, and myself. But as luck would have it, my score of 64%, which equaled the score of my teammate, Charlotte Bredahl with her horse Monsieur, combined with our anchor Carol Lavell and her great horse Gifted's score of 69%, was enough to give us the Olympic bronze medal behind Germany and The Netherlands! Yes, the bar for an Olympic dressage medal was way lower back in 1992, but the lesson I learned was that sometimes when we feel we are failing, we can push on and produce miraculous results, both for ourselves and others.

At the 2000 Olympics in Sydney, I was riding the nine-year-old gray gelding Rainier, owned by Jane Clark. We did a respectable job in the Grand

Prix and helped the win team bronze. At the time, I was dealing with ex-cruciating back pain that traveled down my right leg. Riding, sitting, and even lying down were very painful, so I had a very difficult time sleeping. The Olympic doctors did their best to help me by dispensing medications that were legal but powerful—I took both Tramadol and OxyContin before that first day of competition and still came back to the barn, got off my horse, and proceeded to hop around on my left foot, as it was too painful to bring my right foot to the ground.

Having won the team medal, which was most important, the doctors told me to go ahead and take double the amount of drugs half an hour closer to the time of my test the next day for the individual medals. I did as I was told.

All was going as planned until I got to the middle of the Grand Prix Special test and the walk tour. This was normally the place where the rider and horse could take a big breath before going on to the difficult second part of the test. At that moment, though, the drugs kicked in, and I was virtually flying! I started wandering aimlessly around the arena until suddenly, I heard a voice speaking to me.

"Robert...Robert...what are you doing? You have to go back to the beginning and start again!"

I looked around and saw the person speaking was Axel Steiner, the American judge sitting in the judge's box midway down the side of the arena. Confused, I replied, "You can't talk to me. Only the judge at 'C' is allowed to speak to me!" At which point, the head judge at "C" rang his bell, beckoning from where he sat at the end of the arena.

"You have to start over again," he said.

"From the beginning of the test?" I asked.

"No," he replied, giving me a look. "Just from the beginning of the walk."

I smiled at him, but as I turned around, the magnitude of what I had just done hit me just as suddenly as the drugs had. It was like a hot flash of adrenaline brought me back to sobriety. I proceeded to finish my test without further issues. Naturally, my quest for an individual medal was over, and as Rainier and I walked out of the stadium, the press surrounded us, asking what had happened. My only reply was, "I'm okay."

I went back to my room and fell asleep for six hours, only truly understanding what had happened upon waking up. I felt bad for the Team, and especially Rainier's owner Jane Clark and Chef d'Equipe Jessica Ransehousen, both of whom I was told later were clutching each other up in the stands, asking what the hell I was doing in the arena. It was years before I let anyone know that I was high as a kite during the test. Jane, just as she did for her jumping riders who went off course in their competitions, highlighted the next bill she received from me in yellow and deducted $1,000. Considering what had happened, I was fine with that!

— The Value of Horrible Moments —

I've turned failure into an art form. No one worth anything has not learned how to succeed without many small, if not large, failures along the way. Of course, at the time when they happen, failures are not fun, and we tend to replay them repeatedly—too many times to be healthy—before letting them go and moving on with our lives and careers. It is when we look back that we often see the tremendous value horrible moments ultimately bring to our lives. Now, as a more mature (and yes, hopefully wiser) person, I actually do not fear failure so much as I embrace it and learn from it so as to make myself better, stronger, and smarter.

Consider how trainers of jumping horses will take the young horse that is just learning to jump through the following exercise: A low fence consisting of two rails crossed in an "X" shape—with a third rail on the ground in front of the "X," called a "ground line"—is set up for the horse to trot slowly over. Now, top professionals are great at placing the horse at the perfect spot to jump from and giving the horse all the impulsion and help he needs to clear the fence. But when working with young horses, the smart trainer literally does nothing to help them jump this obstacle, more or less dropping the reins and allowing the horse to do whatever he wishes to do, short of stopping or refusing to jump. The novice horse may leap way too high over the fence, or he may "hang" one or both of his legs and knock down the jump. Rails are usually made out of wood or PVC, and either way, a knock against the horse's leg is a bit of an uncomfortable shock. The jump is rebuilt, and the rider trots right back around and brings the horse to the jump again exactly the same way, dropping the horse's reins and allowing him to jump however he wants. Perhaps the horse now clears the jump with his front legs but hits with a hind leg, bringing down a rail again. He might even shake his head upon landing on the other side of the obstacle, showing a bit of consternation over the discomfort arising from the rails hitting his legs. Again, the fence is reset and the horse is brought back toward it a third time in the exact same way as before; however, this time the horse decides he has had enough of hitting the rails and pulls both his front and hind legs way clear while looking carefully at the fence and beyond to ensure he has jumped cleanly and is ready for what might be next. The trainer has embraced each failure, allowing the horse to (hopefully!) learn from each mistake that caused a small "ouch," until the horse finally succeeded in folding up and properly raising all four of his legs as he jumped. He not only cleared the fence (no "ouch"), he was also praised profusely by his rider.

How does this relate to learning in humans? I use this example all the time when teaching:

Mom comes downstairs in the morning after looking in Johnny's room and seeing the bed is unmade and the room is a wreck. She sees Johnny sitting cross-legged in front of the television and says in a soft voice, "Johnny, please go upstairs and make your bed and clean your room."

Johnny is oblivious to his mother's request and remains seated and staring at the TV.

Mom now raises her voice somewhat and says with more authority, "Johnny, *please* go upstairs now and make your bed and clean your room!"

Johnny, doing his best imitation of a Jack Russell Terrier, totally ignores his mother and remains seated.

Finally, Mom walks over and picks Johnny up by the ear and, lovingly but with no lack of clarity, swats Johnny on the seat of his pants and, with a look that means business, sends Johnny running up the stairs. Mom verifies the bed is made and room is clean moments later, thanks Johnny, and tells him he may now go outside to play.

The next day, the same thing happens—Mom asks Johnny twice to no avail to go upstairs to clean his room. This time, when she begins to walk toward him, before she can grab him by the ear and swat him one, he gets up and runs up the stairs. Again, Mom checks, sees his clean room, thanks Johnny, and tells him he can go outside and play.

Day Three comes and Johnny, having figured out the entire process and really wanting to meet his friends outside first thing, decides to surprise his mom by making his bed and putting away his toys before coming down to breakfast. Mom sees this and not only praises Johnny for his actions but gives him five dollars to get ice cream or candy later in the day.

We can learn from our failures. Corrections appropriate for "crimes" committed and rewards or positive reinforcement for successes are the way people and animals learn best.

Over time I have realized that every one of my failures were enormously valuable in helping me evolve as an athlete in my sport, and more importantly, as a person. I learned that who I was depended on not just how I did in the show arena but how I treated others every day.

I recognized that we do not define ourselves by our actions when we are doing well and winning but rather by the grace we exhibit when things do not go our way. I have been so fortunate to have had many great successes in my life, but today I am just as grateful for the failures that helped me learn to be a winner.

You are probably going to have small and large failures in your life. Having failures does not define *you* as a "failure"—unless you believe you are. You are defined by how you perceive low points: whether you choose to learn from them and show grace and a sense of humor in the process or succumb to them and fall into a deep depression. The old adage, "When you fall off your horse, you have to pick yourself up, brush yourself off, and get right back on," rings true. You define yourself not when everything is going great but rather in the hardest moments. These are the moments where you are tested: Will you show lesser qualities like jealousy, anger, or "sour grapes," or will you find a reason to demonstrate generosity, kindness, magnanimity, and LOVE? ●

Brilliance Lives on the Edge

Establishing and
Expanding Confidence

8

CHAPTER

In 2013, I took over as the Technical Advisor and Chef d'Equipe/Coach of the US Dressage Team. From 1992 through the time that I finished competing in 2005, the United States had consistently been in the medals as one of the three top nations in international dressage competition. In those years, our confidence was very high within our top group of athletes, and our coaches knew that we were a team of professionals they could count on to come home with medals of some color or another around our necks.

Both our horses and some of us riders were aging out after 2005, and at the time, there was not a strong program in America to provide a great pipeline of star riders and horses to take our places. I asked if I could speak to our High Performance Dressage Committee at the annual convention since I was not an active member of that group, and I told them that if they did not make the appropriate changes and create programs from the bottom to the top of the pyramid, meaning all levels of dressage sport, they would find themselves out of the medals in 2008 in Beijing, and it would take years to pull themselves out of the hole they had dug for themselves. Sadly, the coach at that time and the leadership thought they were in great shape because they had enjoyed so much success for so long and did not see any issue in need of change.

As it turned out, the Olympic Team in Beijing was eliminated for a drug infraction, and then the United States was out of the medals both at the following World Championships and Olympics in London in 2012.

My very first job as Technical Advisor/Coach was to produce a four-year plan, which I called, "The Roadmap to the Podiums." This fifty-six-page document, created with help from the other coaches and staff from the United States Equestrian Federation (USEF), described in detail the training and competitive programs we would enact to assure excellent results, including medals. Naturally, such a bold undertaking required an enormous amount of funding for the proposed programs, something which was not a given through USEF or the United States Equestrian Team Foundation (the organization in charge of doing the fundraising for our sport). Therefore, I included fundraising efforts I personally would lead annually to make up the difference so that our athletes would never have to wonder if they could afford to try out for the Team. I also gave myself annual markers, which I had to meet in order to be paid a bonus for achieving the goal or multiple goals of each year.

My first goal? To produce top squads (up to eight horse-and-rider combinations) that would go to Europe each year leading up to the Championships that determined our international team.

These squads competed against the best in the world in their back-yards—and beat them. With each win, the individuals (and thereby the Team), grew in their confidence as medal contenders. There were times when a group of our riders had a win or great placement in a show that I knew had no real significance as an indicator of their ultimate strength against the other top nations in our sport. Nevertheless, I would post on all social media as if they had just won an Olympic gold medal every time, profusely congratulating them on their amazing results while pre-dicting the ultimate success of the team again and again in the upcoming Olympic Games or World Championships. Why? Because it fueled the fire in the riders, their owners and sponsors, and the entire American dressage community, while constantly reminding the rest of the world, including the international judges, that the United States was steadily and convincingly marching toward those medal podiums.

In 2016, we had a squad of super riders and horses in Europe as we prepared for the Olympics in Rio de Janeiro. We started out at the Nation's Cup, a very nice show in France with all eight horse-and-rider combi-nations still vying for the eventual team of four, plus one reserve. Top riders from the actual Olympic Teams from several of the European and Scandinavian countries were taking part, so a lot was on the line for us.

The US Team had a strong lead after the first of what should have been three tests that would decide the winners: the Grand Prix, the Grand Prix Special, and the Grand Prix Freestyle. However, at the end of the first day, it began to rain...and the rain went on and on until the arena became a lake. The Ground Jury made the difficult decision that going on with the competition would endanger the horses, and so the show was over, and the United States was deemed the victor.

Two things happened from this: First, and a bit unexpectedly, Kasey Perry-Glass and her lovely horse Dublet were the huge surprise winner of the class, besting our already-known champions, Laura Graves and Verdades. I loved hearing the other trainers at the show, as well as many of the judges, suddenly comparing Dublet with the famous gold-medal winner Valegro for his power and elasticity. I also knew the win would give Kasey, who was really still quite green at this level, a big boost in confidence. At the same time, Laura, who was used to winning with much higher scores than she received in France due to a few unusual mistakes, was most certainly unhappy with her results, even though she placed second with a score only a point or so behind Kasey. All our other riders did quite well and were happy with their overall results, knowing they were still in the hunt for one of the coveted team spots.

Another happy person was my assistant coach, great friend, and personal trainer for both Laura and Kasey on our tour, Olympian Debbie McDonald. Deb and I worked so well together that we rarely had to finish a sentence before one of us knew exactly what the other was thinking, and we practically always agreed on everything when it came to training and competitive strategies. We also had the luxury of taking turns dealing with issues when one or the other of us was too close to a situation. In this instance, I knew that we had only a few more competitions for our riders before our final selection show in Rotterdam, the Netherlands, where once again, and for the last time, all eight combinations would perform before we named our final Olympic Team and Reserve Rider.

Leading up to Rotterdam, the riders, along with their personal trainers, had listed the remaining shows where they wished to compete, knowing they only had to do two of them to meet the official selection criteria put out at the beginning of the year. While in France, I met with USEF Managing Director of Dressage Hallye Griffin and Laura and Debbie to discuss Laura's plans to not show again until Rotterdam. Understandably, both Laura and Deb wanted to ensure that Verdades would be in perfect shape for the Olympics, so they did not want to show him more than absolutely necessary. I had concerns about this strategy, however.

Looking Laura directly in her eyes, I asked, "What is your goal? Do you want to simply make the Team? Because I am pretty sure you have that in hand. But if you want more—meaning an individual medal in Rio—you cannot wait until Rotterdam where you will be going up against practically all of the international medal contenders without first going somewhere else to make a clear statement that you and your horse are, without a doubt, one of the very top three or four combinations in the world."

This was not exactly what Laura wanted to hear that day. I knew what it was like (so well!) to be told I was not yet up to standard; I also knew the amazing feeling of being told my horse and I looked like top contenders. As a coach, I always promised my riders that I would never expect more than fifty percent of what I expected of myself.

Laura, with her incredible drive and champion attitude, thought for a minute and agreed to show at one more competition in Holland where our experienced team rider Steffen Peters was waiting to begin his tour in Europe with his two fantastic horses, Legolas 92 and Rosamunde. Not only did both Steffen and Laura convincingly win their separate Grand Prix classes, Laura did exactly what I hoped for, receiving a huge score and beating one of the best team riders for Great Britain. Laura was at the top of her game, and now both she and the world knew her and her horse's capabilities *before* our arrival in Rotterdam. All our athletes, and the rest of the international dressage community, could have a high degree of confidence that the US team could, on a good day, challenge all comers, including the extremely strong Dutch team on their home turf.

Prior to Rotterdam, most of us were based at the gorgeous US training facility in Belgium, owned by our wonderful host Rob van Puijenbroek. A couple of our squad riders had opted to live and train elsewhere during the selection period.

Another one of our up-and-coming riders, Ali Brock, along with the lovely stallion Rosevelt, owned by Fritz Kundrun, had been looking like strong team contenders in the earlier shows, as had Olivia Lagoy-Weltz with her super gelding Lonoir. We had a team meeting to discuss the show where, though all eight riders were allowed to start, only four could represent the United States on the Nation's Cup Team, while the other four competed in an equally difficult class as individuals. We explained that the US "Selection Committee" would take the scores from both the team and individual competitions equally into consideration, as well as all the performances throughout the eight combinations' time in Europe. Naturally, those named to compete as individuals felt a bit at a disadvantage as they wanted to do everything they could to make their decades-long dreams come true. As the coach, it felt great to have such a tremendous group of athletes, both two- and four-legged, to mount an Olympic effort, but I could see that Rotterdam was definitely going to test all of their skills as well as their nerves.

No one's nerves, in the end, were tested more than Laura's.

The day we drove to the competition site, a few from our group went ahead to bed down the stalls so that when the riders and their horses arrived, they could go directly into the stabling and relax. I knew the key to managing a successful team was making sure as best we could that the riders had one thing and one thing only to worry about, and that was being great when they need to be—in the big arena! As she always did, Laura took "Diddy" (Verdades' stable name) for a nice walk and hand-grazing around the stable area before her expected schooling time with the others, later that afternoon.

Hallye, Dr. Cricket Russillo, our extraordinary team veterinarian, and I headed to our hotel to check in and catch a bite to eat. We barely made it off the show grounds when all three of us got text messages from Laura. Diddy had gotten bit or eaten something while grazing and his nose was swelling. Before Cricket could send off a response as to what to do, her phone rang—the horse was in real trouble and we had to return to the barn immediately.

We rushed back, and it was hard to keep our horror a secret as we peered over the stall door at poor Diddy, whose nose now looked more like that of a moose than a horse. He was clearly having issues with breathing as well.

It is important to understand the complexity of the situation. Had we not been about to begin an international competition, the vet could simply administer whichever drugs were best to combat such a reaction and tell the rider to not worry about it, the horse would be fine to work again in a couple of days. But we were under strict anti-doping regulations, just as would be the case at the Olympics where there is a zero-tolerance rule. Fortunately, it was only Wednesday and Diddy's first class wasn't until Friday afternoon. And so began the all-day-and-most-of-the-night effort by Cricket, Laura, and all the riders and grooms to do whatever could help the horse and support a fellow teammate. A great team is only as good as every single player within the group, and for us that most definitely included the vet, farrier, grooms, and other specialists we traveled with to ensure the athletes had one hundred percent of everything they needed to be able to shine and achieve personal bests when it was most important.

We were all relieved when Verdades made a perfect recovery. Only a few knew that Diddy had suffered such a scary allergic reaction, which we came to discover was caused by the hairs of an extremely poisonous caterpillar that makes its nest high up in the trees all around the show complex in downtown Rotterdam. No one had informed us that show management annually went through and destroyed the nests of the cater-pillars because of their toxicity. They posed a danger to both animals and people that happened to come into contact with one of their little hairs.

Our entire group looked great as they went for the required "veterinary check" on Thursday, trotting in front of the presiding Dutch veterinarian and the Ground Jury with ease. As is always the case, once we got through the ever-nerve-wracking vet check with all players intact, we breathed a heavy sigh of relief and prepared for battle the next day.

We nominated our Nation's Cup Team, with Laura and Verdades as our anchors to compete last from our group, while Olivia and Lonoir would lead us off, followed by Kasey and Dublet, and then Steffen and Legolas. This is generally the way all Olympic sports teams send in their athletes, especially in subjective sports where judges and the press expect to see the very best competitors going last. The entire team rose to the occasion, leaving the ring with personal bests and showing great self-confidence.

When Laura rode her test, you could hear a pin drop. Debbie and I, along with the rest of the group, stood on the "Kiss and Cry" platform, and movement by movement, we clutched each other harder as Laura and Verdades danced effortlessly and gorgeously around the arena. At the end, we knew she had won the class and helped America take the lead ahead of Holland and all the rest. At that very moment, without saying it to anyone, I also knew, without a shadow of a doubt, that we were perfectly on track to medal in the Olympic Games in Rio later that summer.

The thing is, as I've mentioned in these pages, dressage is a "who beats who where" sport. We had knocked off the Swedes, Danes, Spanish, French, and even the always-strong Dutch on their own home field! Only the British, who had the number-one-ranked combination in the world, Charlotte Dujardin and Valegro, as well as Carl Hester and any horse he might ride, could, on any given day, be just as good as or better than us. That is, other than the Germans, who had won more Olympic gold medals than any other team. They were practically unbeatable. Yet we were now making a statement to *watch out*—we could give them a run for their money.

When you have been on as many select teams as I have, you recognize the feeling of being considered a frontrunner right away. The other team leaders treat you with greater respect, asking for your advice regarding their own teams and congratulating you for how strong your group is. Judges gush about how lovely your horses and riders looked the last time they gave them high scores. The press wants to know all your plans leading up to the Games. But most of all, your team members and all the owners, sponsors, grooms, specialists, federation staff, and fans understand and demonstrate how proud they are to be a part of something bigger than themselves. The excitement they feel and express is contagious.

For me, what happened between my taking on the role of Technical Advisor in 2013 and the Rio Games in 2016 proved once again that we could create a "machine" that, with everyone's help and hard work, would take us from a beginning vision, where we wrote down the Roadmap to the Podiums, to where we one by one, achieved every single benchmark, culminating in watching, teary-eyed, as our brilliant US Team stood on the Olympic medal podium again for the first time since 2004.

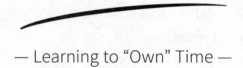

— Learning to "Own" Time —

Up until my thirties, I taught my students the way my trainers had taught theirs. Most male trainers in the Olympic equestrian disciplines back then had come out of the military. We were used to listening to sternly given orders without ever talking back and God knows there was no humor involved! We listened attentively and did our very best to do exactly as we were told. I remember honestly feeling that nothing was more important than hearing my trainer and mentor Colonel Bengt Ljunquist say, "Good job!" It did not matter to me how happy I was with myself or my horse during my lesson, provided my trainer was happy.

I now understand that the true role of a trainer or teacher, like a good parent, is to do such a great job that we make ourselves obsolete. *Through trial and error, correction and reward, and ongoing attention to the details of our craft, the goal of a trainer is to create a student who always knows who they are and what they are expressing outwardly to the universe and all who are in their presence.*

This is the idea.

As I learned with each of my failures, with each competitive success, I was able to hone in on exactly the feelings I was having during those tests and what the horse looked like from where I was sitting in the saddle. I can still remember clearly the look and feeling I had in 1985 with Romantico in the Grand Prix team test at the North American Championships. He felt so uphill and beautifully on my aids, and just as I was about to remark on this as I left the show arena, my Chef d'Equipe, the famous Jessica Ransehousen, said, "Good job, Robert! A pity he was a little above the bit throughout most of your test."

WHAT?

I was *sure* my horse looked perfectly on the bit with flexion just at the top of his head—his poll—and a perfect outline. I always had every ride video recorded, and I sat down to look at it after Romantico was cooled down and put away. Of course, Jess was right on. My horse was about an inch too high in his carriage throughout most of the test.

There are three parts of becoming self-aware: First, the person knows who she is (in relationship to the animal and her own awareness); second, she knows what she is expressing outwardly, as well as what she *intends* to express; and third, she knows what other people are seeing—it's as if she is sitting in a chair, watching herself and what she is doing. Self-awareness means knowing exactly what others are seeing in and of you as you are going through your dressage test...or through your life. Of course, it must be considered whether or not you should care what others see or how they may judge you, but I believe that clarity as to how you are performing, in sport or in life, necessarily depends upon knowing how others perceive you. This is the reason dancers, singers, and yes, dressage riders, use mirrors. We see and pick apart in the moment, every little detail of our movements. We also use video, and ultimately have judges (some kind and some not so much) who critique us, hopefully to help us grow and become more successful. Over time and with countless hours of practice, we gain insight into ourselves, and with that insight, we can better express ourselves outwardly to the world, with our job or our sport or our art, to say, "Look at me! This is my story. This is my 'movie.' This is who I believe I am, and I want you to see and appreciate me!"

Visualization becomes a major key to success as you go from learning a craft to becoming a true "artist" in life. You can learn to paint and understand all the rules and principles of painting, but you'll never create a masterpiece unless you can visualize. Michelangelo did not walk into the Sistine Chapel with a bunch of paint cans and simply toss them up toward the ceiling and hope something worked out. He looked up and visualized the masterpiece in his mind, and then went about the next four years, stroke by stroke, to realize his finest work of art.

Whether we are Michelangelo or not, in order to create beauty or a beautiful life, we have to first see in our mind's eye that which we wish to produce. In dressage, to be successful, you must see the grandest movie you can possibly imagine of yourself and your horse, dancing in perfect harmony together, in the fraction of a second before you attempt to do it. Consider the Olympic diver: He walks out on the diving board or platform and comes to the end. He stops and clears his mind of all extraneous thoughts. Next, the diver goes inside to his "mind's eye" (or third eye, which is said to provide perception beyond ordinary sight) and sees himself crouching down and then leaping up into the air and doing the most perfect dive he can possibly imagine—the "Perfect 10"! A fraction of a second later, the diver attempts to realize exactly what he just visualized, first taking in a deep breath in order to fully oxygenate his muscles, then with lungs full, crouching down in full concentration, directing his muscles to use the amazing physical and mental energy he has prepared over many years of training. Finally, he exhales as he springs upward into the air, so high as to appear like a bird in flight. With incredible precision, the Olympic Champion turns and swirls in the next seconds, before slicing seamlessly into the water below like a sharp knife through the liquid membrane, without sound or splash. To the layperson watching the dive in real time, it is hard to see all the tiny details of the diver's movements, but the judges, like the judges for dressage, have spent their lives practicing their sport, just as the athlete has.

The better you get at any endeavor like these, the more "time slows down." Picture Keanu Reeves in the groundbreaking movie *The Matrix*. In the film, Keanu, a "normal" guy, is seemingly thrust into a parallel universe in which humans are being controlled by computer models that an underground resistance is fighting to overcome. At first, it is practically impossible for Keanu and his cohorts to fight off the much stronger and faster enemy. As they learn and change techniques, however, Keanu ultimately comes to the realization that he is "The One," and that unlike what he thought as he kept being beaten by his foe, time no longer "owns" him, rather, Keanu "owns time." The second he understands this, time slows down, and he easily spars with his enemy and ultimately kills him. With a last grin on his face and spark in his eye, Keanu takes in a breath of freedom, crouches down, and takes off like a rocket, straight up into the sky. The end!

Learning to "own time" is key to reaching the stars.

Each of us has the power to shine, to be "The One," and as we become self-aware, we realize that it is not egotistical to believe in our brilliance, but rather an affront that we would not live up to our grandest potential. It requires a huge amount of work and dedication in seeking the *truth* to reach a state of self-awareness. It also takes risk and pushing beyond fear and boundaries to reach greatness.

Brilliance does not live in safe spaces. Brilliance lives on the edge.

The great downhill skier going seventy miles per hour down the mountain is not thinking about staying safe and comfortable; the skier is asking herself how she can make that next turn sharper in order to shave a thousandth of a second off her time. The great dressage rider knows that the only way to achieve that gold medal is to see where every single point is during her test and go for it, confident that she has achieved such a strong partnership with her amazing horse that what seems practically impossible to those watching is barely scratching the surface of their potential. They make it look easy, as does the great opera singer or dancer. Thousands of hours of practice under the tutelage of top teachers, the never-ending quest for the truth of what they seek and how to reach it, and finally their understanding of their brilliance, produces the enormous confidence and spectacular performance that brings us to our feet with tears in our eyes as we watch them shine on the stage of their lives. We love and admire these stars and set out to be like them, and thus, the process begins again and again.

When confidence is high, success is not only at its most possible, it becomes probable. As I've said, becoming self-aware is a big part of creating what we visualize as our grandest self. It is also the teacher's or coach's job to instill confidence in their student through positive reinforcement as well as well-understood and well-intentioned critiques. With each small success, the next slightly larger one becomes more attainable and comfortable.

Robert Dover

There are certainly moments when compromise in practice may be necessary to get past a blockage in the road. This is true in weightlifting. I had a terrific personal trainer, Bob Gutowitz, who is still a great friend. Once during a workout I thought there was no way I could lift the weight he was setting on the barbell behind me. Bob promised me I could do it and said I should visualize the weight being as light as a feather, take in a deep breath, and as I let it out, *push!* I did exactly as he said, and with great effort and a lot of groaning, I got the weight up and set it down hard on the rack. Bob was not concerned with my imperfect form at that moment. He knew that once I realized I could lift that much weight, I would feel confident enough to lift it again, and as I became more relaxed, I would be able to concentrate on my form at the same time. The same holds true in yoga. Good yoga instructors remind us that we may never achieve perfection but that the true purpose is to stay on "the road *toward* perfection." In doing this, we grow confidence and find harmony.

Confidence and harmony are inevitably intertwined in the nature of all endeavors in life. With improved confidence that any action will result in a reliable *re*action, the result for the person, as well as those who may be watching or listening to the person, is a feeling of harmony. When preparing a student and her horse to compete at a show, we practice the requirements of the test they must do and then rehearse the test itself so many times that the student and the horse are both so confident and harmonious that they exude those characteristics outwardly to the judges and audience. My goal is to make them believe they have already won the class before they even enter the actual arena.

When I competed, I would go around the outside of the arena, greeting each of the five or seven judges seated in their booths, and as I went by, I would give my inside rein forward, just to show the degree of self-carriage and harmony I had with my beautiful horse. I would also do something very difficult for most riders and horses, such as piaffe (a trot in place), to show off one of our strengths. In my mind, I was putting out the vibe of, "You people are so fortunate to be able to now see this gorgeous animal dance around the arena in front of you! To my competitors, I'm sorry, but you might as well load your horses up and take them home because no one will stack up against us."

Confidence, when backed up by the harmonious execution of that which we see in our mind's eye as the grandest version we can possibly imagine of ourselves, results in brilliance! This is why the greatest athletes and teams in all sports, the finest entertainers and artists in all art forms, and the greatest achievers in all endeavors are able to sustain their excellence and go down in history for their accomplishments. ●

Jump into the Great Lake

Surrounding Yourself
with Good People

9

CHAPTER

I love to ski. I actually took up skiing in my early thirties when I met Robert and he and his "second mom," Maryanne, took me to Deer Valley, a perfect place for a first experience on the slopes—that is, if you have the right skis and understand even a bit of the craft before attempting to journey down the mountain behind your loved ones.

I did all the wrong things on my first day of skiing. I wore an old pair of borrowed racing skis that were way too long, and Robert and Maryanne said, "Follow us!" Well, after several falls, I remembered why having a great instructor is so important. I bid my family farewell and journeyed to the office where

I hired a ski pro who helped me to pick out a far more suitable pair of parabolic skis to learn on, and off we went.

What a difference a day made! The following afternoon, as I followed my instructor down a fairly steep slope, Robert and Maryanne were on a lift overhead, saw me, and yelled down, "Hey, Robert, what are you doing already going down a black diamond?"

Of course, I had no idea I was going down a hill of that difficulty. I was just having fun learning from a very good teacher who helped me understand the basics and gave me the confidence to put them into practice. That is what a good teacher does.

There is no doubt that being around successful people helps you to be motivated to stretch toward your goals. Within sports, you will find, for instance, fencers from all around the world converging to live and learn in the south of Germany. The reason for this is simple: like my own sport of dressage, Germans have historically been the very best fencers at the Olympic level. Their upbringing in the sport, from very early on, produces a standard of excellence which results in not only medals but also a national pride that creates an ongoing cycle of greatness and new champions coming up through their pipeline. For many years, Americans saw this same fantastic standard in dressage in Germany as well, and one by one, our athletes would go there to learn and hope that some of the excellence would rub off on them. It took many years, however, before our country as a whole understood and took on the best of the German riding and training methods, while adding our "American flair" to them so that we became an actual threat to their domination of the sport.

When I think back to all the people I surrounded myself with, whether on purpose or by happenstance, each had a role in creating who I evolved into as a person as well as an equestrian and an Olympian.

First and foremost, my family made an impression with their support. My parents and siblings, as well as all my aunts, uncles, cousins, and my grandmother (my mother's mother), gave me a great start. I am so lucky to still have my brother, Al; my sisters, Margo and Dale; my sister- and brother-in-law, Lynn and Bob; and my nephew and nieces, Shane, Morgan, and Stacy (as well as their own spouses and kids now!). Having such a wonderful family to ground and nurture you in spite of all you might face growing up and growing older is a godsend, and I am thankful to have had them all in my life.

In my long career, I have been lucky to work with some amazing teachers: Gerda Friedrichs, Myra Wagener, Margo Kirn, Elizabeth Lewis, Colonel Bengt Ljungquist, Willi Schultheis, George Theodorescu, Herbert Rehbein, and Reiner Klimke. When I read that list to myself, I can't help but think, "What an amazing group of professionals and stars in their own right!" Each had a fundamental and lasting effect on not only my career but on who I have become as a human being.

Just as important have been the incredible people who have touched my life and shaped it in ways they may not even know. So many have been there to help me when I needed it: the Reiley family, who took me in as if I were one of their own during my teens; Patience Priest, who gave me a great place to work as her partner at Sugarland Farm in Maryland; and Linda Zang, Kay Meredith, Caroline Muldoon, Ruth Barish, Bodo Hangen, Lendon Gray, Jack Fritz, Fiona Baan, General Jack Burton, and Dennis Callin, who along with so many others, were dear friends and made a profound and indelible difference in my life.

I have had the most wonderful assistants, including Petra Hofman and Katherine Bateson, who not only made sure my horses were perfectly cared for and managed but were my eyes from the ground at home and at the biggest competitions of my life. They became and still are part of my family. And now I am so lucky to be mentoring Kendall Cox, a twenty-two-year-old superstar who is quickly becoming a great assistant trainer.

I have been so lucky to have fantastic friends, both "horsey" and not, who I could count on during times of struggle or just to give me confidence when I needed it and a stiff kick in the ass when it was called for. They are too many to name them all, but some cannot go without a mention.

Ron Davis has been a huge influence, having brought Robert and me into his life of amazing friends over twenty years ago. His crazy-smart personality, and sometimes aggravating but always reliable honesty, have helped me evolve from a closed-minded and inflexible person to one who (at least I hope) is far less judgmental and most certainly freer and happier. I could not have had a better best friend than Joshua Judge for the last twenty-two years. Without Josh and his fiancé Jory, life would not be the same.

Just as important as surrounding yourself with real, live, great people (in person!), especially in this day and age of social media and literally thousands of people who can become "online friends," is learning to know who is not a positive addition to your life. Robert and I have definitely misjudged people from time to time along the way—and paid a price for our mistakes.

———

Robert and I met Joe Zada in the late nineties through friends, Monica Sinks and Ed Borreson. They were riding Joe's horses at the time and asked if I would give Ed a lesson on one of them. I agreed and went to their farm in New Hope, Pennsylvania. Joe was there and seemed extremely kind and respectful. His demeanor was humble and on the shy side for someone who my students had described as being extremely wealthy and ambitious, both as a rider himself and as an owner of what he hoped would be future Olympic horses in multiple disciplines. I knew he owned horses ridden by David O'Connor, one of America's top event riders, but did not know much more about the guy than that.

When I finished teaching Ed in that first lesson, he and Monica asked me to continue working with them when they came to Florida for the winter, and I was happy to agree to it. As is the case with all my students, most of whom are professionals with owners they ride for, I kept a respectful distance from Joe, ensuring Ed and Monica knew they could trust me never to try to take their client away—one of my golden rules as a teacher and trainer.

For whatever reason, Joe and Monica and Ed ended their professional relationship toward the end of the winter, and Joe moved his horses to Susie and Tim Dutta's barn. Tim owned The Dutta Corporation International Horse Transport, specializing in flying horses around the world, and Susie was an up-and-coming Grand Prix trainer and competitor as well as a student of mine. This new arrangement, like the one with Ed and Monica, ended in almost the same way—abruptly.

During this time, Joe had endeared himself to Robert and to me, while also making a bigger and bigger splash in the Wellington horse show community by taking over the lion's share of sponsorships for both the jumping and dressage shows. Joe stopped renting and bought a fantastic home, which had been built and lived in by the parents of another of my clients, in a gated community inside the Palm Beach Polo Club. The house was on the market for a little over $3,000,000. (Joe had told us many times that he was worth approximately $600,000,000!) He also purchased a couple of dressage horses with my help and jumpers for Robert, though none of them were extraordinary or in the price range of the top horses of the world.

Joe wanted to ride and show but was always a bit overweight and suffered from asthma, so lessons were brief and dedication was low. He did seem to have fun though, bringing his friends and family to watch him from time to time and attending all the shows in his private sponsor's tent. He held lavish New Year's Eve parties in Wellington and had us up to his Grosse Pointe Shores, Michigan, home for Christmas, where we watched an endless stream of cars and buses stop on the road out front so people could take in the thousands of lights Joe used to decorate his mansion every year.

Joe became family to us, especially to Robert. They spent a huge amount of time together, and Joe made Robert feel like not only would he always "take care of us," he would also take care of those we loved in return for our friendship and all we'd done for him and his family. He said the easiest way to do this was for him to invest whatever money we might give him with his own family fortune in oil.

It was 1999 and Robert and I had not done well with our money in the stock market. While driving in Europe that summer, I listened to a report on Armed Forces Network on the radio, which said the market was going to stay volatile and to put your money elsewhere—one of the recommendations was oil. I immediately called Robert, and we agreed to give Joe most of our savings.

The first few years were extremely successful with regard to our business and the investment we had made with Joe. From time to time, he would sit with Robert and explain that the $1.4 million we had given him had grown to over $3 million, and he offered the interest on that money whenever we needed it to make a big or small purchase—from a trip abroad with friends to furniture to a condo in Miami Beach. We were all living the life, with a beautiful home in the Hamptons, an apartment in Manhattan, and our place in Wellington.

Joe decided he wanted his own stable, and Robert helped him locate a nice parcel in the swanky Grand Prix Village, directly contiguous to the Palm Beach International Equestrian Center show grounds. He built the most over-the-top barn with three apartments above, one of them intended for him to live in so he could view his horses being trained from his grand terrace. He easily sold his home in the Polo Club, which he had enlarged to 25,000 square feet, for $12,000,000, and planned to rent while the farm was under construction. But then Joe came to us and said his mother was afraid for him to live alone and asked if he could stay in our guest apartment.

Robert and I felt there was no way we could or would say no to Joe's request. We knew each other's families well by now, having celebrated weddings and birthdays as well as the sad moments, funerals of friends and relatives, together. We decided that when Robert and I left for our New York home at the end of the Florida show season, Joe would take over our entire Wellington place as his own until we returned in the winter.

Robert and I loved the amazing home we had built in Bridgehampton, but in 2004, since I had to be in Europe most of the summer leading up to the Athens Olympics, we rented it to a nice couple from Manhattan. The following spring, they again asked to rent it, but we turned them down as we intended to live there that summer ourselves. The couple was so determined to have our house again they offered to purchase it for a whopping $3.3 million! It was simply too much money to say no to, so we went forward with the sale.

Hearing of our good fortune, Joe told Robert and me that if we gave him this money to invest right away, it was the perfect time to make a killing in oil. He explained that because of how the market was, the Saudis' (and his family's) oil tankers were sitting offshore, full and holding until the time was perfect to sell, as oil prices were about to go through the roof. At that moment, our ships would be brought in, our oil would be sold at a huge profit, and our windfall would be enormous! According to Joe, the net results would earn us nearly $12,000,000 from our investment.

Then, in 2007, the Global Financial Crisis began and major financial institutions failed along with those who led them. Loans had been given by banks to people who thought they were secure—but suddenly they were bankrupt and their homes were foreclosed on. Along with CEOs and members of boards who had spent years misleading and basically stealing from their own workers and the public for personal gain, con artists and Ponzi schemers were uncovered right and left. The money they had been taking from Peter to pay to Paul had dried up, and the top of the pyramid scheme shut their doors to protect their own wealth while those who had maneuvered their way to the middle or higher end of the pyramid were discovered by their "investors." This was the case with Bernie Madoff...and our very own Joe Zada.

Month after month, year after year, Joe told us that reinvesting our money would bring a windfall that would allow Robert and me to retire as multi-millionaires. And, for the first few years after our initial investment, we lived like kings, even though we never actually knew, even after asking regularly for documents, how much our investment money had earned.

In the fall of 2007 as the financial world was under siege, Robert and I, based on our most recent conversation with Joe, made plans to go on a fabulous vacation to South Africa. A few weeks earlier, Joe had promised that our payout would come in the beginning of November and be wired directly to our accounts. Based on our discussion, he said that our investments over the years had indeed produced what he had promised: an amazing total of $12,000,000! How could we be anything but thrilled with the returns? Naturally, we were excited to know we could continue with the real estate investments and lifestyle we had been enjoying.

Right before we left for our flight, I sent Joe a text, making sure the wires would come to our accounts on the fifth of November, as promised. Joe's text back was curt, stating the wires would come but for millions less than what he had originally told us.

I questioned the sum immediately, and Joe replied with an angry text that he knew what he owed us and we would get the rest soon.

With our confidence somewhat shaken, off we went to South Africa with our best friends, Ken Berkley and Ron Davis. On the day that our money was to be wired into our account, I contacted our bank repeatedly. No wire had come in.

The following day, I texted Joe again, and he said there had been a wiring error and he was taking care of it immediately. I followed up with my bank at the end of the day. Again, nothing.

Once more, I texted Joe. His reply now was angry for not trusting that he was "getting it done." He said there would be money in our account by the time we got home in two days, and he told me to relax and enjoy the rest of our trip.

On our way home, Robert predicted that by the time we got back, Joe would have moved out of the apartment he had been living in at our Wellington home. I said I had no idea why he would do such a thing, but Robert claimed that was Joe's reaction when his friends acted distrusting or were disrespectful toward him.

Robert proved to be right—Joe had moved completely out of the apartment, save for a pair of shoes and a computer. We tried to reach him to no avail.

And so began a new rollercoaster chapter of our lives as we started legal action to try to get our money. Our attorney also represented Joe at the time. He was adamant that Joe was good for the money—that he himself was equally "invested" and he had spoken directly with the "money people" in Europe and the Middle East and verified they were on the up and up. Joe kept saying our money was coming, almost always "the following Tuesday." It reminded me of the famous cartoon character Wimpy, on the *Popeye* show, who always said, "I will gladly pay you Tuesday for a hamburger today." Just like with Wimpy, there was never any sign of Joe or our money the next Tuesday. He went so far as to send us checks, once for $3,000,000 each and once for $4,000,000 each. Both times, the day we were to go to the bank to deposit the checks, Joe or his attorney notified us that there was a "delay" with his incoming funds and to wait until he got back to us before doing anything. I finally had enough of the waiting and drove to my local branch of the bank the latest checks were drawn on. When the bank's doors opened at nine in the morning, I was the first customer in line. I had my check from Joe and asked for a cashier's check to be made out to me for the amount of $4,000,000. The bank teller looked like a deer in the headlights.

"I need to speak to my manager," she said.

I watched through the glass wall of the manager's office as she approached and spoke to him. I saw him get on the phone. After a few minutes, he hung up, and they both walked out of his office. Only the teller came to speak to me, though. When I asked where the manager had gone, she informed me he had left the building.

"There are no funds whatsoever in the account the check you are holding was drawn on," she said.

Stunned by what I knew in my gut was coming, I turned to leave the bank, just as a local news truck pulled up and two reporters jumped out. I kept my head down and hurried to my car. A story ran at noon—apparently, I wasn't the only one who tried to cash a check that day. A few firefighters arrived minutes after I left and were told, like me, that there were no funds in Joe Zada's account to cash their checks. The news report enraged Joe, who claimed his good name was being slandered.

The FBI got involved at this point in a federal criminal case that seemed to take forever to come to fruition. We took part in multiple depositions, including one I will never forget, with Joe and his attorney, and Joe sitting directly across from me while I did nothing but speak the exact truth as to what he had done to me and Robert.

During the year following our Africa trip and while we were attempting to get Joe to pay us the money he had promised so many times, his story began to change. In the beginning, he had told us that he was investing our funds along with his family fortune in oil in the Middle East.

And during those first years, we were always under the assumption that we were doing fantastic, since every time we needed money for a real estate investment, Joe would immediately give us a check for a house here or an apartment there. He always said that the money we received was purely from the interest on our investment and we never touched the principal funds. Just in case anything ever happened to him and because we were "family," Joe, Robert, and I, all signed a separate document indicating that the principal was a "loan," which upon Joe's demise, would always and forever be immediately paid back to us.

When we were waiting for the sale of our oil that was being held in tankers offshore, Joe came to us and said he had to share something he had kept a secret all this time we had known him. He pulled out a document with a seal embossed on it, demonstrating it was from a Saudi royal family. It said that Joe was to inherit $600,000,000 from a Saudi prince who Joe said he'd had a long affair with, until the prince died suddenly. The family of his lover was violently contesting the prince's wishes. And, according to Joe, it was this that had caused the delay in funds.

"You know how those Saudis are about gays!" Joe said.

I looked at the document carefully and noticed at least one typographical error and that pretty much any ten-year-old with a computer and printer could have produced the flimsy reproduction. Joe gave us a copy of the document—and this became a major piece of evidence the FBI ended up using in their case against him, as well as the computer he'd forgotten at our house when he left so suddenly while we were in Africa.

In the end, Robert and I, as well as Sergei Federov (the famous NHL hockey player who Joe had taken tens of millions from), and a number of police officers and firemen, all were subpoenaed and testified in court while a jury listened. Seeing Joe sitting in that defendant's chair as, one by one, everyone told the exact same story of how he made them feel like they were his family and took their money to "invest" it, only to find out that he'd frivolously spent it on his own lavish lifestyle, I felt like a huge weight was lifted from my shoulders. We pretty much assumed we would never get any of our money back and were simply starting over, but when the verdict came back GUILTY ON ALL COUNTS, we at least felt like justice had been done.

I felt sorry for Joe's mother and the relatives we'd met over the years who we never saw or heard from again. I honestly don't think they had a clue as to what he was doing, and they had never been anything but lovely to Robert and me. Joe's mom was never that healthy, and there must still have been one person in Joe's life who somehow believed in him to the end, because we heard someone bought his home in Grosse Pointe Shores and let his mother live there in her own wing of the mansion until she passed away. Joe was to serve three consecutive ten-year sentences, which would allow him to seek parole only after seventeen years. He tried repeatedly to get out early, but each time he was denied.

In May 2020, we were informed that Joe would be released due to COVID-19 risk in the prison system and would spend the rest of the next ten years under house arrest at his home in Michigan. Somehow, it seemed wrong to allow the guy to live in a mansion after all he had done to so many. We must not have been the only ones who felt that way, because the next day the decision was reversed—COVID or no COVID. Karma has its mysterious ways!

— A Tide That Makes All Ships Rise —

Perhaps the very best example of people hanging out with the right friends in order to raise their personal bar and achieve highly successful outcomes is Bill Gates. No one explains the phenomenon of Mr. Gates and his friends better than Malcolm Gladwell in his book *Outliers*. Gates met his friend Paul Allen in 1970 when they were both in high school. The two boys were fascinated by computers, and one's genius drove the other to excel...and eventually create Microsoft. In 1980, there were other American tech geniuses on the rise, such as Steve Jobs, with whom Gates had a true rivalry. This competitiveness ended up being a plus for them both as well as everyone on the planet through the creation and continued evolution of Apple as well as Microsoft. Of course, Gladwell is also famous for saying that greatness comes from practicing (which Gates and Jobs undoubtedly did) a craft for 10,000 hours. Having witnessed people devote a lifetime to their craft without ever realizing greatness, I argue the key is not only practicing untold hours but doing so under great supervision and hopefully being inspired by another's similar genius.

In the television show *Songland*, starring Ryan Tedder, Ester Dean, and Shane McAnally, and produced by Adam Levine and Ivan Dudynsky, five geniuses in their field find and help young songwriters as they hope to get their songs sung and elevated into hits by major stars. What is truly amazing each week is seeing wonderful singer-songwriters come in with amazing voices, hoping they will be one of only three who are taken by the guest star to go with either Ryan, Ester, or Shane to make the necessary changes that will later hook the star into taking a song. While the contestants are all talented, it is incredibly apparent that the three stars are not just good songwriters, they have the entire art down to such a science that it is elegantly simple for them to "play" with the melodies and arrangements to quickly turn good into *great*.

This kind of playful competitiveness creates "a tide that makes all ships rise," and this idea works for all sports, arts, or endeavors in life. You want to be great? Look at who is the greatest in your desired field who is still alive and might take you under a wing as a student or colleague, and spend those 10,000 hours honing your skills and willing yourself to be not just as good as your mentor but actually better! "Shoot for the moon and you will end up in the stars!"

Nothing succeeds like success. Being around highly motivated, successful, and interesting people motivates you to bring the very best out of yourself and reach higher every day. Being the big fish in a small pond may bring you temporary gains, but challenging yourself by jumping into the Great Lake will always bring you greater returns in the end.

Robert and I have been so fortunate that our hard work and dedication have paid off, and we are living a wonderful life. We are grateful every day for the good people in our lives and the lessons we have learned, both those that brought true happiness and also the painful ones that produced growth and understanding. One big lesson that may sound cliché but nevertheless is true: If it seems too good to be true, it probably is!

Most importantly, having family and friends who are honest, positive, and truly care about you is one of the greatest gifts we can have as we go through life. When we are younger, we think this is simple, but as you get older, life has a way of showing you exactly who it is who truly loves you and is your "friend." Cherish those people and make sure you let them know often that you LOVE them.

And if there is anything we've learned from 2020, it's to hug them whenever you can. ●

Touch Your Toes

Maintaining Physical Health and Well-Being

10
CHAPTER

As a child, I, like most kids, thought I was invincible. Whether it was getting on any horse or pony without consideration as to their safety and appropriateness, playing soccer and getting knocked down right and left, or trying to walk on my hands across the back yard, it never occurred to me I might get injured in the process. Naturally, I did get hurt, as most kids do, but nothing really bad happened in terms of injury until I was fifteen and living with my family in South Florida.

I kept my horse at the time in a neighborhood near Fort Lauderdale called Sunshine Ranches. The farm was owned by Mr. and Mrs. Heimer, who, along with their two kids, raised and trained Quarter Horses for show and sale. I was fascinated by all kinds of horseback riding at the time and was always thrilled when asked to ride one of their cutting horses. The Heimers had a large field behind the stable that was home to their herd of Angus cattle, which they both sold as beef and used to train their horses to be competitive at cutting, a sport where a young steer or heifer is separated from the herd, and then the horse has to out-think and out-run the cow as the animal tries to get back to the group. A really good cutting horse can react so quickly that it requires extremely good balance and concentration for a rider to just stay on.

On the ranch there was also a very cute pony that belonged to the young Heimer kids, and I took every opportunity to jump on him. I would practice with the pony and the cows in the field, trying to separate calves from their mothers so I could see if the pony and I could work it like the big Quarter Horses did.

One day I galloped the pony into a paddock where a large cow was alone—well, I thought it was a cow. It turned out that he was actually a huge Angus bull, and he was already pissed off as he'd just been separated from his herd of cows. If you have ever seen a bullfight (I don't recommend it!), you know that bulls can be extremely aggressive, and this one, seeing me and the Heimers' pony running madly toward him, turned around with a loud snort, pawed the ground, and with a big roar began to charge directly toward us.

The pony took complete control. Realizing the enormous mistake his clueless rider had made and that his life was in danger, he whipped around and off we flew, as fast as his little legs would carry us toward the exit gate. We just made it out of there with our lives intact, though both the pony's and my heart were beating a hundred miles per hour. I learned my lesson and avoided the paddock thereafter.

After school one nice afternoon the following week, I took the pony for a ride out into the big twenty-acre field where the cows and their babies lived. I loved galloping across the huge field, the wind in my face, and feeling the power of the pony's body as he ran. Suddenly, down we went, as one of the pony's front hooves hit a cow patty and he slipped, tumbling at high speed together to the ground. I had learned to be very well balanced from all the dressage training I had received over the years, and so, as the pony fell on his side, my body stayed with him, and he came down squarely on my left leg. In a flash, he was up. I also attempted to rise to my feet, only to feel a pain that I immediately understood under no circumstances was a minor injury I could power through. So I lay there in the middle of the vast field, watching the pony run back toward home, wondering what I should do next. The pain was throbbing and sharp when I even tried to bend my leg. I determined the only way to get back to the stable was if I dragged myself by my arms, a good fifteen acres across the pasture.

By then it was late afternoon, and I had only gotten about thirty feet when I felt the first drop of rain on my head. Looking up, I saw a large dark cloud heading in my direction, and a second later it began to pour.

"Could this get any worse?" I thought.

As if on cue, I suddenly heard a loud, *Mooooo!* and saw the entire herd of cows moving toward me. I was not afraid of them since the females and babies usually weren't aggressive. The thirty or so cows milled around me, sniffing and mooing as if asking each other, "What the hell is this kid doing in our field, lying here like a fallen scarecrow?" I honestly didn't know whether to cry from the pain and my general feeling of helplessness or to laugh as I imagined what the whole scene would look like if it were in a movie.

I pulled myself along for what seemed like an eternity when I saw my mother's car coming toward me. The pony had run home, and Mrs.

Heimer had known right away something must have happened and called my mom. They'd searched the ranch together and finally realized that the back field's gate was slightly open—just wide enough for the pony to get through.

I was so thankful they found me!

Off we went to the hospital. As we arrived, I was immediately put on a gurney, soaking wet with my riding pants and boots still on. The nurse asked what happened, and I explained, adding I thought my leg was broken above my ankle.

The doctor walked up and said, "First things first—we have to cut you out of these boots and breeches."

"NOOOOOO!" I cried out in protest. The boots were brand new and so expensive; I knew I could not get another pair.

"Sorry," the doctor replied. "The pain will be excruciating if we try to pull the boot off your already swelling leg, and we have to take X-rays to see how bad the break is."

All business, the nurse took the scalpel and began cutting down the length of my boot as I cried, not from the pain in my leg but over the loss of my beautiful riding gear.

A minute later the doctor announced, "This is going to hurt," and the nurse picked up and held my leg as he took the bottom of the boot and pried it off my foot.

Boy, was he right! As blinding pain shot through me, I screamed.

Once my boots and pants were off, I was taken to radiology where the conclusion was that I had broken both the tibia and fibula in my left leg, about halfway between my knee and my ankle. The doctor said I was very lucky that I'd had my leather boots on, as that was the only reason the bones had stayed in my leg; otherwise, it would have been far worse.

My leg was put in a balloon-like ice boot overnight to take down some of the swelling so the doctor could operate on it and set the bones the next morning. The surgery went well, and I awoke with a cast that went from my hip all the way down to my toes.

About a week later, it was obvious that something was not right with my leg. Normally, once in a cast, bones begin to knit and the pain factor is minimal. This was not the case with me, so my mom took me to see the surgeon who set my leg. Another X-ray showed that the bones had moved slightly in my leg, and he needed to make a small adjustment to my cast to realign them. Very simply, he would saw a small piece from of the outside of my cast and wedge it into the inside, thereby changing the angle of the cast to properly align my bones on my leg.

Easy, right?

A minute later, he had my leg on the table and the saw that doctors routinely use to remove a cast began to buzz. As he began to cut, the pain was immediate and incredible and I screamed. The doctor sternly told me to stop crying like a baby as all I felt was the heat of the saw, and my mother, though obviously concerned, just held me tight as I continued to wail that he was cutting into my leg. What seemed like an eternity ended as he took the wedge out of the outside of my cast, drove it into the inside, and declared we were good to go.

I was still in pain but happy to take my crutches and get out of there. The whole way home, I complained that my leg really hurt, and my mother tried to console me, saying she was sure it would feel better quickly. While the acute pain did subside, the ache lasted, and after a week I woke up one morning to see that my toes were black and blue. I showed my mother, and confused, she took a hand towel, soaked it in warm water, and rubbed my toes with it. The black came off on the towel, turning the fabric dark red.

Blood!

Mom pushed the edge of the cloth a bit up into the cast above my toes, and more blood soaked into the towel.

Off we went to the emergency room where my cast was immediately removed. I will never forget the look on the surgeon's face as he found my broken leg covered in mostly dried blood, but also with a little still oozing out of the gashes in my leg from the saw he had used on me a week before. The cuts were exactly the shape of the wedge he'd cut out of the outside.

The nurse quickly began to clean the wounds as I could see my mother seething with anger. I just looked on, unsure of what would happen next. Mom asked the surgeon to step outside the room, and I could hear her yelling at him—and that was that.

I required a second surgery to reset my leg and properly cast it again, along with strong antibiotics to combat the quarter-inch incisions from the saw. Of course, the original surgeon was replaced with someone competent, and all went as planned. I was in the new cast for three months, and looking back on it, I wonder why my parents decided not to sue the doctor or the hospital. I guess it was just not their way. My parents generally believed that doctors were all experts by virtue of their diplomas and need not be questioned, even when they made an error. Later in their lives, when my mom and dad got sick, I and my siblings had to be their advocates to ensure they did not receive anything other than the very best care.

When I finally had the cast on my leg removed, I felt good as new, and was excited to be back in gym class with my friends. The gym teacher had everyone doing track-and-field events that day, and I was determined to take part. The high jump looked easy enough, and off I ran, leaping up and over the bar. On the other side, though, fear suddenly caught me as I thought, "What if I fall on my leg and re-break it?"

With that, I stuck out my left arm to break my fall and felt the snap as I hit the ground. My arm stung above my wrist, and it felt like I was going to faint, but there was no way I was going to be a sissy so, holding my wrist with my right hand, I walked back to my mat, lying on the floor, and picked it up just as the bell rang that ended gym. My left arm ached intensely as I changed clothes, using my right hand only, and went to my next class. I squirmed in my chair, unable to concentrate, and the teacher walked up to me and asked why I was not doing my work. I showed him my arm, which had begun to swell, and asked if I could call my mother. My teacher asked if I could wiggle my fingers. I did.

"Clearly it is not broken," he said. "Go to back to work."

The rest of the day was excruciating until that last bell of the day rang. I hurried home and showed my mother my arm, now blown up like a balloon, and off we went to the hospital...again! I had a simple fracture above my wrist, and the doctor set it in a cast right away.

This time, my mother was anything but calm as she went with me to school the next morning to ream out the teacher and principal for not immediately calling her about my injury the previous day. Again, no legal action was taken. It was just not my parents' style.

Many riders get bad backs. The concussion from sitting on horses, especially in the trot, can take its toll on our spines. This is the case because, traditionally, equestrians aren't encouraged to cross-train to keep both toned and elastic. We think that riding alone is enough exercise. Of course, this is the case for many people who are dedicated to one sport and don't see the value of getting into a gym or with a good yoga or Pilates instructor.

I was twenty-five when my back was first injured after being hit by a huge wave in Hawaii. I thought it would heal and that would be the end of it. As it turned out, the discs in my spine got worse with age until I was living year to year on painkillers and with help from a pain-management specialist. Between 1999 and 2005, when I retired from competition, I received literally dozens of epidurals to get me through the big championships and major shows. At the Sydney Olympics in 2000, not only did the drugs given to me by Olympic doctors cause me to go off course, by the time I got home from Australia, I was completely addicted to painkillers and sleep aids. I'd wake up at three in the morning in agony and go into the bathroom where I'd look adoringly at my trove of pills. *Should I take one of these, two of these, and one of those? No...maybe two of these, one of those, and three of these.*

I finally could not live that way any longer and just threw the pills out, willing myself to deal with the pain until I could be injected again and hopefully feel a little relief.

Addiction found me again in 2004 during the Athens Olympics. I was determined to ride my best and be successful for our team. I also knew it was likely going to be the last time my parents would see me in an Olympics, and I wanted them to be proud and excited to watch me succeed. The tradeoff? I came home full of pills and had to take myself off the opioids on my own once more.

The epidurals and an Ambien at night were enough to get me through the next few years, and officially retiring from the stress of competing was a physical and emotional relief of sorts. Then, in 2007, Robert and I went to New York City for a weekend holiday in a friend's lovely sixth-floor walk-up. We arrived Friday afternoon with our four suitcases (Robert and I have never been known as "light packers"!) and lugged them up the six flights of stairs to the apartment. We decided to go out shopping first thing, so down the stairs we went, and when we came back that afternoon, it was with several bags each of fabulous new clothes. Up the stairs we went again, showered quickly, and back down the stairs we flew to catch a quick dinner before our play. We got home late that evening after going out dancing with friends after the play was over. It was a great but exhausting day, and we were glad to crawl into bed as we had more fun planned for the remainder of the weekend.

Robert was up and in the shower before me and yelled that I needed to get up and get ready, as we were meeting our friends for a late breakfast.

"Sure thing," I answered and began to rise out of bed—until I felt my body answer with an emphatic, "NOOOO WAYYYY!"

I tried again, and again it was a most definite, "NO!"

So, I said, "Robert, I think there are three possibilities: One, you can help me up and I can hop on one leg down the six flights and get in a cab to the hospital. Two, you can call an ambulance to come get me. Three, you can just leave me here, and maybe it will get better in the next few hours."

I was pretty sure Number Three was out of the question, and I was not thrilled with Number Two either.

Robert quickly finished getting ready and came and lifted me slowly up until I was standing on my right foot and leaning against a chest of drawers. He helped me get dressed, and with one arm over his shoulder, we began the long hop down the six flights of stairs to the street, where he hailed a taxi to take us to the nearest emergency room.

The pain in my back down my left leg to my foot was something I had never experienced, even with all the back issues and sciatica I'd had for years. In fifteen minutes, we were at Presbyterian Hospital, and Robert helped me to the front desk where the nurse asked for all the usual information. I was drenched in sweat by then, but rules were rules, and the forms had to be properly filled out. Every twenty seconds or so I suffered ten-second spasms that literally made me scream with agony. I tried to stretch my left leg out to find relief, but there was none to be had. I created such a scene that not once but *three times* nurses came out and gave me different (and very strong) painkillers—I'm pretty sure more in an attempt to stop my screaming than to relieve my pain! They even inserted an IV to administer doses of morphine while I waited...and waited...and waited. The thing is, on a Saturday afternoon in the city, back problems are in line *way* behind all the heart attacks and gunshot wounds.

Seven excruciating hours later, I was finally examined by a doctor. He took an X-ray and an MRI after I described my back history, and then said I needed to see the surgeon the next morning. They wouldn't admit me, and there was no way I could go home to the walk-up, so we booked a room at the adjoining hotel for the night. The pain meds hardly worked, and I did not sleep at all.

Morning came and Robert took me in a wheelchair to the same emergency room with the same nurse at the front desk. She took one look at me and knew she needed to get me out of the waiting room before I screamed again and scared all the incoming patients. She wheeled me back to "triage," which was just another place for waiting, full of sick and crying people who looked to be in much worse shape than I was. I sat there in the hallway for hours, finally in so much pain that I got out of the wheelchair and laid on the floor while nurses and orderlies stepped over me as if I were an inanimate object that had fallen in their path. I listened to ladies and children crying out for help, as hospital staff continued to ignore them and step over me like I was already a corpse. I called my Olympic doctor, who was also a friend, and asked him if there was *anyone* he knew at the hospital who he could get to help me.

"Hang on," he said. "I'll work on it and get back to you."

Another hour went by. Robert waited patiently in the waiting room, asking every so often if I had been seen yet.

Then an orderly tried to step over me and kicked me by mistake.

THAT WAS IT!

Somehow, I pulled myself to my feet and hopped a few steps into the main triage room.

"Hey!" I began to shout at...well, *everyone*. "Have you people all forgotten why you signed up for your jobs? To help people and ease their pain and suffering? Do you know how many of you have stepped over me as

I screamed for help on the floor in the hall for the last *four* hours? Have you not been hearing me? Or the other poor people pleading for your attention? You need to get your priorities in check and do your jobs!"

And with that, I was on a gurney within a minute and rolled back to a room where a doctor gave me more meds and told me the specialist would be right in. Shortly after, a middle-aged, dark-haired man walked up and introduced himself as the surgeon—he was friends with my orthopedist and was already familiar with my case, and he had reviewed the MRI from the day before. Robert and I were so relieved—until the surgeon described what the procedure he was recommending entailed: Fusion of three vertebrae in my lumbar spine—L3, 4, and 5—with a lattice-like "scaffold" around them to keep them permanently secure. I would spend four days in the hospital and then have four months of physical therapy before I could resume riding my horses or doing any normal activities. It was a lot to take in, but Robert and I signed the necessary forms and took solace in the fact that the surgeon had a very good reputation.

It was Sunday and my surgery was scheduled for Monday morning. However, as the day wore on, I began to feel like I was getting sick with a cold. A couple of hours later, there was no doubt about it—I had a cold. I called up the surgeon and got his answering service, but within minutes, he called back and said there was no way he could operate if I had a cold.

I was sort of relieved, especially since the mediations I'd been given had taken my pain level down from a "10" to a manageable "6."

Robert and I decided we would fly home to Florida, and I would make an appointment to see someone at the spine center at Jackson Memorial Hospital in Miami. Dr. Barth Green and Dr. Alan Levy had helped countless riders we knew, so we pulled a few strings and got an appointment for the day after we got back. Dr. Levy looked at everything and heard what the surgeon in New York was planning to do.

With that he said, "Robert, we are going to take care of you. You will be in and out the same day and need only a few days' rest, and you'll be good as new."

WTF?

I was about to have extensive surgery that would have had me out for months, totally fusing my lower back forever, and now I only needed a minor procedure and I would be fine? Dr. Levy's plan was to remove whatever piece of the disc in my spine was causing pain and clean up all around it—a "discectomy." He would only make a one-inch incision.

"I LOVE YOU!" I replied.

And that is exactly what happened. I was in and out of the hospital. Dr. Levy told me it was good for me to walk as much as possible following the procedure.

Our time in Miami for my surgery piqued our interest in real estate, and there was a terrific building in a great location called The Flamingo that Robert suggested we check for an apartment rental. Sure enough, we found one, and during the next six months, we spent weekends in Miami—an easy getaway from the stress of our jobs.

Then, through his connections in real estate, Robert heard about a condo several blocks from our rental that had just been foreclosed on by the bank, and it sounded like a place that would perfectly suit us. It had just been listed, and Robert found out there was a key left in the stairwell outside the apartment door. I walked gingerly behind him as we approached the young man at the building's front desk. Robert told me not to say anything; he would do the talking. The man could not have been nicer as Robert explained that the bank had given him permission to look at the condo, and he already had the key to it. The guy sent the elevator up, and it only took a minute for Robert to retrieve the key from its hiding place.

Usually, places that have been foreclosed upon look like they have been vandalized when you go in. The owners are often so angry that they literally remove everything, whether it is nailed down or not, and break whatever they can't take with them. But when we opened the door to this condo, for a minute I forgot I had recently had surgery on my back and almost jumped into the air with excitement. There could not have been a more perfect place—two bedrooms and two baths, a lovely living room and kitchen, and all in the finest, move-in condition. But it was really the incredible 280-degree views through floor-to-ceiling windows and sliding doors that sold us: from the city skyline over the bay, all the way around from South Point and up Miami Beach. It had been a very expensive condo, but with the recession and foreclosure, Robert and I put in a very low offer, and to our amazement, it was accepted within twenty-four hours. (We still love it and live in it today whenever we can get away from Wellington. Just looking out at the beautiful water views renews my spirit and takes away the stresses of work or the craziness of our world, if only for a brief intermission.)

My back healed well, barring one lingering issue: In extracting a piece of disc about half the size of my thumbnail from where it was imbedded in my sciatic nerve, damage was done to the nerve, causing me to lose the feeling from most of the front of my right foot. You could basically stick a fork in it, and I would not feel it. This meant walking was now tricky, as I could not properly feel my foot contacting the ground. It took a few weeks for me to feel confident again as I walked around, and it would be months before I took the chance and ran on it. More complicated was that the lack of feeling meant I was constantly losing my right stirrup while riding. I could not feel my foot against the bottom of the stirrup at all. I would suddenly feel the metal hitting my leg and have to look down to help guide my foot back in. The thing was, in dressage—my sport—the best leg and foot position required that the heel be down and the toes looking straight ahead. After my surgery, I had to fight with my right foot to stay correct for dressage (and still do today).

— More Than Working Out —

When you are young, no one can tell you that life goes by in a heartbeat and expect you to believe it. Trust me, though, it's true, and the best way to ensure you have a great life is to maintain your health. This means so much more than just working out. Proper nutrition, making good choices, and maintaining emotional stability and spiritual serenity are all key factors in leading a healthy lifestyle.

Three important words: TOUCH YOUR TOES!

If this seems trite, I can tell you for sure that my life would have been completely different had someone told me be to be sure I could always touch my toes. When you sit on a horse with your knees and ankles bent, year after year, the result is tighter and tighter hamstrings, which ultimately leads to back problems. The answer to this, and most other issues like it, is to work with a good personal trainer with a great gym program. It requires the same commitment that anything else does, but you will be so thankful after a few months when you start seeing your body changing as you feel new vitality.

I have worked out seriously since 1988, focusing on creating more muscle and keeping toned. Elasticity was never my strength; it has been a continuous challenge for me over the years. Without the muscle I have built though, with my spine issues and the arthritis in my joints from wear and tear over the years, I would crumble into a heap of dust like a vampire thrust into the sunlight!

My quest to become muscular and fit was inspired by three things: First, I had met Robert Ross—gorgeous and looking like a Greek god— and thought, "Robert, you had best get in shape if you want to land him and keep him!" Second, I was hugely inspired to work out daily, and sometimes twice daily, when I went to the Olympics in Seoul, South Korea, where I was surrounded by all these amazing athletes and had a fantastic gym and pool to train in the Olympic village. Third, the onslaught of AIDS, with one symptom seen in so many guys being "wasting," as their inability to keep fat or muscle on their bodies meant they slowly became like walking skeletons, had led to a fitness craze in the gay community. The use of steroids (by some), working out, and health-conscious living created a new generation of men who strived for that "fitness-magazine look."

I have a very strong regimen of daily vitamins and minerals, exercise with attention to both cardio and weightlifting, and of course, my riding. However, that only deals with my physical body. To be truly healthy, you must also consider your emotional, psychological, and spiritual well-being. These three are intertwined with your physical well-being and must be nourished and cared for along with your body in order for you to become and remain healthy.

As we go through life, we are thrown things that test our strength and resilience again and again. As children, we almost immediately fall down and get hurt, but with a little help and nurturing from our parents or others, we get back up and on we go until the next time we fall down. But when our minds take a big fall, finding our way back up onto our mental feet may take more than a brushing off by a loved one. This is when professionals, trained to help us find our way back to mental and emotional good health, are a vital resource.

There was a time when US Olympic coaches did not want to hear that an athlete was having mental or emotional issues. Their reply to the mention of an athlete needing professional help from a psychologist or therapist would be, "If an athlete needs help like that, why would I want that individual on my team?" In the coach's mind, that person was a liability to the overall success of the team, even if the athlete brought the most talent. Athletes with such "issues" were considered the "weak links"; it was commonly thought back then that we had to be mentally and emotionally tough and not show nerves or fear under any circumstance. Only in the last twenty years have top sports recognized the positive results attained by enlisting sports psychologists and therapists to work with both athletes and coaches.

I could never have produced the medals I won, both as a rider and a coach, were it not for Laura King and Mark Rutherford, both top professionals in their therapeutic fields. Having a great therapist—whether you are an athlete, a performer, a business person, or a kid in school going through the normal challenges of growing up—can make all the difference in becoming a success, whatever your endeavor, and is also a key to finding true happiness and joy.

Let me reiterate: therapy is "a key." It may not be necessary for everyone, but the higher the degree of stress in your life, the more important it is to have someone you can trust to help you navigate through hard times. Naturally, most of the time, for kids, parents are the ones who help guide their children toward becoming healthy, self-aware adolescents and young adults. However, more and more, we see that kids are less inclined to tell their parents all they are going through, and issues at school or after-school activities are left for teachers, school counselors, or coaches to handle. Any great coach must also be a therapist in order to create an athlete or team of athletes who come to their "big moment" with the highest degree of self-confidence possible that they can and will achieve their personal best.

Nothing is more gratifying than seeing yourself or your students, as Whitney Houston sang it, have that "One Moment in Time"! ●

Say What You Need

Communication and Getting Professional Help

11

CHAPTER

A few years ago, I received an email from an anonymous person who claimed to have been highly successful in the competition arena as a Young Rider but suffered from terrible depression and had already tried to commit suicide once. The individual was thinking of making it "final" the next time, which by the tone of the email, sounded soon. I was given a little background and why things seemed impossible to go on. When I asked if the individual would consider speaking with a professional, I was informed that plenty of parental money had already gone to psychologists and psychiatrists. I asked the person to reconsider as I had a great friend who was a sports psychologist, Dr. Jenny Susser, who I was sure would be able to help.

A few days went by and I got a new message, this time making it clear I was corresponding with a young lady. She still would not give me her name but said that she was glad she could talk to me and felt that some of the stories I told her about my own difficulties as a young, gay, Jewish horse-crazy kid were helping her feel less alone. I contacted my friend Dr. Susser, who told me she thought I was doing the right thing. As scary as it was to read notes talking about suicide and "just wanting the pain to go away," Dr. Susser felt confident that this young woman was screaming out to be heard, to have her feelings validated, and to seek help. The next correspondence was indeed a breakthrough when I finally found out the woman's first name, and she promised me she would reach out to Dr. Susser to talk. I am extremely happy to say that this same individual is now doing great, happily competing, and has her own successful business.

I have spent most of my adult life in therapy and am not the least bit embarrassed to say it. The pressure of competing at the Olympic level was something that—on top of being a young, gay, geeky, socially awkward mama's boy—was often too much. But it wasn't until I met Robert and was in my thirties that I sought professional help. The US Equestrian Team was just beginning to advocate for using sports psychologists for athletes. This didn't go over well with some of the team coaches at the time. I recall the famous show jumping coach Frank Chapot gruffly responding to the memo with, "What the fuck is this about? If one of my team riders needs a fucking psychologist to deal with the pressure, why the fuck would I want them on my team anyway?"

Now, to be fair, Chapot's generation of trainers almost completely came from a military background, as did mine. We were expected to have "grit"—a quality of mental and emotional toughness that is an essential part of being successful in international sport. However, what many did not understand back then was that "grit" is not only something people are born with; it can be learned and acquired with the help of an excellent therapist. I had horrible show nerves that I tried to swallow and hide during the first decade of my international career. Once I began speaking with a sports psychologist and learning methods of coping with and channeling those feelings in more positive directions, I learned a huge amount about myself, on and off the horse.

Many of my fears were coming from the "what ifs": What if this happens? What if he does that?

My therapist asked me, "Robert, so what really is the worst that could happen? Would you survive it?"

My answer was always a firm, "YES." I would and did survive each and every one of the "disasters" in my life and career, and came out better and stronger for them.

I learned at a very early age that to get what you want, you have to say what you need. That may sound selfish, but nevertheless, it is true. As babies, we cry for attention so that we are fed, changed, or simply held and played with.

My horses and dogs have taught me how better to relate to people, for they communicate their most basic emotions and needs almost entirely through body language: "I am content." "I am hungry." "I am afraid." "I am unhappy." "I want attention." We share these same basic needs and desires with all other animals; we just make communicating them so much more complicated than our pets do.

Fear is the main reason why we begin, early in our childhood, to lose our ability to communicate with others honestly, at all times. Fear of being hurt or rejected is as powerful an influence as learning that placing your hand on a hot stove is going to burn and bring you pain. Once or twice burned and you begin to make choices to avoid the hurt, even if you know it means being less than truthful with others or yourself. And so we go through life attempting to be good people who others are attracted to as friends, or more, and our personalities are formed, layer upon layer, like the many skins of an onion. With every good and bad experience, another layer coats our true and authentic selves. Our relationships with others, both humans and animals, can bring us closer to or farther away from who we truly are, but in the end, each of us make the choice whether to search or not, and whether to pay attention to the clues life puts in our paths to help us make decisions to communicate our truest feelings and desires to others in our lives.

With every single breath we take, as we exhale, we are redefining and proclaiming to the universe who we believe we are! The problem comes when we forget that we bring with us all the baggage we have acquired since we were born—the relationships we had with our mothers and fathers, as well as others, are always there in our subconscious, sometimes helping us to succeed, while other times causing failure. When you discover that you can't seem to move forward in life and feel like you are being "blocked" by something you cannot put your finger on, it may be time to seek out professional help with an excellent therapist.

I watch people come into my arena these days and can many times tell immediately what their home life is like. If a kid walks in on his horse with slumped shoulders and eyes down and no smile, I know he is not happy in life *off* his horse and lacks self-confidence. If a woman comes in wearing an oversized shirt and no belt, I know she has issues with her weight and believes she is being judged in that regard. If a person rides in looking disheveled with a dirty horse and tack, I know that there is negativity in that individual's life that requires work to figure out. I am pretty good at pinpointing the issues and dealing with them in a positive way with my students, but there are some issues which require top professional intervention.

I have loved my therapy sessions, whether hypno-therapy with the amazing Laura King, who truly helped me navigate six years as coach of an incredibly successful Olympic Team, or my work with Mark Rutherford, who opened up a new world for me in my relationship with Robert and others. Communication is everything in relationships, whether with intimate partners, friends, those we don't know but are trying to hear, or even animals. We tend to think we already know what others are thinking or going to say, and we are so ready with our "pre-recorded" responses that our minds do not truly listen. This is, much of the time, where things go wrong in our relationships. I often see riders become very aggressive with their horses, and when I ask why they have done so, they say that they know the horse is about to do something "bad," and they have to act a certain way to prevent it. The problem with this theory is simple: If every time a horse is put in a certain position or place, he is hit with a whip or the bit in his mouth is yanked on, then whenever he is about to be put in that same position or place, he will assume he is going to be hurt. He will then either try to run away or otherwise defend himself from the impending pain. Sensing this undesirable response, the rider then does exactly what the horse was afraid was going to happen—and the cycle continues.

Great riders try at all times to "think like the horse" so the animal becomes confident that the trainer is his "dance partner" and will never ask him to do something where he cannot succeed. Naturally, like with kids, it doesn't always work, but also like with kids, when you listen, truly listen, and try your best to understand their feelings, both good and bad, you have the best chance to communicate and nurture a positive relationship.

I meet people all the time, introduce myself, and then walk away and realize I have no idea what they said their names were. I *heard* them when they spoke their names, but I wasn't *listening*. Does it matter in the long term that I forgot their names? Perhaps not. But then when I am walking my dog and meet the same person day after day but can never remember the person's name, I think, "Why didn't I remember it *the first time* we introduced ourselves?"

These days, when meeting someone for the first time, I try to always look attentively at the person's face and say the name three times in our conversation. Repeating the name three times makes a huge difference in recalling it the next time I see the individual.

In the same way, when Robert and I have important conversations, we try to make it a point now to say out loud what we heard the other tell us. We repeat it and say we understand, even if we don't necessarily agree with it. Intentional listening, saying another's name when you respond to a statement or question, and making an effort to show you understand and validate another's point of view are all ways of creating a successful path for communicating.

— Communication Is the Keystone —

Today's America has never been more polarized, with people using social media and watching television that caters to like-minded factions. I prefer to channel-surf and listen to both ends of the political spectrum on issues. But from the pandemic to the 2020 presidential election, the divide has broken up families and friendships in ways never before thought possible.

What is the answer? I would say that the most important thing is to be true to your heart. This *does not* mean that you have a knockdown, drag-out, fight with a friend or family member with different views, but rather that you can choose to really *listen*, and then agree to disagree.

In life, there are moments where not standing up for what you believe in is not possible. If remaining silent means being complicit, you owe it to yourself to speak your truth, and let the chips fall where they may.

I have always been known to have very strong opinions and zero fear when it comes to voicing them. Too many times to count, I could have taken the path of least resistance, and I know Robert and others in my life would have given a sigh of relief had I done so. But I would not have been true to myself had I remained quiet in certain scenarios and I knew it. With my students throughout my coaching career, I have always tried to tell it like I saw it (while hopefully not hurting anyone's feelings). I am a very passionate teacher, and there have been times when my intensity has been too much for a rider. Some were kind enough to tell me when I crossed a line, and I was thankful in those instances and immediately changed my tone and presentation. Sue Blinks, one of our Olympic medalists and a long-time student, told me early on that shouting just did not work for her. At the same time, I had people who were offended if I did not raise my voice, as they thought I was not taking enough interest in their efforts. As you have heard in these pages, it was when I took up skiing that I learned I could keep teaching fun, and yes, still be intense at times, but never with anger or frustration. Skiing changed my teaching forever.

Finally, it is important to know that, the vast majority of the time, what you believe people are thinking or saying about you is mostly inaccurate. Many times Robert and I were certain that a specific person or group of people had a negative opinion of us, only to find out they were simply afraid to speak to us. We tend to form opinions about people based on how they look or speak without knowing their "story," and once we meet them and have a conversation, we may reach the opposite conclusion. In today's world, however, social media has seriously reduced the necessity of really communicating with people and learning the truth about them before assessing their value in our lives. We see snapshots and make assumptions based on background information on social profiles. Facebook, Instagram, and other platforms know what attracts us and use that to keep our attention and maybe persuade us to purchase what their sponsors are paying them to advertise.

I have had to learn, many times and the hard way, that trying to hide from the truth only prevents you from creating and maintaining healthy relationships, whether friendships or intimate affairs of the heart. *Honest, open, two-way communication is the keystone to a successful relationship.* ●

Think of It as Rain

*Finding Love
and Giving It Back*

12
CHAPTER

I was so lucky to be raised in an extremely loving family. The importance of loving and nurturing others, both two- and four-legged, was instilled in me from the time I was old enough to understand it. Other than my immediate family and closest relatives, my first understanding of unconditional love involved our Wire-Haired Fox Terrier Skeeter. Despite the fact that my brother and sisters would chase me, knowing Skeeter would join in and gleefully grab ahold of my pants, pulling them down and leaving me crying on the floor, that Terrier was still my best childhood friend. He would cuddle and sleep with me, and I knew then as I know now that the look of your dog, peering directly into your eyes right before he gives you a big lick across your face, is most certainly and undeniably the definition of LOVE! A dog's devotion shows us how love should be given and received. And we undoubtedly search for that same kind of love with other human beings.

The next time I loved someone like I loved Skeeter was my first horse, Ebony Cash. I spent every waking hour I could grooming him, riding him, or just playing with him in his stall or paddock. I would arrive at the stables and call out a very slow but very loud, "C-A-A-A-S-H!" After a few calls, I would hear my riding instructor, Myra Wagener yelling back at me, "ROBERT, ENOUGH WITH THE HOLLERING!"

I couldn't help it. I loved my horse! The kind of trust we had in each other stemmed from the love a kid gets from bonding with a pet. I knew my horse would always try to please and protect me, including regularly finding our way back home when I would invariably get us lost out on the dirt roads, which all looked exactly alike on Grand Bahama Island.

Leaving my beloved horse when my family had to move off the island broke my heart for the very first time. Without a doubt, the hardest part of falling in love is, for whatever reason, when it is over—especially when you are still in love. The thing you learn, though, through heartbreak, is that it is not only possible to love that deeply but to heal from loss and fall in love again. It's even possible to love many individuals, be they people, animals, or even things, at the same time. Our capacity to love knows no boundaries other than those we place in front of our hearts.

———————

My first romantic love was when I was eighteen and at the University of Georgia. Until then, I'd had my share of dates with college girls one of my riding friends, Kathy, would set me up with. This was the end of the seventies—the time of "sex, drugs, and rock and roll." While I loved (almost) all kinds of music, including rock, and sex, like with most guys (if not all kids my age) was constantly on my mind, drugs were something

I had no interest in at all. Perhaps because of my father's issues with smoking and alcohol, I had an aversion to all things I deemed "unhealthy." I most certainly was *not* a partier. One hundred percent of my time was spent between school and the barn. I had found a private farm a few miles from campus, owned by a sociology professor, Dr. Nix, whose son Alan also was a dressage rider. Dr. Nix and I bartered: My horse's board was covered by me giving lessons to Alan. I was up early every morning to see and take care of my horse before classes began and was back at the barn to ride, groom, and feed him at the end of the day, before returning to my campus dorm room where my homework awaited.

That is, until I met Lisa, a senior from a high school near campus. We met through our mutual love of horses. She and her mom Jean were and still are important players within the Arabian breeding and showing scene—Jean was a breeder and judge, and Lisa a top rider. The two had won many national championships.

Lisa invited me and my friend, also a rider, over for lunch one afternoon to see her family's horses. My friend was from Westchester, Connecticut, known for its opulence, and he lived up to his address. He was a slick character, and upon seeing how beautiful Lisa was, he immediately honed in on her while I spoke to her mother about my love of horses and dressage, and chatted about my major—philosophy—a department that, coincidentally, had been headed by her now late husband.

I will never forget that after my friend left, the first thing both Lisa and her mom said to me was that they were pretty sure he was gay. I remember replying that I really did not think so, but naturally, looking back, it is pretty funny!

Things clicked between me and Lisa, and I fell madly in love with her. I spent every moment with her when we were not in class or working with our horses. I loved everything about her: She was beautiful, very smart, extremely mature, and always made me feel confident, even when there was really no reason I should. Little things made me love her even more: The way she bound her two big toes together with a rubber band to keep her feet upright when she tanned in her back yard. Her Southern twang and boisterous laugh. And her unwavering passion for animals, which we shared. Most of all, the fact that this talented, smart, and beautiful lady could love a skinny Jewish kid with a big nose and crooked teeth—basically a geek in every possible meaning of the word—was to me a miracle!

Lisa was only sixteen and living at home with her parents and little brother, while I was two years older but definitely awkward, so navigating our budding relationship, the first for both of us, was both exciting and scary. But her family accepted me with open arms, and the next couple of years were amazing. Lisa and I rarely fought and spoke of eventually getting married and having kids—hopefully they would get her looks, but for sure they would be smart and born to ride horses!

We had been dating three years and I was twenty-one when a friend of mine, Francie Dougherty, who was in vet School at UGA, said I could borrow her horse to compete in my final National Pony Club Rally, which was taking place in Lake Placid, New York. The US Pony Club was the major source of training for kids twenty-one and younger, was responsible for launching the careers of the vast majority of our equestrian Olympians. So, competing at the highest level achievable in this organization, as an "A" Pony Clubber, was to be the highlight of my life up until then. I asked Lisa to drive up with me and Francie's horse for moral support, and I was thrilled when she agreed. Off we set on our great adventure.

Lake Placid was gorgeous, and the stage was set for a week of top competition. Lisa helped me where possible, but the nature of the Rally was that Pony Clubbers had to be responsible for all their own grooming and care of their horses and equipment, as it was judged as the "Stable Management" part of the competition. Written tests were also part of Rallies, and points or deductions of points from these phases, as well as the ridden competition, determined the overall champion. As for riding, we had to perform three disciplines: The first was dressage at a Second or "Medium" Level. Next was a cross-country test of technical difficulty over a course of up to thirty-four obstacles and an array of combinations and questions that demanded superior skills. Finally, the third day we rode a stadium jumping course, which, with fences at a maximum height of 3'11" (comparable to a 1.20-meter jumper class), was a test of how responsive and fit your horse was after a hard cross-country course.

I was confident that I would do a good job in dressage as I normally did. Francie's horse was also a very good, brave, and clean jumper, so I was pretty sure we could have a fine stadium jumping day. The problem I historically had was with cross-country. It was not that I feared falling or running out at a fence. No, my problem, if you recall, was that I always seemed to get lost somewhere out on the course. Once I got going faster than a brisk walk, I was famous for having *zero* sense of direction.

I decided that there was *no way* I was going to get lost in this, my very last Pony Club Rally. I walked the course not one but two times. Then, I was so determined that I actually ran it as fast as I could so that I would be prepared to make decisions more quickly as to which routes and turns to take. By the end of the day, I was exhausted but absolutely confident that I knew the course inside and out.

The next morning was the dressage test, and Francie's horse went great, winning the class and setting us up in perfect shape for our cross-country day. A crowd congratulated me afterward, and I beamed at Lisa when I saw her fleetingly. She seemed to be enjoying herself socializing with people in the spectators' tent. When I was competing, even back then, I was totally self-absorbed. Honestly, you need to be if you want to win.

The morning of cross-country, the horse and I were ready. But I had neglected to consider the one other phase of the competition, which mirrored three-day event competitions back then: "Roads and tracks" consisted of a very simple, brisk trot around a mowed track that was a very obvious square perimeter of a ten-acre field. It was basically meant to warm and loosen up the horses before they had to gallop and jump. Easy enough, right?

Not for Robert Dover.

Off I went on my trot, noting as always the red and white flags that riders were to stay between on their ride around the field. As I came to about the halfway point, I clearly saw a red flag hanging from a tree and a trail going off into the woods. Not having walked the track, off I went into the trees. A few minutes later we were heading down a ravine, and I eventually stopped at a rocky creek. I could barely see the path on the other side of the water, and the creek did not look easy to cross, but I was determined to win the competition and every second over the time limit to finish roads and tracks would cost me points. My horse was not happy about the crossing, and we only made it halfway before he reared up, whirled around, and took me back the way we came. Deciding he had more "horse sense" than I did, I trotted him back up the hill, exited the woods where we'd entered, and saw plainly that we should have just stayed on the mowed path. We broke to a canter and then a slow gallop as I wanted to make up the time we'd lost but did not want to overtire my horse before the major test ahead of us on cross-country. A few minutes later we finally finished, and my friends asked what had happened to me. I chose not to think or talk about my mistake, and instead prepared my horse to enter the start box where the next phase would begin. As the steward counted down, adrenaline coursed through my body. I was hot and sweating, nervous but determined as never before to go clean.

Francie's horse was wonderful, taking each jump in stride with ease, and we finished the cross-country with no faults. He also jumped perfectly the last day during the Stadium Jumping. Had we not gone wandering during roads and tracks, we would have been the clear winner; however, the time we took to complete that simple trot around the field cost us...
ONE HUNDRED TIME FAULTS!

ONE HUNDRED TIME FAULTS!

I was embarrassed and not a lot of fun to be around the last twenty-four hours of the event. Lisa obviously knew this, but she was enjoying herself and had made friends with a lot of kids, including a very handsome, Ivy-League rider named Tad from a well-known equestrian family. Tad was well over six feet tall and pretty much the polar opposite of me in every way. Under usual circumstances, I would have been jealous of their friendship, but I was so single-minded and exhausted from the competition that it wasn't until we were loaded up and on our way back home that Lisa and I finally had any time to really talk. We'd always been great at talking, and we covered everything—from the competition to getting back to Athens and school.

Hours into our drive, Lisa told me she had spent a lot of time with Tad over the weekend and that he had asked her out.

"I will always care about you, Robert," she said quietly, "but I think it is time we faced the fact that our relationship is over. I want more."

I was absolutely crushed and cried on and off the rest of the long drive home. Lisa was also upset, but she had made up her mind; I couldn't talk her out of breaking up with me. Arriving back in Athens, we unloaded Francie's horse at the barn, then I dropped Lisa at home, went back to my double-wide trailer, and fell into my bed, crying myself to sleep.

The next day, I was a wreck. I called a guy who rode at my barn, Steven, and asked if he could take care of my horse as I was just too upset to do it myself. Hearing the sadness in my voice, Steven asked if I wanted to go for a drink later that evening. I said no but he was determined to get me out of my trailer, and after all that had taken place that weekend, the thought of getting drunk felt like maybe not such a bad idea.

Steven picked me up in his station wagon that night...and the rest was a blur.

I woke up the following morning, my head pounding, and rolled over to find Steven asleep next to me in bed. As pieces of the evening's events rushed back into my mind, I pushed myself out of bed, stumbled into the other room, slid down the wall onto my butt with my hands around my knees, and cried.

What did all of this mean?

I was confused...but I was also filled with a flood of other thoughts and emotions. The fact was, I had liked what had happened.

Moments later Steven came out of the bedroom and saw the look on my face right away. He tried to comfort me, promising he would not talk to anyone about the fact we'd slept together. He also said that if I wanted to go out again sometime, he would show me that there was a real gay community I could discover and be a welcome member of.

I needed time to think everything through. I was still broken-hearted over Lisa and ashamed of our failed relationship as well as afraid of what others would think of me.

On Friday I saw Steven at the barn, and he asked me again if I wanted to go out with him again, this time to Circus, Athens' gay dance club.

I made a decision.

Steven picked me up about ten that night, and we arrived at the small club, which had a raised, square dance floor with a large disco ball hanging above it, a bar in the back, and tables filled with guys and a few ladies in front. It was crowded, and Steven told me to find a table while he got us drinks. My eyes bugged out of my head as I moved through the room and tried to take it all in. Guys were dancing with and making out with guys everywhere. The music was pounding, and the DJ kept shouting out, "Have a great time and tip your waiters!"

I saw only one table with two empty seats but was shy about asking if they were free. A couple of guys were seated there already, along with a large Black woman with big hair and a bright red dress. Seeing that I looked like a fish out of water, she lifted her hand and spoke in a deep, baritone voice.

"Baby," she said to me, "if you want to sit your ass down, go right ahead. No one here's gonna stop you. You're fine!"

I had never seen a drag queen, much less sat with one at a bar. Was it HE or SHE? I felt flustered. She waved again, and I obediently sat my ass down and nervously waited for Steven to come back. I was asked my name and responded, adding that it was my first time at Circus.

"VIRGIN!" she cried out.

Drinks arrived with Steven, and as he said hello to everyone, it became obvious he was a regular who knew virtually everyone in the bar.

This was my introduction to my new life as a gay boy, and with that, my life separated into halves: my riding life and my gay life. Days were spent as the "straight-acting Robert" while nights from Thursday through Saturday were devoted to my gay activities—dancing, drinking, and finding boys to share my bed for the night. I had no desire to have a relationship. I was at the "gay buffet" and wanted to try it all.

For a few months I juggled my school and horse life with my new social life. It was exciting to go out, both in Athens and when the group of gay friends I had made would take a caravan of cars to Atlanta to try out the big city bars and clubs. Atlanta was known as the New York City of the South, and it did not disappoint. The clubs were packed with wild and incredible people. One night we even ended up at a bar where Elton John was holding court with his groupies.

After the initial excitement of my self-discovery, I toned down my night-life and began putting more energy back into my riding and school, which were beginning to feel at odds with each other. School was important—my parents had put so much money into my education that I felt obligated to become something they and my other relatives would be proud of. At the same time, I was doing well with my riding, and my progress required that I take off time from school to go to Maryland to train with the Olympic Coach, Colonel Ljungquist.

I decided to move to Arlington, Virginia, to the apartment of a guy I had dated a few times. I was too immature to realize that the guy was thinking I was coming up to be his boyfriend, and he spent a week trying to get me to sleep with him while I stayed on the couch in the living room. His roommate was actually way more appealing, and I eventually started seeing him! I was twenty-one, a kid looking for my dreams as a dressage rider and trainer to come true while also experiencing the big city of Washington, DC, by night. At that point, no one would have been enough for me. The fact was, *I* was not enough for me!

I made a lot of new friends. Among them one in particular: Rick had a big smile and a nose even bigger than mine, and one night he came over and started talking to me in a bar called The Lost and Found in southeast DC. Rick was *not* my type, if I actually had one at that point, but he was relentless, and at the end of the night, I went back with him to the trailer he shared with his ex-boyfriend. We got into bed without saying much, and he looked into my eyes...and...we both simultaneously burst into hysterical laughter.

And so began a friendship that spanned decades.

Rick was outgoing and a prankster, the polar opposite of me at that time, which made us perfect roommates, and we found an apartment to share in Alexandria. It was an easy commute to the hotel where Rick worked the front desk and close enough to the highway for me to get out to Linda Zang's farm in Davidsonville, Maryland. Weekend nights were spent out with Rick and friends at the local bars and clubs. Rick was always the ringleader, whether taping a napkin with "CHEAP" written on it to some poor guy's back or hooking one end of a chain that blocked off a doorway to my belt loop and laughing hysterically as I took a step and found myself chained to the wall with my pants almost coming off.

I was also friends with a small group of guys who all were roommates in downtown Washington. The four of them shared a very cool house in a neighborhood that was slowly being "gentrified" as gays started moving in when they saw how much more house they could get for their money. Two of the guys, David and Keith, had once been boyfriends, but they had broken up the year before I met them. Well, David took a liking to me and we started dating.

This was David Number One.

I couldn't help always feeling there was something wrong when David and I were together. The closer we got, the more he seemed to push me away. I was going to his place several days a week, only to be rejected when I wanted to be intimate with him. I kept finding myself involved in fights between David and Keith. Finally, one night when the five of us were having dinner together, it became clear to me that David was using me to make his ex jealous. That was enough for me. I broke up with him.

Around this time I was hired as the trainer at the farm in Pepperell, Massachusetts, near the New Hampshire border. The day before I was to leave, there was a knock on my door. Opening it, I found David, crying on the front step. It was cold and dark out, so I invited him in, concerned about what could have caused him to be in such distress. David dashed through the door and threw his arms around me, sobbing, telling me how sorry he was to have acted the way he did and how much he missed me.

"I will do anything to be with you again," he pleaded.

I was confused but still had feelings for him. When I told him I was leaving for Boston in the morning, he begged to come along and start a new life with me in Massachusetts. I gave in, and off he went to pack.

We left the next morning in my car, pulling a U-Haul trailer behind it, loaded with our belongings. When we hit the very snowy outskirts of Boston, my car began to slide on the slick roads, and we crept along, very slowly, for the last hour of our drive. The farm owners were waiting when we finally arrived in Pepperell, and they showed us to a tiny apartment over the barn. The bathroom was a porta-potty, outside.

As I began unpacking, David lamented that this was most definitely *not* the lifestyle he thought he was buying into when he came crying to me. By the time night fell, he said he wanted to go home and was booking the first flight back to DC he could find. What could I do? I took him to the airport in the morning and never saw or heard from him again.

Within a few weeks, I briefly dated another David (David Number Two) who I shared little in common with, other than his friend—also named David. David Number Three was in still in college and a little, cute Italian with a big personality and a bigger temper. We began to date and soon were living together. We both got to know each other's families and the first six months were a lot of fun—he even moved with me back to DC when I accepted the position at Chestnut Lawn Farm in Virginia.

Our problems began when I started showing my horses and had to leave for extended periods of time. Once David had graduated and taken a job, he could not go with me, and he was incredibly jealous of both the horses and anyone else he thought I was paying attention to.

I began to sense things were not working out as his jealous behavior escalated, and I tried to end things with him, but David threatened to hurt or even kill me and himself if I left him. He chased me around the apartment with a butcher knife, and once when I locked myself in the bathroom, he punched a hole in the wall next to the door. His temper scared me so much that it took three years before I had the nerve to finally leave him.

In 1984, my mother came to visit us in DC. She stayed in a hotel, but when she came to our apartment, she saw that I was sleeping on the couch and asked if things were okay. I broke down and told her all that had happened with David. Startled by my confession, she urged me to separate from David, saying it was the perfect time. I had just made my first Olympic Team and we were to fly out to Los Angeles three weeks before the Opening Ceremonies to train with our coach at the equestrian venue—the famous Santa Anita Park. Mom suggested I move all my belongings into storage before I left and tell David he could keep the apartment, which I would still pay half the rent for until he found a new roommate or a smaller place.

David was hysterical when I told him, but my mother was there to give me courage, and there was nothing he could do with her poised to call the police. I left with my mom and had movers come the next day to take my belongings.

Unlike David Number One, this was not the last I heard from David Number Three. Less than a year later, his mother called me to tell me he was ill. When I asked what was wrong, she broke down, saying through sobs that it was AIDS. They were doing all they could but he had already been hospitalized twice.

David was one of the many thousands of victims of AIDS, and I made sure I either saw or spoke to him on the phone weekly over the next six months before he, like almost all the others at the time, succumbed to the disease.

I had started doing clinics, one of which was in the Boston area again, when I met David Number Four. He was tall, handsome, and five years younger than me. I was immediately interested in him. He was a dressage rider, too, which was new territory for me.

David was quiet and not as outgoing as I was, but we hit it off, and soon we were living together. Looking back, I recognize now that our relationship had horses in common but lacked both communication and passion. At the time, however, I only knew it was better with David than it had been with boyfriends before.

David was not easy to keep happy; he constantly wanted to live elsewhere, and so we moved from Washington, DC, to California, from there back to Boston, from there to Germany (which was really my choice, as after the 1986 World Championships, I wanted to live in Europe to hone my skills as a top competitor in my sport), and then back to Gladstone, New Jersey. We spent five years together, and during that time, slowly grew apart.

One afternoon I had returned from a trade show and brought him some nice shirts and other gifts to give him. I went to take a shower, and when I got out, David had neatly folded his new clothes and packed them in his suitcases, laid out on the floor near the door. Toweling off, I asked where he was going, and he calmly told me he was leaving. Confused, I asked him *where* it was he was going, and he clarified by explaining he was leaving *me*. David said he had been having an affair with one of my students, and he was going to go live with him. I sat down next to him and was taken aback by the very quiet and deliberate conversation we had next, listing what he wanted to take from the relationship: the Mercedes, the two-horse trailer, his two young horses, and all his clothes, jewelry, and material belongings.

I said yes to it all and that was that.

From the moment I walked into the arena on my horse and saw Robert Ross setting jumps, I somehow knew what I felt was more than just physical attraction. Robert was and is stunning in so many ways. He is beautiful, for sure, on the outside, but he is also magnificent and complex from within.

When we first met, it was becoming clear that my relationship with David Number Four was not right for either of us, and meeting Robert—with his brilliant blue eyes and his smile that could stop traffic—cemented that fact. More than that, Robert had an intellect that came from being on his own far too early, street smarts that I, coming from my sheltered upbringing, could not entirely understand but knew were formidable. At fourteen, Robert had managed a restaurant (using his older brother's work permit), at fifteen he managed a trophy shop, at sixteen he was production manager of a large graphic arts company, at seventeen he moved with his boyfriend (an ice skater) to New York City, and by eighteen they were in South Korea together, where Robert managed the ice show. By twenty-one, he had found and purchased his own townhouse in West Hollywood and was working for a printing company. He had his own horse and was pursuing his passion for show jumping, which is how he came to be at Olympian George Morris's farm in New Jersey, Hunterdon, for a weeklong clinic when we met. In a strange coincidence, I had conducted a clinic the weekend before at the barn in Los Angeles where Robert kept his horse, and his trainers there—our close friends Jeff Katz and Budd Wolf—had told Robert I was someone he should meet. Fate? Maybe, as I was certain I wanted to be with Robert. Nevertheless, he was smart enough to tell me that I had to be one hundred percent available if he were going to go on a date with me.

That was in July. It wasn't until the following March that my breakup with David was complete, and Robert and I went on our first official date.

We went to Key West together, where we lay on the sand and talked for hours about everything. We became lovers, and I knew that with him it was different than it had been with any other relationship I had ever been in. I always say, being with someone should not be to "fill a hole" in yourself; instead, it should be an outlet for you to share and allow the love you have inside to "overflow" outwardly into someone else's life. Robert allowed me to share all of myself, strengths and flaws alike. He has truly seen me as no other person has, even my mother. Certainly, my mother loved me unconditionally, but Robert has not only given me that, he has also challenged me to keep evolving and becoming a better and better man.

Robert has always been a smart business person who understands numbers and details in ways I have never been good at. In our first year together, he saw so many issues with my tax returns that he enlisted his agency from California, which he'd trusted for years with his own returns, and saved us almost $250,000 that I would have simply paid without a second thought. In the following year, Robert came along with the US Dressage Team on our European tour as our "unofficial business manager," and for the very first time ever, our fully funded dressage squad not only did well, we came home with a surplus for the US Equestrian Team Foundation from our winnings at the international shows. We did so well with our budget, in fact, that from that point on, the system was changed to giving grants, normally about $35,000, to each rider on the squad, and then allowing them to keep their personal winnings from the shows. This evolved due in large part to Robert showing Fiona Baan, the director of dressage at USET headquarters, that we could and would make our tours remain within a budget and produce far greater results, including medals at Olympics and World Championships in 1992 and 1994. By 1994, we were running like a true machine.

I was crushed when we found out that year that Fiona had terminal cancer. I adored her, and Robert was my rock to lean on as we dealt with her prognosis. We knew she did not have much time, and so our team decided to ride in her honor that summer in The Hague. Tragically, Fiona passed away before we left for Europe.

She left me a note:

Robert, you have always been my shining star!
Love, Fiona

With Robert and his dad there, as well my family members, I will never forget riding into the arena in The Hague with Devereaux, knowing I was going to make them—but more importantly, Fiona—proud. We got our personal best score and led the US Team to the bronze medal. However, more etched in my memory is a photo someone took of me at my last halt with the most amazing rays of sunlight shining down on me and my horse, as if from an angel above.

Two years later in Atlanta, another picture was taken with me and Jessica Ransehousen, both of us among Fiona's best friends, with similar rays of sunlight shining down on us as we left for the black-tie engagement right before the opening day of the Olympic Games. Both photos are incredibly special to me as they will always remind me of Fiona and the true power of LOVE.

––––––––––––

Robert always instinctively knew when to give me the space I needed to concentrate on my competitions and was also a great influence on the spouses of my teammates in the days leading up to our major championships. He made it look easy to support me, even though I always knew it was anything but that. Athletes are similar to artists, who become so self-absorbed leading up to a big moment that being around them is simply not fun. For this reason, when I coached teams, I produced a set of rules and boundaries for the team members in order to ensure they had the space they needed while buffering them from the stresses and spills of family life and friends. Rules like mine were not around back in the late eighties and nineties, other than at Olympic Games, where athletes lived in the Olympic Village and away from pretty much everyone, other than at designated times. Robert took all of it in stride; he instinctively knew how to be there to support me while keeping my family and others from distracting me at important moments.

Robert also took care of our business, Romance Farm, Inc., while becoming a better rider and trainer as a hunter-jumper professional. He trained with Joe Fargis and Conrad Homfeld, both Olympic medalists, and unbeknownst to most people, the first gay partners ever to stand on a gold medal podium together at the 1984 Games in Los Angeles. Through Joe and Conrad, Robert was able to purchase two wonderful, older Grand Prix horses from another of their students, Denise Cowanga—Black Eyed Pea and Kidd Gloves. While their best years as top competitors may have been behind them, each horse gave Robert the incredible experience he needed both to move up the levels and to become a better all-around horseman. Committing to his business one hundred percent, Robert evolved very quickly from an amateur rider into an elegant and effective professional.

Robert was and is both a perfectionist and a tough competitor with the instincts of a natural winner. That is a double-edged sword at times. He would sometimes have an excellent warm-up, then enter the competition arena and head for the first fence with grace and softness. The problem was that older horses like his could be rather careless with their legs with a "soft ride" to jump number one, so they would knock down the top rail. Immediately, Robert would grit his teeth and gallop on with enormous determination to be both fast and clear over the rest of the course, and most times, that is exactly what would happen. Still, he would finish the course, pat his horse on the neck, and walk out of the arena feeling like he had let his horse and his coach down.

I said, "Robert, go into the arena next time with the thought that you *already* had the first rail down, and ride like you usually do *after* that happens."

With small adjustments like this, Robert began to win more and more, and his confidence grew. He brought along younger horses and continued to lease some older ones to stay in the Grand Prix arenas. He did really well, especially considering we could never afford the quality of horses that so many of the other Grand Prix riders were on. What he had going for him, other than talent, was that everyone loved him and wanted to help him and see him succeed. He also has an incredibly strong work ethic, and to this day, it makes him a great success in whatever he chooses to do.

In the late eighties, I bought a very lovely, three-year-old gelding named Dunhill at the Hanoverian auction in Verden, Germany. He looked so smart and had a beautiful face, and I thought he would be perfect for me to bring along. Of course, I met with the auction veterinarian after I tried him to make sure he was sound, and the vet showed me each X-ray, saying each one was perfect.

Now, auctions are strange animals. Before the bidding began, the head auctioneer told me he wanted it to appear that I was purchasing the horse for much more money than I planned on spending—close to 100,000 Deutschmarks. He knew I only had around half that. The auction-eer explained he would continue to raise the price, and at 90,000, I would raise my hand and he would knock down on that price. The auction house would make up the difference from the 40,000 I had promised to pay. The feeling was that the positive press would be worth paying the balance for me to have him.

I was very excited to now own this lovely horse, who I renamed Darien, and I brought him home to Boston, where I was living at the time.

Less than a week after he arrived, one of my favorite students, Gwen Blake, fell in love with my horse and offered me double what I had spent on him in Germany. Well, there was no way I could pass the chance up, and I sold him to her. My wonderful vet at the time, Dr. Marty Simonsen, did the pre-purchase exam, which I was sure would be a slam dunk since I had just bought him with a perfect vetting overseas. A day or two later, Marty called me up and said, "Robert, Darien is a lovely horse and clinically he looked fine, but there's one big problem. Your three-year-old horse has the X-rays of a nine-year-old with arthritic changes that are simply not okay for a horse this age."

Shocked, I replied that the vet in Germany had showed me the horse's films, saying each one was perfect. Marty asked that I request the films so he could compare them with the new ones, so I called the Verden Auction office and asked for Dunhill's X-rays. After a long hold on the phone, I was informed that they were sorry, but the horse's X-rays had been burned in a fire.

Well, I immediately knew what was happening, and I made my displeasure plain.

"Listen," I said angrily, "I do not have the money to be able to take you to court, but what I do have is a pen and paper, and I am going to write all about my experience with the Verden Auction and send it to every equestrian magazine in the world. We'll see how that works out for you!"

Flustered, the auction representative tried to reassure me.

"Mr. Dover," he said. "We don't want you to be unhappy with us. We will work something out with you. Please do not write about the auction in that way."

The auction's concession was to give me 15,000 Deutschmarks toward any Hanoverian horse I might like in one of their future sales, so I went to the next one, but I could not buy one leg of a nice horse for that amount of money.

While I was living in Germany, my horse Federleicht won the Grand Prix Freestyle at my last show in Aachen. I was sitting in the lunch area, taking with friends and saying how unhappy I was that I could not find a suitable Hanoverian to replace Darien, who because of the issues with his films, I'd ended up selling to Gwen for exactly what I'd paid for him, rather than double the price. A jumper rider, Guido Brunninx, overheard our conversation and said he had a very special yearling that was branded Hanoverian but had amazing bloodlines from the famous Belgian breeding farm Zangersheide. When I heard the bloodlines—Cor de la Bryère, Almé, and Ramiro—I looked at my friends and off we went for the hour-long drive to Guido's place.

As we neared the Belgian border, I realized that in my haste to check out this horse, I had left without my passport. In those days, the border patrol were very strict and would take me to jail if they caught me. My friends put me on the floor in the back seat of the car and threw a horse blanket over me.

We made it across the border and arrived at Guido's farm as it was getting dark. He brought out this black colt with two white hind legs and a star and stripe on his face, and he turned him loose in the small indoor arena. The colt looked around for a second and floated off with a beautiful and elastic trot before breaking into a lovely canter. I was sold on him right away, but then Guido said, "Just wait, and I will show you something even better!" He constructed a free-jumping chute, consisting of a little fence followed by a slightly bigger one. The colt trotted in and flew up *way* over the jumps. Guido made the second jump bigger and bigger, and no matter how big it got or how many times the black yearling jumped it or how tired he was, he still flew up a mile over the obstacle, with his tail almost hitting him in his head.

The very next day I arranged for the Verden Auction representatives to pay Guido the 15,000 Deutschemarks they promised me with the agreement that if I sold the horse again before he was six years old, I would have to split the profits with them.

When he was three, this young stallion, who we had named Cor d'Alme Z, was ready to break, and Robert took him and did all the work. He was quite a strong stallion at first, but Robert was fantastic with him and over time began to walk and then trot him over rails and tiny jumps. The stallion was so careful, he would leap five feet over a puddle and did not want to touch anything he was pointed at. At four years old, we took "Corde," as we called him, over to George Morris's Hunterdon, and Robert took a lesson and jumped the fences in George's indoor arena. After only a few jumps, from the chair where George was sitting, came a resounding, "I LOVE THIS HORSE!"

He showed the same star potential he had shown as a baby when I bought him.

The next year, Robert continued to work with him and did some dressage to improve his rideability. At five years old, Joe Fargis took over the ride from Robert, and Corde began winning immediately in the low jumpers. Slowly but surely, Joe moved the stallion up, and every step of the way, Corde stepped up to the plate and showed his top-class potential. When he was seven years old, Joe showed the horse in three Grands Prix and won all three as I nervously watched, holding my breath and lifting my legs with each fence he cleared. The offers then started to come right away, and within a few weeks, the great John Whitaker was in New Jersey with a Norwegian client, a young professional named Geir Gulliksen. He loved the stallion and his sponsor, a shipping magnate also from Norway, purchased the horse from Robert and me for a whopping $1.3 million! Even after paying out commissions, Robert and I, having already sold Federleicht a couple of years earlier for $500,000 to Ireland, were officially millionaires.

We had been fixing up our first house in Tewksbury, New Jersey, for quite some time. It was cute and on five acres with a little two-stall barn in the back field where I had put a baby horse that kept leaping out over the fence and ending up at the Thoroughbred breeding farm across the street. We sold that house and bought a very cool, sort of ski-lodge-style home, built two-thirds the way up a very steep foothill in Hunterdon County, within a mile of our best friends Ken Berkley and Scott Stewart (who still live in their gorgeous home there, which we love to visit). The driveway at the bottom had a bridge that crossed over a small creek before taking a left and going up a very steep angle for a few hundred yards and then bearing left and up again to the house. It was a split level: When you came in on the landing, there were steps down to the first-floor great room and kitchen and up to three bedrooms and two baths. The nicest thing about the house was the twenty-foot-high ceiling and wall of glass that looked over a very large deck down through thirteen acres of woods to the creek which rambled below. Above the house were more wooded acres with trails that led to an open twenty-acre field. In other words, it was very private and lovely.

Right away, Robert and I set out to make our new home exactly what we dreamed. First, we added an additional family room, glassed in on three sides from floor to ceiling, and added another bathroom with it on the first floor. Above, we blew out the master bedroom and created a fabulous suite that also had a deck to step out onto and sit and look at what was to become the *pièce de résistance* of the home: our pool. We cleared and dynamited into the mountainside to create a fifty-foot, natural lagoon-style pool, with huge boulders and a dark gray bottom. At the far end, we created a stone creek that we brought down from forty feet up in the woods through the lush plants and trees we planted that ended as a twelve-foot waterfall into the pool. At the near end, tucked into the hillside, we built a spa, surrounded by rocks and tall grasses and flowers and its own small creek, out of which hot water could flow and fall into the pool. Of course, both "creeks" could be turned on and off with a switch and we recirculated the water.

The renovation was finished right in time for our tenth anniversary. Ten years together called for something really special, and Robert and I pulled out all the stops, inviting one hundred and fifty of our best friends and family members for a catered event the Saturday of July Fourth weekend. Robert and I put up a lot of our family members either at the house or in local hotels, and friends flew in from all over for our big occasion. The most complicated issue was getting people up to the house, since the driveway was not conducive to traffic and there was nowhere to park a hundred or so cars. We hired a limousine company to transport our guests from a field a mile or so up the road, which we were kindly loaned to use as a parking lot.

The party could not have gone better—it was so good, in fact, that many people stayed on partying through the night and the next day, sleeping on the chaise longues by the pool or the couches downstairs. It was *definitely* one of those weekends! Monday morning, I woke up and raised the blinds that looked out to our pool to see there were still a few stragglers that had not left! I just closed the blinds and went back to sleep, happy it had been such a success and everyone had (and was still having!) such a great time.

That winter, Robert and I decided to rent the place out since we were heading to Florida and would not be back until late April. Very quickly we met a nice couple who had one older child and seemed like they would be perfect tenants, as they were both well employed and seemed very respectful. A few months later, we asked a friend to stop by to check on the house. He called us immediately, informing me it was a wreck and I had to come up.

Arriving at our home, I knocked on the door; it was opened by an elderly lady I had never met. I took one look around and realized the house was being lived in by no fewer than eight people with several dogs (and who knew what else!). It was a disaster from top to bottom: Expensive rugs had been urinated on, furniture moved around, and a baby's playpen was in the middle of the great room. Our yard and all the grass and plantings had died of lack of water or the dogs, which appeared to have been chained up to a pole outside by a trampoline they had erected. I asked the woman where the tenants to whom I'd rented the house were.

"I don't know," she replied. "But my daughter-in-law should be back with the baby soon."

"Whose baby?" I asked incredulously, as the woman we had rented to certainly hadn't had one when we had met her prior to renting out the house.

We ended up having to get lawyers to evict the family, although we never got more than the security deposit back, as they did not have the money to pay for the over $50,000 in damages they had done to the house and grounds. It was a huge life lesson for us!

The summer of 1999, I left for another European tour to prepare for the 2000 Olympics in Sydney. Robert called one night and said he was out in Southhampton, the very beautiful and exclusive area at the tip of Long Island where his trainers, Joe Fargis and Conrad Homfeld, had their facility.

"Can we move out here?" he asked excitedly. "It's really beautiful!"

I immediately answered that we had just finished getting our New Jersey home perfect again, and I was so happy there. But Robert was and is so smart that he already had his answer ready, one that he knew I could not resist.

"It's only thirty-five minutes from the ferry to Fire Island!"

And that was all it took for me. The sign was up to sell our home, which we did easily within a few weeks. We looked for a rental in the Hamptons so we could take time to figure out exactly where we wanted to live and found a nice house not far from Two Trees Farm, an amazing facility on over a hundred acres with several large barns, one of which we rented for our horses and clients. Robert and I both had our separate training businesses going, and the farm had superb arenas for jumping, while the owners, David and Jane Walentas, put in a lovely dressage arena for me with great footing and a gazebo to sit in when I taught. Life was great.

One day, I was in the arena teaching and looked around and saw a man and two women sitting in my gazebo. I kept my attention on the horse and rider I was training, but when my student and I finished, I walked toward the gazebo where I saw our friend Kelly Klein, the rider-artist-photographer-awesome human being (who we love to this day)! With her were two people I immediately recognized—actress Kate Capshaw and her husband Steven Spielberg. I apologized for making them wait so long as Kelly introduced us. After a few pleasantries, Kate asked if I would come to their place in East Hampton to teach her, as she was interested in exploring dressage, and Kelly had told her I was the one to help her.

Flattered, I nonetheless explained that I was not the best trainer for someone beginning her dressage career. I was not the most patient person, and more importantly, I said, "I don't do house calls."

They were nice, though, and persistent! So I finally made a deal with them. I would come out to their farm, an estate I had heard had five homes and a lovely barn and arena, and I would teach her one lesson, provided I could go into every single room in every house, including the closets! I mean, it was the Spielbergs, for God's sake! I wanted to see her collection of shoes and his collection of gadgets, which I knew he was a huge fan of. (I think Steven had drones before there were drones!) They agreed, and that began a long-term friendship with their family that I cherish. Their family, with seven children in total—now mostly grown up—was the perfect example of kids who are brought up to know that being of service is hugely important, and especially since they were living lives of great advantage. It showed me that the most successful people can still lead the most authentic and generously loving lives. I have never forgotten that lesson.

One other thing that I will never forget is a particular lesson I gave to Kate on a lovely Grand Prix horse I helped her find. Shortly after he arrived from Great Britain, I could see that she was afraid to push herself to ride him the way she should. He was big but not at all fractious; still, she was easily frightened as a person who was learning to ride advanced dressage later in life, just as I was with skiing.

That day, she was almost frozen with fear, and I had to figure out how to calm her enough to try what I was hoping she could learn on her horse. Suddenly, it hit me.

"Kate," I said. "I want you to imagine you are playing me in a movie and become me up there."

The look on her face changed immediately, as it only can in a great actor, and within moments, Kate was on her way forward with her new horse. Over the next fifteen minutes, with a look of determination and total concentration on her face, she did every single movement perfectly in the Grand Prix, as if she had done it a hundred times before.

This whole thing is truly between our ears!

The next spring, Robert and I and my parents shared a table at the final selection trials for the Olympics in San Juan Capistrano with Kate and Steven, and I was so proud to have a personal best result with Kennedy in front of them all. Robert, as usual, let me have both my moments of self-absorption before my competition as well as those of glory after, in which I was the "star of the show." He never complained or sought to take the attention I was getting away from me.

What, I ask, could be a more obvious act of LOVE?

Robert continued over the next few years to take good but not great horses into the ring and do well due to his talent and determination. We bought a few nice horses in Argentina, where prices were considerably lower, and Robert got them all to the big arena successfully. However, it became more and more clear that to be truly competitive in the

Grands Prix, you needed to be extraordinarily wealthy or sponsored by someone who was. We were neither, and having just gone through the Joe Zada debacle, experienced issues similar to mine with his back, and a desire to invest in property, Robert decided to take the real estate exam. After passing it, he became an agent with Keller Williams, the largest agency in America. As with everything, Robert was determined to excel, and within a couple of years, because of his incredible honesty and work ethic, he was at the top of the list of agents in Wellington and South Florida. Today, Robert has, year after year, been one of the most successful agents in Florida and is a force to be reckoned with in the industry. He has also steered us toward purchasing and flipping many homes and parcels of land, from New York to Miami Beach— including over twenty in Wellington. His success allowed me to slow down a bit in what was for a while a nonstop and full-on training stable, a radio show (*Dover's World*), a reality television show (*The Search for America's Next Equestrian Star*), and now, Robert Squared, our vegan equestrian-wear company.

I had always hoped my parents would be there to see Robert and me legally married, but this was not to be. My mom passed away in July of 2012, and my dad's Alzheimer's had progressed to the point that he was in a living situation catering specifically to people with his condition. I know how much they would have loved being with us to celebrate our wedding, but they always knew how dedicated we were to each other and said we were more "married" than most straight people they knew! Robert and I ended up having a very small ceremony on the third of September, 2013, out on Fire Island, and our best friends Ken Berkley and Scott Stewart decided to make it a double wedding, joining us on the beach at dusk. As the sun set and the waves crashed against the sand, we said our vows, and our justice of the peace, who looked and spoke very much like Barbara Streisand, sealed the deal and pronounced us MARRIED!

The party for twelve of our best friends and Robert's mom was held right after at our home, just a few feet off the beach. It was perfect! And the next day, we went to Ken and Scott's place in New Jersey, where a couple hundred of our mutual friends celebrated again with us, long into the night.

Soon after, it was made abundantly clear that members of my family and Robert's who lived on the West Coast were unhappy they had missed the celebration, and they demanded a regional do-over. The following spring, we all met in Palm Springs and had our second wedding, with my brother Al, the judge, presiding over the ceremony. It was as fun as the first time around with more of those we loved sharing in the special moment.

Robert has, both literally and figuratively, navigated me through my life. We can be anywhere in the world—for instance, Stuttgart, Germany—after twenty or more years of not having been back, and Robert will know exactly how to get to the gym from our hotel! I, meanwhile, have to look right and left and pause a moment when leaving my hotel room to remember which way it is to the elevator—and much of the time, I am still wrong. But Robert has also always been a huge factor in the biggest decisions of my life and ours together, as it should be. His moral compass and compassion for others drives his actions every single day. He is far more emotional than I am. I consider myself more "mechanical" than him. By that, I mean that I begin each day with my breakfast and then go to work, and with the first horse and rider that enter the arena, something clicks in my mind and I begin to train. My passion and energy take over and I literally give one hundred percent to each and every moment while teaching, but it is not from something I have to will myself to do. *This* is what I mean by saying I am mechanical. I know, verbatim, every lecture I have given for the past thirty-plus years, and I never second-guess myself while training. I always say there are only three things I am certain about in my life:

• Love is the most important thing and our highest priority.

• I know and understand what goes on in the "sand box" we call a dressage arena.

• I am one hundred percent positive that I am not one hundred percent positive about anything else!

Everything else resides in the enormous gray area that is the mystery of life, and I feel enormously liberated by living this way, open to being surprised by new information, experiences, and belief systems.

In the end, Robert has been the reason for my evolution toward being a better person over the years. His grace in literally being in my shadow for twenty years while I competed on and coached Olympic teams shows his amazing patience and love for me. Just as importantly, Robert's gradual growth in his self-confidence and feeling of empowerment, enabling him to say what he wants and not yield to my wishes, have forced me to look at myself and try to listen better and be more malleable and willing to compromise. This has not been easy for me or simple for us as a couple, and we both continue to work with our therapist to help us get through the hurdles that all couples have in their relationships, especially those that have spanned decades, like ours.

Robert Ross and I have now been together exactly half of my time on this earth. It hardly seems that I could have had a life before him, even though I have the memories, and now this book, to prove it was so.

I am more in love with Robert today than the day we first met.

— The Only Thing We Are Here For —

There is nothing more important than LOVE. I believe we were put here to love and be loved and that everything we do is an expression of our love...unless it is not. When it is not, it is an expression of our fear, or worse, negative or even evil things.

I was born into the Jewish religion, and though I do not consider myself a religious person, I do have a strong sense of living by the Golden Rule: "Do unto others as you would have them do unto you." As kids, we were taught that the stories in the Bible were not necessarily to be believed as factual and historically accurate. In other words, there probably weren't literally "forty days and forty nights." I grew up to believe that they were written to teach the difference between right and wrong and create laws in communities and civilizations in order to more or less keep people in line. Most importantly, humans have always sought the answers to the "Big 'W' Questions": Where did we come from? Why are we here? Where do we go when we die? Religions all attempt to answer these questions in order to allay fear of death and produce faithful, obedient communities where otherwise chaos might reign. The faithful are easier to control: "Do what the Bible says or God will punish you, and if he doesn't, we most definitely will in His name."

I do believe that many good deeds also are done by virtually all religious groups; amazing charities and positive activities abound within them all. Still, historically, many of the worst atrocities know to man have occurred in the name of religion and the "otherness" and hatred caused by it. And so, I am not religious, but as I have said in these pages, in my own way, I am very spiritual. I believe in a force, whatever you might want to call it, be it God, love, or the universe. I come to that conclusion first by asking myself a simple question: What started everything? Naturally, I get the answer from friends: "Robert, of course you know that the Big Bang started it all." And when I hear it came from "X" before that, well, then I want to know what created "X," and so on.

What was there before EVERYTHING?

Perhaps before everything there was *thought,* and just perhaps that is what everything still is.

Robert Dover

We may never have all the answers, but I do feel in my heart that love has incredible power, and collectively, it has created all there is, all there ever was, and all there will ever be! Here is how I believe it works. (Be patient and go with me on this one, whether you are religious or a total nonbeliever.)

Since the beginning of civilization, humans have looked up to the heavens and prayed, whether to the sun, moon, stars, or to a god or gods. They believed that there was a power that was greater than they were, worthy of their praise. Religions were created to explain and answer the big questions. Science has now given us explanations of how the universe was created, but questions remain: What created the thing that created the thing that created it?

Both science and religion require, at one point or another, a leap of faith. Scientists will tell you that they can prove their theories with math. But who created that math? People did. Quantum physics says that a particle can be proven to be able to inhabit multiple places at the same time, using mathematical formulas to do so. Still, no one has ever actually seen this phenomenon. We are asked to believe it on what? Faith in math!

My belief is that the universe is made up of energy, which equals God, which equals love. I don't care which word you use; they are all fabulous to me!

Love, in the form of energy or light, shines down on us, warming us, nourishing us, and giving us life. It allows us to flourish and find our true purpose, which is to love—to find love, share love, and show others that *love is the most important thing*. In every action of doing this, we emit energy from ourselves that may go unnoticed but is measurable. People gravitate toward couples who are in love. Congregations of people who come together to pray for love create a spectrum of positive energy. If you believe in a god who is all-knowing and shines her light of love down on us, the love we all give emits the same light energy, and literally, as well as figuratively, is our gift back to her. Or, stated another way, energy does not cease to exist; it merely changes hands.

Think of it as with rain: It comes down, soaks into the earth, and is consumed by us to give us life, and then goes back into the atmosphere through evaporation, forms clouds, and rains again. Love shines down on us all and through our acts of loving, we send it back into the world in a never-ending circle.

Regardless of whether you are a devout Christian, Jew, Muslim, or an atheist, LOVE is the most important thing. It is truly the only thing we are here for. ●

55. One of our first all-gay Atlantis vacations to Punta Cana in the Dominican Republic. We loved playing volleyball and made some lifelong friends. ●

56. I purchased this Hanoverian, Darien, at the auction in Verden, Germany in the late eighties. He went on to become a lovely Grand Prix horse for Gwen Blake, also the owner of Juvel, who I took as my alternate horse to the Olympic Games in Seoul, Korea, in 1988. ●

57. In a rental on Fire Island. It was and still is a place to kick back and completely relax with friends and loved ones who could care less about my sport! ●

58. In 1990 we met Joe Zada (left), shown here with the late Gene Mische. Joe became a client and friend. He was a lavish star sponsor of the shows in Wellington—we just didn't know he was using our money to do it! He would later be the cause of a great deal of financial and personal heartache. ● *Photo by Ken Braddick/ dressage-news.com*

59. Parties at Joe's mansion were the events of the year in Wellington, and they all had a theme. Can you guess this one? ●

60-61. Robert and I had our own parties. We hosted Christmas parties for children in hospitals, as well as the children of migrant workers. We continue to send presents every year to kids all around the world who otherwise would not get Christmas. ●

62. At 15, Katherine Bateson (now Bateson-Chandler) was determined to work for me, despite my telling her daily that she was too young. She persisted and eventually became my assistant and finally took over as Jane Forbes Clark's sponsored dressage rider, where she still is employed. Katherine is the closest thing I have had to a daughter, and I love and admire her every single day! ●

63. When I moved to Mülheim, Germany, in the eighties, I was so lucky to have the most fantastic lady as an assistant, Petra Kasseberg Hofman, seen here many years later holding my godson, Niclas. Petra along with her husband Dieter and Niclas are my beloved German family. ●

64. My godson Niclas was born to ride and was on (and sometimes off!) ponies from the time he could walk. He now has his own stables in Germany where he trains and rides jumpers. I could not be more proud of him! ●

65–66. I am so thankful to Robert for introducing me to the amazing fun of skiing. Robert has skied since he was a kid and is super good at it, as is seen here with him catching some air. ●

67. 1992 was the year of the Barcelona Olympics with Walter and Mary Anne McPhail's Lectron. He had done so well at all the shows leading up to the Games and then got his tongue over the bit as I started my Grand Prix test. Amazingly, our team still got the bronze medal! ●

68–69. Our bronze-medal-winning team at the 1992 Olympics in Barcelona: Charlotte Bredahl-Baker on Monsieur; I'm on Lectron, owned by the McPhail family; Graf George, owned and ridden by Michael Poulin; and Carol Lavell and her very own Gifted. We were led by our fantastic Chef d'Equipe Jessica Ransehousen, herself a three-time Olympian. ●

70–71. Sitting in the stands in The Hague, site of the 1994 World Equestrian Games, with family and members of our squad from that year: (left to right) Melinda McPhail, my parents Jean and Herb Dover with Chef d'Equipe Jessica Ransehousen behind them and me beside them; Carol Lavell, Jane Savoie, and Gary Rockwell. I bet we were all there watching our teammate not pictured: Kathleen Raine. ●

72. On the Bronze Medal Podium with Gary Rockwell, Carol Lavell, and Kathleen Raine. To our right, standing proudly, is Klaus Balkenhol, one of the team gold winners from Germany, who went on to coach our American team through our medal-winning years from 2000 until 2008. ●

73. 1994 was another medal-winning year, this time with Susan Dansby's Devereaux at the World Equestrian Games in The Hague. My family was there, along with Robert, as we proudly rode in for our medals. ●

74. I am with Kathleen Raine, Carol Lavell, and Gary Rockwell, and we are led by our Chef d'Equipe, Jessica Ransehousen. ●

75. Back in the stables at the 1994 World Equestrian Games in The Hague with a bronze medal around my neck and a magnum of champagne in my hands, ready to pour for Robert, Jessica, and Team USA! ●

76. Mary Ellen Purucker had Katherine Bateson, shown here with Mary Ellen, and I bring Devereaux out to Kansas City for the Kansas City Royal Horse Show, a big indoor event she helped sponsor. The "Grand Dame" of her community, Mary Ellen is now 105! I was honored to have her speak at my birthday in 2021. ●

77. In 1995 the World Cup Finals were brought to the Los Angeles Equestrian Center. Though Devereaux ended up having a quarter crack in his hoof, resulting in my withdrawal from the competition, we still had fun at the many parties. This one, at the home of Ken Kragen—who secured the talent that appeared on the hit fundraising single and album "We Are the World"—and his wife and my student, Cathy (between me and Robert), was chock full of television and movie stars—and of course, all the dressage stars from around the world (Monica Theodorescu is on my left). ●

78. A fun shot of my folks and the lovely Kate Capshaw. She rode dressage and has a great farm with her husband Steven Spielberg and their kids in East Hampton, New York. ●

79. With the beautiful and amazing Katherine Bateson-Chandler, my right hand for sixteen years, in 1995. She was so keen on grooming for me that I finely had to kick her out of the nest to my great friend, Carl Hester, or she might never have left the stables. Katherine has gone on to become a top rider and trainer with her own clientele. ●

80. 1996 was another Olympic medal year, this time in Atlanta, where I rode Anne Gribbons' gelding Metallic, leased by my sponsor and friend Jane Forbes Clark. ●
Photo by Arnd Bronkhorst

81. In 1994, right before leaving for the World Championships in The Hague, the fabulous director of dressage at USET headquarters, Fiona Baan, passed away from cancer. She and I had a very special and close relationship, and I told the team we would ride in her memory. As I came out of the arena, it was late in the day and cloudy but somehow a photo showed me on the jumbotron being soaked in rays of sun from above. I took that as a sign that Fiona was shining down on us, and amazingly, two years later in Atlanta, as Jessica Ransehousen and I left for a party the night before the Grand Prix, this photo was taken. I LOVE IT! ●

83-84. In 1998, Robert and I had our ten-year anniversary at our home in Flemington, New Jersey. My very happy mom and dad had a photo op, floating in our pool. (The truth is, my mom never went in the sun much, protecting her perfect skin and youthfulness.) We really enjoyed entertaining good friends, like Scot Evans (shown on the left with Robert Ross), at this house. ●

82. How handsome is Robert Ross in this shot in our spa at our home in New Jersey in 1998? ●

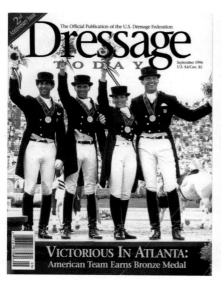

85–87. From the end of the 1980s to the mid 2000s, the United States was consistently in the medals almost one hundred percent of the time, and just as often we made the cover of the major equestrian magazines. Top left: The 1996 Atlanta Olympics with my great friends and teammates Guenter Seidel, Michelle Gibson, and Steffen Peters. Top right and bottom: Federleicht was the top American horse from 1987 until I sold him in 1989 to Ite Young of Ireland, who went on to compete him through Europe in the years that followed. He was retired and lived well into his thirties, cared for by a lovely family in Germany. ●

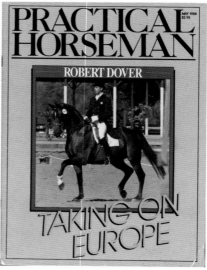

88. Lennox, owned by Kenn Acebal and leased for me by Jane Forbes Clark, was my mount for the World Equestrian Games in Rome in 1998. Our team ended up just out of the medals, in fourth place. ● *Photo by Karl Leck*

89. At the 1998 World Equestrian Games in Rome, with our Chef d'Equipe Jessica Ransehousen and her groom, cheering on Sue Blinks and Flim Flam, owned by Fritz and Renata Kundren. ● *Photo by Karl Leck*

90. Atlantis Gay Vacation, circa 1999, in the Bahamas. The resident hypnotist did his work on a group of us on stage and declared us all ballet dancers. Naturally, I was all in! ●

91. Rainier, owned by Jane Forbes Clark, was my mount for the Sydney Olympics in 2000. Rainier was both talented and tricky, a trait I have learned over the years is associated with many gray dressage horses! They tend to be extremely sensitive, smart in a way that can be difficult, and complicated to keep steady on the bit. And with all that, I still love them! ● *Photo by Arnd Bronkhorst*

92. Rainier wasn't always easy but he was photogenic and the right horse to take into the award ceremonies—even if he and I had actually placed second to my other horse at the time, Everest! ● *Photo by Charles Mann/arnd.nl*

93. Two of the best teammates and riders a guy could ever hope to have: Steffen Peters (left) and Guenter Seidel (right). ● *Photo by Charles Mann/arnd.nl*

94. At the Olympics in Sydney in 2000, I rode through pain but was thrilled to win a team bronze with my teammates Sue Blinks, Guenter Seidel, and Christine Traurig. ●

ROBERT DOVER
EQUESTRIAN SPORTS
BORN: June 7, 1956
HOMETOWN: Wellington, Florida
EVENT: Dressage
OLYMPIC HONORS: Three bronze medals
(1992, 1996, and 2002); 1994 U.S. Olympic Committee
Male Equestrian Athlete of the Year

When you're as famous as Robert Dover is
in the world of equestrian-dressage competition, every step—
or "pirouette"—you or your horse makes is big news.
But this summer's Olympics are especially meaningful for Dover,
who formally retired after the Sydney Games, in 2000.
Several factors—including his parents' failing health and the opportunity to
ride a horse, 15-year-old F.B.W. Kennedy, that he's admired
for years—have lured him back. Just one more reason, perhaps, that
he's been called the Michael Jordan of his sport.

95. Leading up to the 2004 Olympic Games, famous photographer
Bruce Weber took photos of US Olympians from many of the sports
for a feature in *Vanity Fair* magazine. I was lucky to be picked
to be among them. ● *Photo © Bruce Weber*

96. Coming out of another one of my many retirements, this time in 2004, to ride the best horse of my career, the fantastic FBW Kennedy. I was literally amazed by Kennedy's heart and reliability. Here, I'm praising him after our Olympic ride, knowing he truly could have gone out of the ring, come right back in, and done it all again with just as much brilliance as the first time. ●
Photo by Arnd Bronkhorst

97. With Kennedy and our 2004 Team coach, Klaus Balkenhol, during a training session. ●

98. The thumbs up from none other than Steven Spielberg at the final selection trials in Cota de Casa, California, for the 2004 Olympic Games in Athens, Greece. Steven and his wife Kate Capshaw were and are wonderful friends and have been incredibly great supporters of the Equestrian Aid Foundation. ●

99. Okay, I admit that I was not thrilled about wearing the "Athenian Crown" for the medal ceremony in 2004 in Athens; however, it was definitely one of my proudest career moments. ● *Photo by Arnd Bronkhorst*

100. As Coach/Chef d'Equipe of the Canadian Dressage Team, I was determined to get the squad to Europe to compete and grow. This was the group in 2010 (left to right): Wendy Christoff, Bonnie Bonello, Shannon Dueck, Ashley Holzer, and Belinda Trussell. ●

101. In 2011, Mark Bellissimo, with the help of "Founders" like Kim Van Kampen, pictured here with us, inaugurated the Global Dressage Festival venue that has gone on to literally change the game for American dressage. I am so grateful to them and all of the GDF sponsors over the years for making one of my dreams come true! ●

102. On early mornings at the Winter Equestrian Festival show grounds in Wellington, Florida, after a night of rain, there still had to be a way to get to the warm-up arena to help a student prepare. Here, I was caught by my wonderful friend and top photographer Mary Phelps as the sun was coming up. ● *Photo by Mary Phelps*

103. In 2015 gay marriage was legalized in the United States, and Robert and I wed on the beach in Fire Island, New York. ●

104. The goal to be back on the medal podiums became a reality in 2016 at the Rio Olympics. ●

105. A final photo of the US Olympic Team for Rio de Janeiro in 2016 at Rob Van Puijenbroek's beautiful Stal Begijnhoeve in Belgium: riders, farrier, team veterinarian and physio, and our fantastic grooms, all of whom contributed to our eventual bronze medal.●

106. My great friend for over thirty years, the amazing Carl Hester. ●

107. Over a decade ago, Lendon Gray and I got together to create The Emerging Dressage Athlete Program for riders twenty-one years of age or younger. We produced the Robert Dover Horsemastership Week, an intensive and free week of training with top Olympic trainers and other specialists for the top twenty youth riders in the United States, from little kids on ponies to our elite Young Riders. This program was taken over by the US Equestrian Federation and is still a great program today. Here I am earnestly teaching one of the young participants. ● *Photo by Mary Adelaide Williamson for PSdressage.com*

108. You don't get better than these two as teammates, trainers, or friends: Debbie McDonald and Steffen Peters. ●

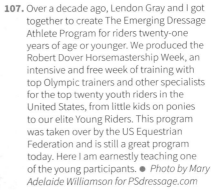

109. US Olympic Team members Kasey Perry-Glass and the great Michael Phelps, getting ready for the opening ceremonies in Rio de Janeiro in 2016. (I had no idea Michael was such a fan of Kasey's!) ●

110. Training Kasey with her wonderful horse Dublet at the gorgeous, Gut Ising riding school in Germany in 2015, leading up to the Pan American Games in Toronto. The pair went on to win an Olympic team bronze the following year in Rio de Janeiro. ●

112. With my favorite sidekick Simon, the best Schnoodle in the universe of dogs! ●

111. Robert and I have been very active with the Democratic Party and worked to help with Mayor Pete Buttigeig's election campaign for President in 2020. We are so happy he has an important role as Secretary of Transportation in the Biden administration. ●

113. At least once in every clinic I give I can always be counted on to make a fool of myself while trying to demonstrate how I want a rider to visualize the way the horse should move. No one will ever say I lack passion when teaching! ●
Photo by Ilay Zahavy

114. Praising Salvino after a great ride with the always amazing Adrienne Lyle, here in Rotterdam, 2017. ● *Photo by Shannon Brinkman*

115. The six years of watching and cheering on our riders and horses from the "Kiss & Cry" area—along with the fabulous Debbie McDonald and the best grooms, owners, vets, and staff—could not have been more exciting and gratifying. ● *Photo by Shannon Brinkman*

116. Another Nation's Cup victory in Rotterdam, 2017. Laura Graves, Kasey Perry-Glass, and Olivia Lagoy-Weltz were outstanding. We were so proud as the American flag was raised and our national anthem played! ● *Photo by Shannon Brinkman*

117. The 2018 World Equestrian Games made my dream as a coach come true when our silver-medal-winning team gave the Germans a real run for the gold, and Laura Graves and Verdades had a strong silver win individually, as well. ● *Photo by Shannon Brinkman*

118. In 2018, right before the World Equestrian Games in Tryon, North Carolina, here pictured in front of my medals for *Sidelines Magazine*. ● *Photo by Isabel J. Kurek*

One Good Thing

Being of Service and
Paying It Forward

13

CHAPTER

I recall as if it were yesterday the first guy to tell me he was going to the National Institutes of Health to find out why he had "something strange going on with his blood." It was the very early eighties, and within a few years, many of my close friends, along with people across our country, were coming down with what was called at the time "The Gay Plague." Religious zealots shouted that homosexual sinners were getting what they deserved, and sadly, much of America was willing to turn their backs on thousands of boys and men whose only desire was to find love in a world where we were told we were unworthy of it in the eyes of God.

I was still living a life in which I shook the hand of President Ronald Reagan as he congratulated the US Olympic Team, even though I knew that he refused to even utter the word *AIDS* until the death of his friend, actor Rock Hudson. Pressure from icons in the entertainment industry in which Reagan had found his fame, such as movie star Elizabeth Taylor, forced the President to finally take action to mitigate what had become a pandemic, affecting more and more people around the world regardless of their gender.

Acknowledging my incredible luck in dodging the AIDS bullet myself, I knew that I had to do something to help those not so lucky. In 1989, I was asked to ride one of my Olympic horses, Juvel, in a dressage exhibition at the Washington International Horse Show. The most well-known organization doing research on HIV/AIDS at the time was the American Foundation for Aids Research (amfAR), being led by Elizabeth Taylor. I told the show organizers I would be happy to participate but asked for an appearance fee of $5,000, all of which was to go to amfAR. The management agreed to my fee. Then, before I performed in Washington, I was told that while they would give me the money, they did not want to "bring the crowd down" by announcing I was riding to help people fighting HIV and AIDS.

Frustrated by the management's reaction, I told all the show jumpers I knew what was going on. The show jumping classes were the heart and soul of the indoor shows. Word spread quickly in the barns, and less than an hour later, I was summoned to the show office. With a shrug, the manager said I must have really great friends in the equestrian world because all the top show jumpers had gotten together and told officials that if the announcer did not read what I had written about my donating my performance fee to amfAR to fight AIDS, they would boycott the show and refuse to jump that night. With the riders all on my side, the management gave in.

Juvel and I did three demonstrations under a spotlight to "One Moment in Time" by Whitney Houston. We brought down the house with each performance.

After the demonstrations, Robert and I continued to raise money for amfAR by putting on clinics with top Olympic equestrians, but we discovered that our donations were, for the most part, going to pay salaries and administrative costs. We felt we had to do better.

One night we were having dinner with our friend and lifelong horseman Mason Phelps, Jr. His brother had died of AIDS a few years before. We started talking about creating our own relief organization—a 501(c)(3) that could allow people to donate and receive tax deductions. The three of us decided to call it The Equestrian AIDS Foundation. We would provide financial support to anyone in the horse world living with HIV or AIDS. Mason, Robert, and I went to our great friends in the business—Scot Evans, Kim Tudor, Gene Mische, Janice Gray, and the husband of a client of mine who was very well versed in creating nonprofits. In 1996, our vision became official.

Ten years later, with so many drugs and vaccines to help manage HIV, the EAF expanded to become the Equestrian Aid Foundation, providing grant-based support to horse people suffering from any catastrophic illness or injury. We broadened our mission again in 2018 to offer a helping hand to those in the horse world suffering from devastating natural disasters.

I am most proud of this Foundation and what it has accomplished over time. We have given millions of dollars to help people in the equestrian world in their times of need.

My ultimate belief is that we are out here on this earth to share LOVE and to leave this place better off than when we arrived—if we possibly can. The footprint each of us makes on this planet is far larger than most of us realize. Touching one life, indeed, has a ripple effect that is exponential, regardless of whether we are ever made aware of the almost infinite ways in which so many can be impacted by one tiny action on our part. Decades later, I have been told by individuals that something I said or did when I was a teenager changed their lives for the better. What could be more gratifying or make it more clear that this should be our daily goal—helping someone or something? Doing something kind does not require great wealth or advantages. It only requires a desire to make an effort. Some of the least-advantaged people I have known have led lives of service. "There but for the grace of God go I."

When I was in my twenties, Pony Club was about to go under in Fairfax, Virginia. Kids needed it, and of course, I had my personal connection given my years involved in the organization as a young person. So I decided to become the District Commissioner of the Arlington- Fairfax Pony Club, and in one year, it went from seven members to over *seventy*. Giving back to kids became a hallmark of my life as later in my career, with the help of Lendon Gray and then the US Equestrian Federation, we produced the Robert Dover Horsemastership Clinic, an annual event that brings the top kids in the United States, ages twenty-one and under, together for an intensive week of training and lectures by great US Olympians and equine specialists. The Horsemastership week is now going into its eleventh year and has helped enhance the equestrian careers of hundreds of young people.

In an effort to help more kids who showed that "X factor" through their innate talent, personality, determination, and general worthiness, I created the Christian Kennedy Future Stars Scholarship Program, named for a young man who died in a tragic car accident the year after he participated in the first year of the Future Stars program.

Robert and I understand how very fortunate we are, and many years ago, we discussed and agreed upon other ways we could give back, particularly to children. We have sponsored many children around the world in disadvantaged places and received heartfelt letters from them and their teachers. We have also had a longstanding tradition of making Christmas about giving back to those less fortunate by taking gifts to kids in hospitals and later to the kids of migrant workers, as well as sending presents to families in countries suffering from devastating poverty.

As an equestrian coach, I have looked up to some of the great team coaches of the last hundred years from all sports, including American football. I did a lot of reading and learning certain coaching philosophies and have applied many of their techniques in my own training. One of the great Vince Lombardi's best quotes is, "The measure of who we are is what we do with what we have." He was one of the most inspirational coaches in history, and I continue to look up to him as a mentor, even though I never met the man.

I am lucky to know a living football coach, Charlie Weis, who has mentored me by helping me not only deal with tough situations with athletes but also navigate through negotiations with owners and federations. His straightforward, honest advice has truly been a gift to me in the last decade.

I believe mentoring is one way to be of service to others, particularly in the equestrian community. I look back on the people I consider to have been my mentors and appreciate so much their loving commitment, helping me over the years to try to become the best version of myself. I have told you about the magnificent Anne Reiley, who was like a second mother to me in my teens. She was always ready with sage advice and comfort in my times of need, and provided me with security when I was trying to find my way as a young professional. Having been a world-class ice skater, she knew how to push me while also helping me keep my feet on the ground as I became more successful. She also gave me great tools to decrease my tendency to be nervous in competitions. Who knew that a drop of spirits of ammonia in a cup of tea would almost immediately bring a feeling of calm and well-being over you?

I think of Colonel Ljungquist as my greatest mentor because he not only taught me everything I remember today as to riding techniques, he also provided me with my overall philosophy of horsemanship and the moral compass I have followed my whole life. The colonel taught me fairness, humility, determination, logic, honor, methodology, and to keep a sense of humor. Many, many of his words are indelibly etched into my memory and will remain there and be invoked for the rest of my life!

My other trainers, who I've named throughout this book, all enriched and enhanced my life with their knowledge and love. And just as important have been the students I have been privileged to mentor myself along the way. Katherine Bateson-Chandler, for one, has been like a daughter to me, and I proudly watched her in 2010 at the World Equestrian Games in Lexington, Kentucky, from the ingate, behind the American delegation, because I was coaching the Canadian Team that year. As she entered the main oval, I thought I would be fine, but I swiftly became incredibly emotional, crying with joy that this young woman had come so far, achieving dreams that were always mine for her too!

Watching students ultimately become my teammates—from Guenter Seidel and Gary Rockwell to Jane Savoie and Gwen Blake (to name just a few)—has truly been one of the great joys of my life. Beyond the fact that I was so proud of them for their achievements in the competitive arena, I was equally proud of them for being the awesome people they were and are.

It is our responsibility and a great privilege to mentor, and I wish there was a "National Mentoring Program" in our sport; it is something I have been lobbying for, for many years now. Lendon Gray's Dressage for Kids and my Christian Kennedy Future Stars Program are both excellent ways to encourage and coach young riders; however, a true National

Mentoring Program would be a game-changer for America. It would start with a "registry" of sanctioned, top trainers from one end of the United States to the other, all of whom would agree to give two clinic days a year for free. People would then receive information on the dates of the clinics in their region and could apply to go one or more days to be trained for free. The trainers would keep detailed information about each of the riders and their horses, and this information would go to the US Equestrian Federation NMP (National Mentoring Program) subcommittee for review. The review process would identify the most promising young athletes, both two- and four-legged, from across the nation for future training with not only these volunteer mentors but official USEF coaches in their programs.

Not only would the National Mentoring Program be a win-win for the riders and the local mentors since it would encourage them to continue training with each other, it would also create a spider-web-like network that would find and identify young people who might otherwise fall through the cracks because they live in outlying or obscure places where they do not have access to top training. Once identified, they could be afforded more training and assistance from the program to ensure they have the best chances to succeed. Such a program would truly be enormously helpful for a country as big as the United States.

I have done my best to be influential in the process of both my sport in my local community and my country as a whole. A few years before Gene Mische, "Mr. Stadium Jumping," who created the modern show jumping scene in the United States, as well as the Winter Equestrian Festival and its home in Wellington, passed away, real estate developer Mark Bellissimo and his Equestrian Sport Productions took over. The show grounds became too full and busy with hunter and jumper competitions and horses to allow for dressage to take place, especially since it had not shown to be as profitable as the hunter-jumpers. Dressage shows had been relegated to other venues nearby, which, while they did an admirable job, did not achieve the international environment or acclaim that could entice the world to come and compete with American riders.

Just up the road from the hunter-jumper show grounds, now called the Palm Beach International Equestrian Center, was fifty acres, which for many years had been a venue for polo as well as jumping competitions. After the polo fields were relocated to a new spot a mile down the road, the old polo stadium sat unused and an eyesore. But I looked at it and saw the most beautiful dressage venue in my mind and knew it could become a great success.

Dressage had flailed by itself for over two years with very few highlights, and I lamented that fact. By chance, I got to chatting one day with my friend and one of Mark's Wellington Equestrian Partners, billionaire businessman Roger Smith, and told him how short-sighted I thought it was for Equestrian Sport Productions not to use this piece of land, which they owned outright, for an international dressage venue. Roger was not only kind enough to listen to me, he promised he would ask Mark to meet and discuss the idea.

The three of us had lunch a couple of days later, and I actually drew on the white paper tablecloth the picture I had in my mind of what now stands on that fifty acres—the Global Dressage Festival and Equestrian Village. I am so grateful to Mark, Roger, and Kim Van Kampen, as well as the other many wonderful and generous friends of the dressage world who came forward to become the official founders (sponsors) responsible both for the building of the venue and sponsoring the many classes, to the tune of over $600,000 per year, at the nine international competitions held there annually. Top riders, trainers, and vendors, and fans from around the world come every winter season, many of them now having bought homes and farms locally, to watch dressage riders and their horses dance during "Friday Night Lights," where up to 5,000 people regularly cheer their favorites on. Not only does this make me proud, I also know that having such a venue and atmosphere has made American athletes better prepared for international championships. The US riders have consistently brought home medals in the last decade.

I've tried to be forward-looking in my life and have been politically active for many years in an effort to influence the direction of my sport, equestrian sport in general, American Olympic sport, and the greater social community. I feel like the hard thing about doing what I've done for so many years is that a part of me has always felt that I've made a living helping people who really don't need anything. What is the value of what I do beyond helping people prance around an arena wearing a top hat and tails? This is why I needed other outlets to set and achieve goals for the greater good and the greater world. There is a certain amount of guilt when you are me and you have made a career and become financially successful through a subjective sport like dressage that requires a lot of advantages in order to participate. I want to make the people in my life proud of me by virtue of the fact that I do more than that.

We are in the age of social media, where so many people have become "influencers"—a title given to those who earn money from telling their many followers to consume whatever their advertising sponsors are using their platform to sell. I use my own social media platforms to share my opinions on causes I am concerned with, whether political or societal. Being a gay man, I do my best to speak out on subjects of equality and justice, and when the United States had a president who emboldened the worst impulses in Americans, I spoke out and will continue to do so in posts like the following one I shared the day after President Joe Biden and Vice President Kamala Harris were projected to win the 2020 presidential election.

Things I would like to apologize for in advance:

• *I apologize for not listening more closely to your legitimate worries or frustrations with the Democratic Party that caused you to vote Republican and for Trump.*

• *I apologize if my being so outspoken made you feel that I did not respect or care about you or your loved ones.*

• *I apologize for grouping you into a box that made you think I did not wish to remain friends or friendly.*

• *I apologize for not making it clear that I actually agree with many fiscally "conservative" Republicans while disagreeing with most of their socially "conservative" beliefs.*

I truly believe that President Joe Biden will seek compromises in the best interest of America and find common ground in places where that is possible, and I hope to follow that ideal.

That being said, I want to also apologize for the following:

• *If you are making more than $400,000 a year and have been using loopholes or enjoying not paying your fair share of taxes, I'm sorry, but...*

• *If you are a person of white privilege and are worried that people of color might gain more equality, I'm sorry, but...*

- *If you are a civilian and want to keep your semi- and fully-automatic guns, even though you have zero need for them to defend yourself or your family, I'm sorry, but...*

- *If you are against women having the right to choose what they do with their bodies, I'm sorry, but...*

- *If you want to pollute our air and water and strip our world of endangered animals for your own pleasure, I'm sorry, but...*

- *If you were hoping to keep America walled off from all other countries and prevent Dreamers from having a path to becoming legal citizens, I'm sorry, but...*

- *If you did not care about having US allies believe in American values and US leadership as a guiding light in the world, I'm sorry, but...*

- *If you have enjoyed the daily chaos and unrest in our country and were hoping for four more years of it, I'm sorry, but...*

- *If you are homophobic and are afraid LGBTQ people are going to gain more rights, I'm sorry, but...*

I am incredibly happy and relieved that we now have President Biden and Vice President Harris for America!

So many have the world literally right at their fingertips, and prying them away from self-indulgence and an attitude of entitlement so they can grasp a life of service to others can be extremely difficult. That being said, life with horses has a way of producing people who see that nurturing another life, albeit a four-legged one, is a beautiful thing and something that requires true dedication. I have seen firsthand how this kind of dedication bleeds through into the rest of your life and becomes, like in mine, an integral part of who you are.

There will never be a shortage of ways to give to others. Figure out something that makes you feel good by being of service; I promise you will immediately understand the reward that comes from helping others. Being a part of something that is bigger than yourself, whether working with organizations that help humans, animals, or the entire planet, enhances your own life in remarkable ways.

In the end, as I said at the beginning of this chapter, we are all here to spread LOVE and hopefully leave our world a better place than when we arrived. I, for one, will continue to listen to my mom and do at least one mitzvah every day for the rest of my life. ●

Be a Star, Not a Victim

Making Every Single Day
a Joyful, Fabulous Adventure

14

CHAPTER

E ven in times when our lives seem extremely complicated, if we try, we can see those moments as simply part of the adventure and even find joy in them.

In the summer of 1987, Gabriela Grillo asked David Number Four and me to ride a *Ross Balet* (a ride to music done in the feudal times for the courts of the kings and queens) during the Summer Fest in Salzburg. We were excited about riding in the show, and Gabby choreographed the entire ride to classical music. The day before our exhibition, we were told that we were to attend the *Gala Abend,* a black tie dinner event in town, held annually for the festival VIPs. Well, David, my fabulous assistant Petra, and I had brought nothing but our blue jeans and riding clothes, so we immediately called around to see if any store would rent us black tie attire. Much to our chagrin, there was no such thing in Salzburg. After all, if you were invited to such an event, well of course you owned many appropriate outfits.

After searching everywhere, frustrated, and in despair that we'd be unable to fulfill our required appearance, Petra called a local costume shop where actors rented outfits to play roles in local plays. Desperate for options, off we went to the shop, which was more of a warehouse, where the very kind proprietor listened to our situation and did his very best to make us look respectable. For David, he found a "smoking jacket," black pants, and a decent white shirt and bow tie. The only issue was that the fly in his pants was broken and could only be closed with a safety pin. He found a similar costume for me, but the only white shirt was way too large, forcing me to keep my head and neck perfectly still so that my collar would remain above the lapel of my jacket. And for Petra, he found a lovely gown, something that might have been worn by Julie Andrews in *The Sound of Music*. The bustline was very low and loose, however, making it highly probable that leaning forward, even a little, would find Petra more out of her gown than in it! But we were off to the ball, and as we entered the great hall and saw everyone, clad gorgeously in the very finest attire, all we could do was look at each other and burst out laughing.

Gabby came up to us and we told her of our adventure, and she chuckled with a glance to her mother across the room, who was looking not nearly as amused by the picture we were making. The three of us found a way to shake off our embarrassment and enjoy the night. We would have danced but for my collar, David's fly, and Petra's...well, you get the picture. We ended up having one of our best and most fun evenings in our time together in Europe. What could have been an awful and mortifying experience became, instead, a wonderful memory that I will never forget.

— Flip the Script, Be the Director —

"We are all making it up as we go along!"

"None of us are coming out of this alive!"

I've employed the first phrase for many years in my teaching. The second one my mom told me as I cried beside her deathbed, to make me laugh and think differently about her situation.

If you ask people who they are, they will probably reply with their names. Ask them a little more about themselves, and they might tell you their ages, where they are from, and what they do—their schools or their jobs. We define ourselves through our family heritage and the path we have chosen. We use prefixes such as, Doctor, Father, Sister, Professor, Rabbi, and even Pope, to describe who we are to others and ourselves. The effort to "become" who we wish to be can be painstakingly difficult or as easy as making a decision and hanging a shingle on our door. We become who we desire to be, and if not, who we believe ourselves to be.

This is why I say, "We are all making it up as we go along."

So remember what I talked about in chapter 8: If you think of your life like a movie that you are directing and play the starring role in, it is up to you and you alone to make that movie the most fabulous and joyful one you can possibly imagine. When people say, "This is not a dress rehearsal," nothing could be more true. It feels like yesterday that I was marching into the Opening Ceremonies at my first Olympics in Los Angeles in 1984! Life goes by in the blink of an eye.

The question is, if this is not your movie, then whose is it? There is no doubt that people go through terrible events in their lives that cannot be prevented. Suffering is real and an inextricable part of human existence. But becoming a "victim" in every single moment is also a choice.

I am not in any way discounting the tragedies that befall people. What I am saying is that, by acknowledging the "bad" and the "challenging" are real and an inevitable part of our existence, we can choose how we decide to perceive them.

The best example of this is Elie Wiesel, the famous Holocaust survivor and author. In his book *Night*, he explains so incredibly how, in the middle of the most horrific situation, surrounded by death and torture, he still chose to see beauty. He was not blind to what was happening at all, but survival meant that he needed to see a different movie in his mind, one where hope, serenity, and LOVE still ruled.

No matter what, each of us lives our movie, either as a star or as a victim. If it is the latter, the answer is to take back your role as director and start again. *The truth is that every time we breathe out, we are redefining who we think we are and announcing ourselves to the universe, and most importantly, to ourselves!*

I ask my students all the time as they are riding, "What are you seeing right now?" Most of the time, they are perplexed by the question, wondering if I mean what they are seeing literally, with their eyes. I then explain, "What are you seeing in your imagination, in your mind, your third eye?" Too much of the time, we think in words: "Faster," "Slower," "Bigger," "More sideways," "More energetic." With dressage, I see the most fabulous movie of my horse and myself, dancing over the ground from movement to movement, and a fraction of a second later, I create, as best I can, that exact look for those watching from the ground to perceive. This is how people in sports, arts, and virtually every endeavor create the "grandest version" of themselves and then go for it.

Of course, with all things, "perfect practice makes perfect" and producing your movie will require many thousands of attempts, trials, and errors, and small (and some big) failures. No matter what, keep going, searching for your finest version of yourself, and then create and realize that movie!

Morning meditation and writing affirmations or creating a vision board are all fantastic ways to begin each new day. *Putting your positive thoughts into words and expressing them outwardly into the universe calls forth those words to become your reality.* It may take time and patience, but the act of practicing seeing yourself in the grandest role you can imagine creates positive energy that you and those around you will feel. Such a positive aura attracts others who feel you and want to be a part of your energy. There is an infinite number of doors which may open to those who do the work, show the dedication, exude the talent, and express LOVE in every moment. Fear has no place in this world you have created and disappears altogether as you step forward into your greatness.

GO FOR IT! ●

Memories and Drinking Stories

Being Conscious
of and Thankful for
Every Revelation

15
CHAPTER

The moments that stick with you as you journey through life are sometimes the last ones you would think, at the time, might eventually be unforgettable.

I remember...

When I was about five years old, my parents took us to Kiddieland, an amusement park in Melrose Park near our home in River Forest. My older sisters and brother were all about the rides, especially the "Little Dipper"—a super roller coaster attraction there. But for me, it was the pony rides. I clearly recall my dad putting me up in the saddle and watching as a handler led me around and around a circle. The merry-go-round drew me, too, with more fabulous horses to ride.

I remember...

David, my best childhood friend, and I, walking together to school and home again when I was around six. I had a transistor radio, and one day after school the most amazing song came on: "I Want to Hold Your Hand" by The Beatles. In no time, I wanted to have the haircut and look like them, and become a star like them, just like millions of other kids around the world.

And I remember...

David's second oldest brother, almost out of the house by the time David and I were old enough to know anything, and the ways he exploited my lack of understanding as he sexually abused me.

   And then there was the "Sitter from Hell." Our parents left the four of us with a babysitter who decided that her favorite dish, macaroni and cheese, would somehow be turned into a tool of torture. Now, how she managed to take such a "normal meal" and get four kids to start screaming in unison, I honestly can't recall. But I do remember the arrival of an ally to battle the horrid enemy sitter, Grandma Fey! My mother's mother appeared as we were in full protest and cast out the evil witch in the blink of an eye, much to our relief and subsequent pleasure. We adored her even more after that!

I remember...

Alex Konyot, a true horseman in the way we rarely see anymore, putting a group of jumps up: a small one followed a couple of gallop strides later by another set at the very top of the standards, about five feet high! I was riding around on one of his Spanish dressage horses and had not even shortened up my stirrups when Alex yelled, "Bobby, go ahead and trot him into the first jump and then take the second one, too." I had never jumped a fence even close to that high, no less on a dressage horse that I had never sat on before. But I was always an obedient student, and I did as I was told, flying up into the air, and just by luck, landing back in the saddle on the other end! It was a huge rush and made me realize just how powerful and agile horses are.

Perhaps among the most exciting parts of any Olympics is living in the Olympic Village. Imagine being one of 15,000 athletes and coaches, all inhabiting a town built expressly for you with everything you could possibly want or need available at your slightest whim. One look into the "food tent" (and you should know "food tent" simply does not do this temporary cafeteria—open for literally thousands of hungry athletes from all around the world every hour, 24/7, from all around the world—justice) and you understand that the Games are set up to ensure people from all cultures and ethnicities are thought of and catered to.

At the Los Angeles Games in 1984, I was standing in line with our coach, George Theodorescu, when he tapped me with his finger and gestured to me to discreetly turn around. As I did, I came face to—well, not so much face to face as face to navel—with the bare midriff of a lady. I slowly lifted my glance higher and higher, and at the very top of this seemingly impossibly tall woman was a head no larger than a grapefruit. So astounded was I that I couldn't help but stare for what was clearly too long—my coach all but slapped me back to attention. I just had to know more about her and so, looking upward, asked what sport and country she was representing. In broken English and a huskier voice than mine, she pointed to the emblem on her shorts that showed she was from Yugoslavia (now Serbia) and said she was on the volleyball team.

That day I really began to notice how incredibly specific just about all Olympic sports are with regard to athlete body types. Tree-like volleyball and basketball players, tiny gymnasts, and enormous Greco-Roman wrestlers who, like weightlifters, in the last days before they competed, ate an army's amount of food in order to gain as much weight as possible. I could not help but think it was so fortunate that we all had our sports, for otherwise, in another time or place, we might only have found a home in a circus. However, I found that the athletes I came to know would not have wished their lives to be anything different. They were the very best in the world at what they loved and were born to do. If anything, I saw myself as old and weak by comparison.

In 1992, I was with my team at the farm of Herbert Rehbein, one of the finest trainers who ever lived, in the north of Germany. Herbert loved life, horses, and drinking.

One day, before my lesson, he yelled, "Robert, come with me!" I followed him dutifully down the hill to the barn reserved for broodmares. There, in a small kitchen, he pulled a bottle from the tiny fridge and took a couple of shot glasses shaped like riding boots off the shelf. He poured a pair and handed me one as I complained that it was just around eleven in the morning and I still had to ride.

"Nonsense!" Herbert responded. "We will both drink and then go back up to the ring and train!"

With a "Zum wohl!" we both swigged down the shots, which tasted like one-hundred-percent pure grain alcohol to me. I felt a buzz within seconds.

"Ready to go back up?" I asked hopefully.

I could not be that lucky. Herbert replied in German, an old saying that basically meant, "Robert, you can't stand on just one leg!" This obviously meant we had to drink two-boots-worth of the dreaded liquor.

With the second swig down, he said, "Right, let's head back before my wife knows we're down here drinking."

Well, I could barely walk, never mind ride my horse. I was so unbalanced in the saddle that his wife, Karin, shot me a look that made it clear she was not thrilled.

Shortly afterward, it was my birthday and we were showing in Wiesbaden; it's a gorgeous show with the arena in front of a castle. My horse and I did very well in the Grand Prix, and Robert and I went out to celebrate at a local restaurant, which all the riders frequented when in town for the show. Somehow, it got out that it was my birthday, and the shots and drinks began arriving to our table.

At first, it was rather a sweet gesture, but soon it became more of a sport for my colleagues, who were obviously trying to see how much liquor I could withstand (I've never been a drinker!). Though I made it through the night, the next morning as I mounted my horse, my hangover was so bad that every bouncing step of trot was like a knife to the back of my head. My equilibrium was totally gone, and what I had hoped would be a successful ride was more like an episode of *Survivor*! When the press came out later that day, one journalist had written, "Robert's riding seemed to be very unsteady today when compared to his usual elegant form. His hands were unsteady as well as his head, and this resulted in multiple mistakes. Too bad!"

Captain Mark Phillips was the very successful rider and trainer who coached the medal-winning US Eventing Team through multiple Olympic

Games. Mark is also a great guy who I admire very much and consider a friend to this day, so I hope he does not take offense to my story about our adventure together that I will never forget. In 2008, the year the Olympics were in Beijing, he asked me to work with his top riders on their dressage. We got off to a very good start, with his riders and horses coming to clinics and me helping them warm up at major competitions.

One such clinic was at a farm in Kalispell, Montana, a place I had never heard of. Getting there required two flights and a couple of hours of driving. I am not sure why eventers tend to gravitate to the more obscure places in America, but this most assuredly took the cake.

I had just reached the little motel where I was staying, threw down my bags, and was getting ready to go to bed early when there was a knock on my door. It was Mark, of course, welcoming me and saying I had five minutes to change, as we were off to have dinner with the farm's owner. As much as I did not want to go, I got myself ready, and Mark, in some old clunker he had rented, drove us a full hour on one very boring, flat road, until we came to a lively area on a lake, where he stopped in front of a beautiful home.

A few minutes later, we were sitting with the woman who owned the farm; she explained they had built their home apart from the farm because her husband liked being on the lake. I could see why. It was gorgeous!

We were drinking white wine, though I was unaware of how much Mark had consumed before we met at the table. He began to tell a story while holding his wine glass up with his elbow on the table, when in mid-sentence, his eyes closed and he began to snore. I truly had no idea that such a feat was possible—falling asleep with your hand firmly on the stem of a glass below the goblet without the hand falling or losing its grip! Well, I panicked. *What must the farm owner think right now?* I kicked the table with my right foot, jarring Mark back to consciousness, and to my amazement, he started up again, *exactly* where he left off with his story! AMAZING!

I knew there was no way I was letting Mark drive the hour back to our hotel; I mentioned I could drive and he tossed me his keys before we began the journey back on the flat, straight, boring road home. Mark immediately fell asleep in the passenger seat, and as there was no such thing as navigation in a car or on a cell phone back then, I became anxious after an hour of driving with no hotel in sight and my usual complete lack of direction. When I saw a light at an intersection coming up ahead, I looked at Mark, snoring away beside me, and slammed on the brakes. Mark had his seatbelt on, but his head bounced forward onto the dashboard in front of him, and he opened his eyes.

I asked, "Mark, is this the light where we are supposed to turn?"

"Next one," he said without hesitation before again closing his eyes.

I sighed with relief but also had to hold back a laugh. What a night it had been. We finally arrived back at our hotel and I, for one, was extremely thankful!

— Every Story Counts —

If you start at the beginning and try to list in order those events or moments that truly changed your life or way of thinking, you may really surprise yourself with what comes up. As I began listing my "moments" when I started writing this book, I had to stop for a second to rewind and recall that I was a very happy and very loved kid. The reason for my need to pause and do this is that, like so many of us, my strongest recollections from my life may be the painful ones, which left indelible scars on our memories. But as my stories of riding lessons and drinking demonstrate, there are other, funnier moments that remain clearly imprinted on our brains, too. And all of them taught us something.

Consider my meeting with the towering Yugoslavian volleyball player. My first thought was to judge her negatively: "Oh my god! She's a freak!" But then I asked her what sport she did and what country she was from and discovered a nice and humble athlete, who, like me, was just so very excited to be at her first Olympics. That was a life-changing moment for me, as I recognized that we all have qualities that make us special, and if we are very lucky, they help us find our niche in the world. It's so interesting that we come into this world, as the Jewish religion teaches, with our hands clenched into fists, ready to fight for everything we can get, but we leave the world with our palms open, taking absolutely nothing with us. At the end, if we are lucky, what we have are our memories and LOVE. ●

"DOVERISMS"
and Special Memories

I asked friends and acquaintances if, sometime during the many years I've been lucky to be here, they and I shared a moment they remember well (whether great or not), that they please send it to me. Here is a collection of those memories and "things Robert says."

● *from* **JANE SAVOIE**:
"You have to act like a champion before you are a champion."

"I turned losing into an art form."

● *from* **CARL HESTER**:
Robert, you dispute this recollection, but I stand by it. You couldn't make it up and it's one hundred percent "Doverism." This is the whole thing from my book *Making It Happen*. Robert, I can't wait to read yours.

Robert has been part of the dressage world for decades. Nutty, intelligent, successful, terribly political, and one of the most interesting people in the sport, Robert was to become a great friend, mentor, and someone I can even now ask any question about dressage and he'll always have an answer. Back then it looked as if he was conducting a "Robert séance"

255

outside the warm-up arena. *All the US riders were standing around in a circle holding hands as Robert intoned, "Melindurrrr, I wan' it awl and I wan' it now." Poor Melinda [McPhail] looked absolutely terrified, her eyes nearly popped out of her head, and off she went and did a disastrous test! Robert would ride her horse Lectron in Barcelona while Melinda herself would be named reserve on him for the 1994 World Games.*

That was at Wiesbaden CDI, 1992, my first year at international Grand Prix and the year of my first and Robert's third Olympic Games. What adventures we've had since then.

• *from* **BERNADETTE HEWITT:**

Robert, I probably could go on! *It was at the World Equestrian Games in Rome, 1998, that I first remember the knockout sight of Robert "riding" every stride of Guenter Seidel's test on Graf George. There wasn't a Kiss-and-Cry stand, so Robert was at the edge of the arena. Hilarious, yes, but a signal of how Robert was so invested in his teammates' tests you got the feeling he'd happily have been in there with them. There's a Werner Ernst photo in* L'Annee Hippique *of Robert there beside Jessica Ransehousen, Chef d'Equipe and, as Carl christened her then, "The First Lady of American Dressage." It might be a still but you can see the movement!*

I'm proud to call Robert a dear friend, but for me as a journalist, Robert was always so great to interview. I'll always remember him in the mixed zone at the Athens Olympics, Robert's best to date and sixth Olympics, in 1994: "On my God, I think I just gave another sermon." I've still got the profile for Horse International. *I wrote his opinions aren't just black and white but full Technicolor. They are and the world's the richer for it.*

• *from* **INGRED KOONAN:**

I remember you on a flight with horses from Amsterdam to New York with KLM. I was on the flight as an animal attendant.

You had been training in Germany. We spoke a long time during the flight, and you gave me a wonderful white, thick, cotton saddle pad—which I still have! I was impressed by your riding and still am! And by your kindness!

● *from* **JANE SKEELS:**

I have a ton of Doverisms, but my favorite two are:

"If you can't compress your horse in the canter on a short side, he will never compress in a pirouette."

"Every corner is a quarter pirouette so why are you blowing through your corners like a twenty-meter circle?"

● *from* **GWEN BLAKE:**

Robert, you expected perfection. Every detail had to be taken care of. Every training session required tremendous focus. But... many times I experienced the most common phrase you would yell during our lessons. It was... "Half-halt! Half-halt! " I was trying so hard to rebalance my stallion Juvel. I never doubted you, but one moment...I broke focus to look at you and saw you were calling for your dog—whose name was Half-Halt! And now you have a dog named Simon.

● *from* **PATTY MAYER:**

I had the pleasure and honor of scribing for you at Lendon Gray's Youth Dressage Festival. You said, to heck with the schedule, it was important to take time to speak with each of the riders after their tests and you were going to do it. Every one of those kids will cherish the comments you wrote on their tests; however, taking the time to share your knowledge and guidance with them, with eye contact and spoken words, left a lasting impression on their hearts and minds, and demonstrated how to treat others. I love when judges do more than just say thank you and add a few encouraging words. There's another funny side to this story. Because we were behind schedule, you judged straight through our break. There came a point where your bladder was screaming. You got up to leave the judge's box and apparently one of the test runners had mistakenly locked us in. We were trapped! You jumped out the window, ran and jumped over the stone wall to the restrooms! You ran back just as fast! I'll never forget seeing your athleticism in action—you had great form going over that stone wall! It was a long, wonderful day. Thank you for all you do and for leading by example.

● *from* **ROBYN AYERS:**
My favorite "Doverism" is, "I don't even know what that was." That one could make you laugh or cry! I always loved how tough you were on all of us. It showed how much you cared.

● *from* **KATE MOORE:**
There are so many things you have done for my life—where should I start? For me, as I continue to teach and watch the half-halt, over and over again, I am so grateful for the education you provided. On a lighter note, remember when you gave me that t-shirt that said, "Award- Winning Actress in Her Own Soap Opera"? And all my memories of the magic of Romance Farm.

● *from* **MYRA WAGENER:**
Brian and I bought Pinetree Stables in 1967. I was trying to sort out who would go in which group to teach. You were heartbroken that I had you in the "B" group and pleaded with me to try you with the others. I said I would give it a try, and of course you proved your worth

on Sugar and Candyman. (Sugar was the gray mare and Candyman was a small, pinto pony I used to jump and play polo on.) Remember how I used to take jumps down to the beach so you guys could get some idea of cross-country jumps? Then Cash arrived—we were all very impressed. I remember you renamed him from Cassius Clay to Ebony Cash. He was such a nice horse—and perfect for you. That is where the dressage started! You were so enthralled by it—getting the right rhythm and making sure Cash was properly warmed up. You'd ask, "Mrs Wagener, how many times should I trot round before I can canter?"

● *from* FELICITAS VON NEUMANN-COSEL:
I have so many memories, but one that sticks out is running the gauntlet of your Jack Russell Half-Halt's teeth to help you to get out of your boots. I guess before zippers the good old boot jack had to do, and I had to step on your toes!

● *from* ELISABETH WILLIAMS:
I remember you always checking your test sheets to make sure scoring got it right—and they were sometimes very wrong! You and I did not always see eye to eye but respected each other nevertheless! In the end, many fond memories.

● *from* MONICA SINKS:
I have in my list of "Things I have learned from the Masters: Robert Dover taught me a horse cannot lean against nothing." In other words, give versus take. I quote you in all my lessons.

● *from* WANDA J. SILAS:
I may have been the first one to put dressage on the radio. When I interviewed you, I was not a reporter; however, I worked in audio

production at a major-market, all-news radio station and I loved horses. The Associated Press radio aired that interview, and a friend of mine heard it in Chicago, so I had proof that it was broadcast across the country. I remember you and the Jack Russells, hanging out with Carol Lavell (she let my trainer and I watch Gifted while she ran off to do something). Then, there was that time I had press passes and brought a friend who grew up riding horses to see you ride that Freestyle to Whitney Houston. It was when I saw dressage for the first time. My friend said to me, "He's just sitting there. The horse is doing all of the work." I looked at my friend and replied, "Yeah, but he's riding. We're just standing here watching...." Fortunately, I learned a great deal about dressage after that, and of course I know now that you weren't just sitting there!

● *from* SUE GAUDETTE:

I had just come home from Genn Farm in Ontario, Canada, with my first upper-level horse, Filius. I was lucky enough to get into one of your clinics. We had a great day, and at the end you said: "Okay...now do ones." My jaw dropped. "How? " I said. "Just collect him and ask," was your reply. "Slide alternate legs back and keep him collected and straight." My heart racing, off we went. My first ones! I will never forget that day.

● *from* JENNIFER CONOUR:

I tell people all the time that I often had to completely stop riding during my lessons with you, as I would be laughing so hard. The story I tell of you all the time is about that time Michael Kohl was riding and you were working on changes. He did fours. "They need to be 'archier,'" you said. He did them again. "Okay, now threes....more forward!" "Now do seven twos!" Well, that was a hot mess. There were ones, twos, and threes in the line. "Ride them more clearly!" Now he just had a bunch of ones and twos. "AGAIN. More clear. One, TWO! One CHANGE, one CHANGE." And we had more ones and twos. "AGAIN." Now we had good twos. "Okay—now let me see the ones."

Michael: "I don't do ones."
You: "Just do five ones."
Michael emphatically: "I don't DO ones!"
You: "I just saw you do ones."
Michael: "That was a mistake."

You, without pause: "Then show me another mistake. In fact, show me fifteen mistakes in a row."

I had to stop trotting. It's hard to sit the trot while laughing! Thank you for all the joy you brought to my riding—both through education and just *joie de vivre*!

● *from* **MICHAEL RIPPLOH:**
I remember...it all started with Romantico. We only had a few days at Chestnut Lawn to get ready for Devon, your first big outing at the Grand Prix! You came in second twice! I'll never forget it—a very special weekend.

● *from* **NICKY GREED:**
I will never forget being the only non-riding *Equestrian Idol* contestant and you encouraging me to continue when I wanted to give up. You told me of how much the relationship I had with my mother reminded you of the relationship you had with yours. Since that time I've founded two companies and my music has gone around

the world a few times. Thank you for being a light when I was still finding my way.

● *from* **MARY ANNE MCPHAIL:**
Those group lessons that we all had over in Wellington were always interesting...particularly when someone did something not very well and you would yell, "WHAT WAS THAT?"

● *from* **JONATAN COOK-BALL:**
"You need to be the one wearing the top hat and he needs to be the one wearing the saddle."

"Canter up that centerline looking the judge in the eye. And when you halt and salute, keep eye contact and tell the judge that you are going to win the test."

"Tell him 'Good Boy.' Am I the only one saying 'Good Boy'? 'Good boy!' Pet him."

"You need to be able to ride with that sweet aid."

"Add like he is going to extend for two steps and then hold; as you bring him back, make him want to keep going."

By the time I was seventeen, I had been very successful in 4-H, Pony Club, and on the Quarter Horse circuit. I felt overfaced by the cross-country part of eventing, but the dressage always intrigued me. My parents had read of an up-and-coming superstar named Robert Dover and decided to contact him. It just so happened that you were looking for working students for the summer, so off I went to a farm in Maryland owned by Patience Priest.

I was there for one week and you came to me and said, "I've entered you into the first intercontinental Young Riders championships," and I thought my heart was going to bust with nerves! I had never ridden above Training Level, and this, (back then) would be the equivalent of Prix St Georges. You brought out this big beautiful horse named Glen and introduced me to him. Then, after you had ridden all the horses for the day and all my work was done, you told me to get Glen and get on him. Thus started my first lesson learning how to sit the trot to this big-strided horse. Now, I had seen flying changes, half-passes, pirouettes, and extended trots, but had no idea how to perform them. I had very little confidence, but you seemed to have enough for both of us.

For two months, and with a ton of patience from you, we worked and worked and worked. One week before the competition, you came to me and told me you could not go with me, but all the arrangements had been made. My parents came from Massachusetts to travel with me, and off we went to Wayne, Illinois.

Day one was the warm-up, which we were not judged on. Day Two was our first test, but no scores would be posted until the final, Day Three test. I looked around and watched the other competitors on their horses, and I thought I would die when I saw how good everyone was. I was like a fish out of water.

My first test was, I thought, terrible. My second test I figured couldn't get any worse than the first, so I let Glen do his thing and became a passenger. Oh sure, I did what you had taught me, moving my leg here, and my other leg there, bending his neck to the left and right and using my seat. Hours after I had ridden, the scores were finally posted. Out of twenty-four horses, I came in seventh. I was used to winning—I had over two-hundred championships from 4-H and Pony Club, plus a World Championship won at the Quarter Horse Congress when I was fifteen. But I now was in a totally different world.

I came home with my tail between my legs feeling like I had let you down. The next morning, it was business as usual. I got to the farm early, fed the horses, mucked out the stalls, and started getting your first horse ready for you. Out you came from the tack room, and when you saw me, you started laughing and clapping and said, "Way to go, Jon! Awesome job."

That one statement changed my life, and I realized it was a pivotal moment. My parents bought your young stallion named Chandon (brother to Chablis), and I finished the summer with both of us breaking him. Then, off I went to finish my senior year in high school. The next summer, you moved to Pepperell, Massachusetts, right near me, and I once again became your working student, only this time, you allowed me to warm the horses up for you, and riding so many horses clinched my love for dressage. I went on to have a fabulous career, winning on my own horses and teaching and competing and winning on clients' horses.

In 1991, back home on Christmas vacation, I got into a bad car accident when a drunk driver crossed the median strip and hit me head-on and broke my back, which ended my career. After I learned to walk again (that took two years), I took over my parents' hair salons and spas and became a hair designer and color specialist. I met the man of my dreams in 1994. After fifteen years of doing hair, Hollywood came to call, and I became Debbie Reynolds hair designer, did the hair of Cher (and her wig maintenance), as well as the boy band, One Direction. I had never thought I would or could meet such famous people, but every time in my life that a little voice says, "You can't do this," I always remember that pivotal moment when I was seventeen and you saying that it wasn't win or lose, it was that you put yourself out there and tried and did your very best. That is how much of an impact you had on my entire life, both personally and professionally, and I will be forever grateful. ●

Robert Dover

ACKNOWLEDGMENTS

I want to thank my friends at Trafalgar Square Books: Martha Cook, who talked me into writing this book and made me believe it would be fun, and Rebecca Didier, my editor extraordinaire, who patiently guided me through the process and helped me in more ways than I can adequately describe.

To my brother Al—thanks for ensuring that what I thought I recalled from my youth was, in fact, accurate and factual.

To Tami Hoag, Cyd Ziegler, Mark Rutherford, and Carl Hester—thank you for your friendship and kind words.

To Robert Ross—thank you for patience, your help, and your encouragement, not only with this book but for everything in my life and our life together.

Thank you to all of my family and friends, within and outside the equestrian community, who have encouraged me in my life and my career.

Finally, thank you to my four-legged friends who have unconditionally loved me and changed my life in the most extraordinary ways I could ever imagine!

INDEX

numbers noted in *italics* correspond
to image numbers in the photo insert pages.

INDEX

numbers noted in *italics* correspond
to image numbers in the photo insert pages.

INDEX

numbers noted in *italics* correspond
to image numbers in the photo insert pages.

INDEX

numbers noted in *italics* correspond
to image numbers in the photo insert pages.

INDEX

numbers noted in *italics* correspond
to image numbers in the photo insert pages.

INDEX

numbers noted in *italics* correspond
to image numbers in the photo insert pages.

INDEX

numbers noted in *italics* correspond
to image numbers in the photo insert pages.

INDEX

numbers noted in *italics* correspond
to image numbers in the photo insert pages.

INDEX

numbers noted in *italics* correspond
to image numbers in the photo insert pages.